"JACKIE"!

BY IRVING SHULMAN

NOVELS

The Amboy Dukes ⎫
Cry Tough ⎬ A Trilogy
The Big Brokers ⎭
The Square Trap
Children of the Dark
Good Deeds Must Be Punished
Calibre
The Velvet Knife

SHORT STORIES

The Short End of the Stick

BIOGRAPHIES

The Roots of Fury
Harlow
Valentino

AMERICAN CULTURE

"Jackie"!

"JACKIE"!

The Exploitation of a First Lady

by IRVING SHULMAN

TRIDENT PRESS
New York

SBN: 671-27052-4
Library of Congress Catalog Card Number: 75-105865

Published simultaneously in the United States and Canada by Trident Press, a division of Simon & Schuster, Inc., 630 Fifth Avenue, New York, N.Y. 10020

Printed in the United States of America

For Scott and Sidney Meredith

AUTHOR'S NOTE

SOME years ago, as I took my aisle seat in the first-class section of a plane bound for New York, I saw that both seats across the aisle were reserved but unoccupied. Passengers continued to embark and as the stewardesses welcomed them and checked their reservations, they too glanced at the empty seats and wondered, I believed, if both passengers had canceled their flights.

Scant seconds before departure the tardy passengers appeared in the cabin. They were a mother and her physically precocious daughter, whom I judged to be no more than fifteen. Both were breathless and the mother was vocally angry with her daughter, who carried about a dozen fan magazines which had taken her too long to buy at the newsstand in our satellite. The plane cleared the airport, and as soon as safety belts could be removed, the mother left her seat for several coffee-table magazines carried on the plane. The daughter flipped fleetingly through the magazines on her lap and discarded them in the aisle, to the annoyance of passengers and stewardesses. I asked to look at them and soon found myself reading about President John F. Kennedy and his First Lady, two "stars" who were not to be found in the *Academy Players Directory*, which is the principal casting book for movies and television.

However, not until some several years later did it occur to me that fan magazines were considerably more than a trifling symptom of American malaise, and this symptom could explain the American public's conditioned acceptance of such obscenities as genocide, favorable kill ratio, nuclear fallout, murder, a geometric increase of violent felonies, starvation, slums, denigration of the human condition, fine print in consumer contracts, demagoguery, venality and stupidity in public office, and a spate of social violences which imprison juveniles in a delinquent society of adults. However, these obscenities are accepted without question—they are even defended with patriotic fervor—by the very same majority of American citizens who become fearfully exercised by any use of sexual substantives of four or more letters. To this segment, *these* are the obscenities.

In this case, to bear out my thesis, I have used a particular to prove a universal. The particular chosen is the fan magazines. Along with relevant précis and quotations, I have done my best to reproduce faithfully their carnival use of typeface for titles, taglines, and coverlines. If there are instances where my reproduction is faulty and I have failed to duplicate the original fire-sale fonts, capitalization, and random punctuation, forgive me.

I am grateful to friends and peers who helped me during the discussion meetings and the recording of their data. I also thank them for helping me fill in runs of fan magazines. And I am particularly indebted to Professor Lewis Yablonsky for his assistance in the composition of a research questionnaire, its distribution and for his advice on how best it be presented and interpreted. I am also grateful to the people who completed their questionnaires, wrote letters, and agreed to the publication of their comments. Last but not least, I thank my editor, Bucklin Moon, for the considerable advice he gave me during the time we worked together on this investigation of an American subculture which has become in the sixties a quite normal and standard example of too much of the "respectable" American media.

IRVING SHULMAN
Sherman Oaks, California
May 9, 1969

CHAPTER ONE

The Lady on the Red Velvet Carpet

CERTAINLY more than a million Parisians and tourists declared June 1, 1961, a holiday to welcome the new President of the United States, who was accompanied by his nation's most gracious ambassadress—his wife. From the Salon d' Honneur at Orly Airport, where the press and media crews waited, a red velvet runner almost a hundred yards long stretched to the landing area. There *Air Force One* would cut its engines after the flight from Washington. This, the first visit of the newly elected president of the world's most prestigious democracy, was of unusual importance to the free world and the communist bloc nations, too, whose political analysts would study the reception accorded the President and his wife for diplomatic insights and appraisal of NATO unity. And in Vienna, where Nikita Khrushchev awaited President Kennedy to clasp hands amiably and discuss nuclear testing, treaty possibilities, Cuba, Red China, and the current tensions between the eastern and western sectors of Berlin, the tone, thrust, and advantage of their discussion would be determined, in meaningful part, by the reception accorded the American President by the French.

For more than a month, the American Ambassador to France, James Gavin, had assured Secretary of State Dean Rusk of the French intention to make the visit one of the year's more eventful state occasions. The French press had vied in their publication of pro-American articles and editorials, and the night before, French National Television had broadcast a complimentary program about the Kennedys. Significantly, a fifteen-minute segment was devoted solely to Mrs. Kennedy, who was interviewed in French. Now that the show had been broadcast and assessed by the public and its professional spokesmen, an overwhelming majority opinion held that the President's wife, a poised young woman, at ease with cameras and interviewers, had made a positive impression on everyone. A quiet but certain majesty of presence, an authentic but modest self-assurance, an intelligent ability to make the most of questions and choose the proper nuances in phrasing her replies—these had impressed the French, a people with considerable experience with royalty of all degrees of importance. The unaffected dignity of Mrs. Kennedy had made itself felt whether she pushed a baby stroller along a park path, attended the opera or later, when she conducted a televised tour of the refurbished White House.

All agencies of the French government had been instructed to do everything possible to secure the health, comfort, and safety of the important visitors. Although there were as many guards in plain clothes as there were in uniform, President Charles de Gaulle did not have to employ the elaborate security precautions later utilized by Dr. Carlos Andres Perez of Venezuela in 1961, who jailed four thousand political suspects and massed twenty thousand troops to insure the safety of the American President on a visit to Caracas. Quite likely, even if there had been anti-American protest groups in Paris dedicated to embarrassing the American visitors, those who thronged the airport and lined the parade route would have squashed any unfriendly demonstration.

A sudden cheer arose from the crowd as *Air Force One* appeared in the early-morning sky, executed its approach, and landed easily at the end of the runway. Engines cut, the bright plane taxied into the landing area and positioned itself at the end of the long red carpet. Some seconds later the door opened and President Kennedy strode forward to wave at the crowd as his wife joined him. Poised, handsome, groomed, the two stood at attention, as protocol demanded, while a deep roll of drums alerted the crowds beyond the airport that they would soon be called on to extend their welcome.

After the tattoo of drums ended, sound hung for some moments over the stilled heads of state, then President de Gaulle and his wife raised their hands in welcome. In response, the President and Mrs. Kennedy descended the stairs to join the dignitaries grouped around the French President. As children waved little flags and shouted their rehearsed welcomes, the color guard saluted smartly, the Garde républicaine snapped to attention, and the band offered a rather sentimentalized rendition of the "Star-Spangled Banner" before they played a rousing "Marseillaise."

While batteries of cameras recorded every movement as the President and his wife acknowledged introductions and exchanged pleasantries within the Salon d' Honneur, two little girls as pink as their dresses presented Mrs. Kennedy with bouquets of spring flowers. Quite touched, the First Lady whispered, *"Merci bien."* Her accent was good, and as French guests spoke in simple French to Mrs. Kennedy to which she responded with easy assurance, their delight was unbounded. The lady spoke French. She was beautiful. She was cultured. She was elegant. When was the last time all of these could have been said of an American First Lady?

With regret, for the First Lady was charming, the guests gave their attention to President Kennedy. His statements were translated readily into polished, literary French, and as they listened, and were delighted, many observers were convinced that Mrs. Kennedy had contributed considerably to her husband's remarks. Genuine warmth was in evidence throughout as the requisite amenities were concluded and the French President escorted his guests to waiting Citroëns. De Gaulle rode with Mrs. Kennedy while Madame de Gaulle accompanied John F. Kennedy in a second car to the Quay d' Orsay where the American head of state would stay while in Paris.

The procession, which included Mrs. Joseph Kennedy, the President's mother, the Secret Service, diplomats, military officers, Dr. Janet Travell—the President's personal physician—and the press corps, was cheered with Gallic enthusiasm as it moved down the Bou'l Mich', across the Seine, and into the heart of the French capital where stands of colorful flags complemented the crimson and white Harvard banners waved by French and American students who chanted the Kennedy football countdown in cadence.

Enthusiasm for Mrs. Kennedy rivaled that for her husband. At first the cheers were correct and formal. *"Viva, Jacqueline! Viva, Jacqueline!"* Then a bolder group called, *"Viva, Jacquee!"* As the crowds struggled for a better look at the beautiful woman at the side of Charles de Gaulle, informal chants of welcome and affection increased in volume and strength. Evidently the enthusiasm of the crowds in the street was for Mrs. John F. Kennedy. More often now, as the chanting became more general, the crowd called to her as one of their own—not merely the wife of an American President. She was a Parisienne. She had come home, as the French always knew she would. Twelve years before, had she not attended the University of Grenoble and the Sorbonne? Had she not lived for a time as a guest of the Comtesse de Renty? Was not her love for the City of Lights universal knowledge?

If the Citroën in which "Jacquee" rode had lacked an engine she would have been drawn through the streets by people who would have been honored to pull her car, as their fathers and grandfathers before them had pulled the carriages of Rachel, Mistinguette, Bernhardt, Réjane, and Printemps. Never again during the thousand days of the Kennedy administration would the President and his wife ever experience such an outpouring of enthusiasm and affection.

Freeze the moment of panache, the procession of triumph, as is done in a tableau or movie. Permit the young, handsome President and his wife—America's noblest couple—to enjoy their brief, companionable glory. In recent history, few modern monarchs have received so warm and genuine a welcome by the people of a foreign nation. The Parisians cheered the President of the United States, but the lady at his side was more than his wife and First Lady of the United States. She was "Jacquee"— the people's queen. Her hat was a powder-blue pillbox, but the French saw it as a crown. Once again, as stylists to the Western world, Paris had set the international tone, for soon the rest of the world called her "Jackie" too.

Some thirty-four months after the inauguration, the nation joined the young widow in grief and admired her courage under stress. After her year of mourning, Mrs. Kennedy again became "Jackie" in the public press and mind. Then—most unfortunately, but quite normal for the level of American gall—the movie-fan magazines, one of the more banal and preposterous forms of modern journalism, would enforce their claim to "Jackie" and make that claim pay off. As other magazines that could be kept on domestic coffee tables without embarrassment began to suffer a loss of sales, they too altered their editorial purpose and began to imitate their inferior contemporaries— but on better paper stock. "Jackie," born of admiration on that June day in Paris, would be shaped by an irresponsible press into a combination of idealized nymph and beautiful widow. She would be treated as the common property of a swinish multitude and the press they favored, whose concern was that she be made to love again—and marry. As long as it was profitable to sell this image to the fat-witted readers of fan magazines who managed not to misspell more than half their shopping lists, there was nothing Mrs. Kennedy could do to assure herself of privacy. She was a public figure: therefore, she could only have as much seclusion as the public was willing to grant.

All news media realized this could be used to influence sales and ratings and advertising. The invention of news about Mrs. Kennedy was enjoyed by the reader. If a comic strip became so insipid it had to be canceled, if a sports season happened to hit a dull week, if a sensational murder, divorce trial, or case of public malfeasance failed to occur at a time when the public demanded relief from realities, the press, and particularly the movie magazines, could always turn to Mrs. Kennedy, sigh for inspiration, and make delicious news. As historians ponder the present and recent past, they may wonder—was there ever a Mrs. John F. Kennedy? Could they, from press accounts of her time, reconstruct a real woman? With good reason they might conclude that she never existed at all—that Jacqueline Kennedy was just another demigoddess created for the fevered pages of mean-spirited magazines. Between 1963 and 1968, Mrs. Kennedy was featured as often as, if not more than, Debbie Reynolds or Elizabeth Taylor on the covers of movie fan magazines. Fantastic as this sounds, it is true.

This exploitation of the former First Lady on magazine covers that violated every canon of taste has been made possible by the average American woman who might better serve society if she could be altered to lay eggs like a bird, and then be compelled to sit on them until they hatched. At present she is more inclined to sit on myths until their shells crack to reveal what she believes to be legitimate realities instead of bastard imbecilities.

There are good reasons to explain the current relevance of movies, television, and politics in the United States. The acceptance of what passes for acting and the acting of politicians has strengthened the unhealthy symbiosis between these endeavors. Of course, Jacqueline Kennedy never was, nor is she today, an actress, nor in any real sense was she a politician. However, through reflexive association, her continued press exploitation has vested her with both roles.

Democratic as the position of the president of the United States may be, the very height of the office, its unusual elevation in world affairs, places the man with the keys to the White House on a height far above any contemporary aristocrat. Unlike an aristocrat, the rank of president is impermanent; an ex-president may become an undistinguished private citizen, a thorn to political professionals, even an embarrassment to his party. Certainly the ex-president's wife is stripped of all importance. History has proved this true in the case of many presidents and all First Ladies with the exception of two: Eleanor Roosevelt and Jacqueline Kennedy. Mrs. Roosevelt made news to the very last day of her life. John Kennedy's widow will certainly do the same.

When a young, handsome President with a full head of hair, who was bright, personable, and possessed of a true sense of humor and a beautiful wife, was given a four-year lease to a distinguished mansion on Pennsylvania Avenue, many good citizens whose senses of proportion and comparison had been developed through movie attendance and television viewing to a microedge of stupified insensibility, saw John F. Kennedy as a happy trinity of Sir Walter Raleigh, Dick Van Dyke, and the first citizen of Marlboro Country. Critics—and there were many who lamented the decline of bigotry in the United States—saw the young President as Franklin D. Roosevelt's black heir and forerunner of Orwell's Big Brother.

In one of his columns for *The Saturday Evening Post,* Stewart Alsop listed ten qualities for the successful present and future of a politician in 1968. In order, the aspiring public servant is: (1) handsome; (2) a likeable chap; (3) rich; (4) married, probably to his first wife, with whom he has had a minimum of two children; (5) not necessarily a war hero; (6) a past member of his college's debating team and a man remembered by classmates as a B.M.O.C.; (7) well groomed in the casual style; (8) appreciative of good food but not a gourmet; (9) a hard worker who loves to work hard; and (10) a man with a genuine affection for power.

Lady politicians, in the United States, are still catalogued as women compulsively compelled to compete with men because of some psychic envy explained best by Freud; or because they are cats, love to talk, and are ever ready to take advantage, in all regions of the United States, of awesome ignorance. However, if we were to draw a composite of an acceptable lady politician for 1968, 1969, or 1970, or more pleasantly, a majestic First Lady, what would she be like? As optimum consort for Alsop's successful politician, especially on the national level, she would have to be: (1) young and winsome; (2) beautiful and grateful that she was so blessed; (3) poised and charming, but never patronizing; (4) of good reputation before and after marriage, and the mother of at least two children; (5) modest of demeanor but regal of presence; (6) well educated but neither bookish nor puristic in her cultural standards; (7) a linguist with a good accent, who only uses a foreign language when it will enhance the prestige of the United States; (8) reasonably athletic, outstanding only as an equestrienne; (9) a tasteful homemaker and a pacesetter of style; and (10) a lady who also loves power.

In 1961, with the unhappy sweep of twentieth-century history in full view of the American public, they had to see how the larger world had been at war since 1914; how American military involvement had begun some four years later and had never ended; how the nation's unhappy history of institutional racism was responsible for quantum increases in disaffection, crime, delinquency, and normlessness; how inflation, seemingly beyond control, swelled income taxes; how, throughout the land, there were endemic pockets of poverty resistant to all amelioration, with a significant number of American citizens—their families' third generation—on the public welfare rolls. These problems inspired a national hedonism that was evidenced in many ways, and one of the most significant was the growing affection for beautiful people in general and beautiful politicians in particular. With a "Jack" and "Jackie" in the White House, with old politicians looking for young candidates possessed of good looks and manners who might be logical personalities to occupy the White House *after* it was vacated by the Kennedys, demographers recognized what professional party politicians accepted with a demurrer before they surrendered to the popular will: *new* political candidates and their wives had to be possessed of the ability to star on the rostrum and more importantly—on film and television.

Currently, fifty percent of the American population is under the age of twenty-six, and actuaries agree that by 1970 this figure will be at least seventy percent. Even improvements in Medicare or a relaxation of immigrant quotas will not have a significant effect on this projection. Rather, in the current and future internal conflicts between youth and age, the elder statesman concerned for his own perpetuation, and hence for the only people who would elect him, would be well advised to see that the largest share of the nation's research budget be allocated to gerontology.

The chasm between youth and age broadens and deepens; the worship of the Son rather than God the Father is evidenced by the shift in advertising focus, which now targets its appeals at the teen-ager, the young man and woman, rather than their parents and other substantial elders of the middle class. The nation's emphasis is on youth and an imitation of youth—ergo, in a television commercial an oldster is shown leaping over the door of his Mustang. Middle-aged men ape their sons by an interest in surfing, sports cars, and sexy "center-fold" magazines. Not to slight anyone who can afford to buy—even grandmothers are encouraged to use dentifrices that will give their mouths sex appeal (this bold invitation to oral sexual practice seemingly escapes the self-appointed, constipated keepers of the nation's morality). Golden-age grandmothers establish a sympathetic connection with their daughters and granddaughters by jesting about the Pill, by attempting to look, act, and think young, by devoting themselves to romance, fashion, and sex manuals appropriate to the climacteric years—and movie fan magazines.

Paul Goodman's article "The New Aristocrats," in *Playboy* (March, 1967), observes in part:

> Nor are these young people properly called "youth." The exigencies of the American system have kept them in tutelage, doing lessons, till twenty-three and twenty-four years of age, years past when young industrial workers used to walk picket lines or when farmers carried angry pitchforks, or young men are now drafted into the Army. Thus, another cause of their shared resentment is the foolish attempt to arrest their maturation and regulate their social, sexual and political activity.

In the paradoxical, even antithetical atmosphere of war and pleasure, grave international conflicts and international film festivals, balances of power and trade, which involve a swapping of teen-age models, song stylists, and rock 'n' roll groups, why wonder that young Americans see contemporary American politics for what it is: a theatrical entertainment that ranges from olio to fairly good melodrama. Thus, the movement of actors from the sound stage to town-hall lecterns, and the abandonment by politicians of the savant for a movie personality—or someone who could be made to appear, behave, and sound like a movie star—is proof of pragmatic apperception.

A modern interaction of entertainers and politicians was demonstrated in 1967 by the Los Angeles City Council as it appropriated $16,160 to convert its legislative chamber into a professional television studio, the better to facilitate an increasing number of appearances on home sets; this prompted some dour critics to ask if the community at large had lost the ability to distinguish between a being—truly human—and an infinitely clever machine capable of romantic enlargement. The council, which was properly concerned with public evaluation of its performances, turned—for one of the few times in its contentious history—to Mayor Sam Yorty for instruction in lighting, makeup, and public stance. Inasmuch as the mayor was a master of ceremonies on his own ninety-minute television show, his expertise was beyond question. Why the television critic for the Los Angeles *Times* suggested that Sam Yorty was no better a "TV host" than he was a mayor is explained by the churlish feud between the *Times* and the city's first official.

The trend from politician-as-performer to performer-as-politician became most evident when political life beckoned to Ronald Reagan, who was assured by his friend, Senator George Murphy, that fortune had given him a gold ring on the political merry-go-round—after he had shucked his Democratic affiliation and become a Republican. Inasmuch as Reagan had also been a Democrat who had, during his political development, suffered from a bleeding heart—which to the conservative is more abominable than leprosy—his shift in party allegiance, pejorative abjuration of any political philosophy that made sense, and a full-blown ability to fill this vacuum with simplistic semanticisms was rewarded with the office of governor.

In a letter to *Time* (November 4, 1966), Stephen Longstreet reminisced about a conversation he had had with William Faulkner in 1945.

> [We] were standing outside Warner Bros. studio waiting for our car, both a little glum since we had been working on the screenplay of *Stallion Road*. Bill said: "Who's going to star in this?" I said, "A horse." "I mean human." "Ronald Reagan." Bill thought a while and puffed on his Dunhill. "I don't know. Back home, we'd run him for public office." "Why?" Bill thought some more, then said, "An actor now has to be the part he's playing, but this boy is too much everything, and none of it settles down. You can't go too wrong in politics going from no place to nothing. . . ."

In all fairness to the state, particularly the southern extremity, it should be noted that Albert Dekker was elected a state assemblyman, Helen Gahagan Douglas served in the nation's House of Representatives and aspired to the Senate, and Wendell Corey was a councilman in Santa Monica. However, the success of George Murphy and Ronald Reagan for the Republicans has compelled the Democrats to look toward the movie and television studios for charismatic candidates. Steve Allen, Gene Barry, and Jackie Cooper have been suggested for office, as have Robert Vaughan, Robert Culp, and Chuck Connors, who is the current darling of distaff Republicans. A redoubtable candidate was Shirley Temple Black, whose hawkish sentiments astonished many fans who remembered her as Little Miss Marker, but apparently had forgotten that for the past thirty-five years she has held the rank of colonel in Idaho, was commissioned a commanding colonel in the Hawaiian National Guard, and made an honorary colonel of the 108th Regiment, National Guard of Illinois.

In December, 1932, when Shirley Temple was not yet five, Paramount released *The Phantom President*, a comedy that starred George M. Cohan in the dual role of a presidential nominee who was replaced by a look-alike song-and-dance man from a medicine show. The plot clincher was inspired: secretly, the real politician went on a world tour, and the song-and-dance man generated such overwhelming popular and enthusiastic support through his ability to entertain that he was elected President. This "talking picture debut" of George M. Cohan saw him ably supported by Claudette Colbert and Jimmy Durante. The picture would long have been forgotten had it not been referred to with increasing frequency by students of film history, who now see *The Phantom President* as a harbinger of things to come.

The American public need do no more than see an actor play a role to believe that role is fact; and played often enough, the actor, who solves every problem to the delight of the audience, *and never fails nor suffers defeat,* is considered to be more expert than any real-life professional. One Perry Mason in a city and there would be no need for the homicide division of a police department; one Dr. Kildare reporting directly to Dr. Gillespie would relieve the medical shortage; one Lucy family next door would do more for property values than the most rigid of zoning covenants. In 1932 the suggestion that someone in show business could become President was too far-fetched to make the picture a success. Paramount should take a print from its vault and look again; now—almost forty years later—a remake could become a box-office champion.

An actor's skill is related to his ability to step into his role, his interpretation of personality, and the dramatic investiture that he gives to the spoken word. If the dialogue in a play was memorized, delivered in ringing tones with appropriate gestures—often attained through coaching, then, by God, you had an actor. Today, if your favorite candidate is lighted properly, made up to heighten his appearance, photographed winningly, amplified strongly, ghostwritten intelligently, then, by God, you have a politician.

And take especial notice: in the area of politics, speechwriters work primarily for men, but in their finished addresses the women, who can vote too, are never neglected. Although their political emancipation is still fairly recent history, the literary preferences of women have always had the weightiest influence on domestic fiction in the United States. A student need only refer to the subject matter of the very first American novels to hear familiar Pavlovian rings which still draw the ladies to fiction, for then and now they were and still are enthusiastic about adultery, seduction, incest and suicide; so much so that contemporary readers of *The Power of Sympathy* (1789), *Charlotte Temple* (London, 1790; Philadelphia, 1794), and *The Coquette* (1797) might have found themselves cozily at home if they had been offered what passes for entertainment in the movie fan magazines. From then until now, their literary preferences have indicated a great liking for gossip, scandal, and certain titillations that writers of any given period in American history sought to accommodate, inasmuch as these fictions offered psychological pleasure as well as promises of factual freedom.

As women gradually divested themselves of successive layers of undergarments, made their dresses more revealing, and raised their hemlines higher and higher above the ankle, their reading habits became almost totally concerned with material written to emancipate them from the moral bondages of unrewarded sex and insincere sympathy. Thus, as she freed herself from the stays of corsetted convention, twentieth-century woman accepted the publicizing of feminine hygiene as she accepted instruction in postured bedroom conduct. Her new candor and poise, immediately evident after World War One when she began to drink socially with men while the practice was illegal, reflected a sophistication that could be dismissed neither by pulpit nor cash register. Rather than ignore this sophistication —or prurient interest, as it was identified by some social Gothics —the *new* women's magazines took advantage of the tastes and interests of their emancipated readers. Circulation soared and advertisers were quick to subscribe for space in publications that

catered to the ladies, their increasing control of the nation's finances and burgeoning purchasing power.

Insight into private problems became more evident in the
magazines favored by women. Where insight was thin, conjecture and fantasy sufficed, and by the sixties, mothers and daughters were companions as they associated themselves in delicious
fantasy with Debbie Reynolds, Elizabeth Taylor, and finally,
with Jacqueline Kennedy. The television set takes modern
woman outside herself, the women's magazines take her inside
all the women she would like to be. And as she dreams in the
semidarkness, awaiting the arrival of Mr. Kleen, the Man from
Glad, and the White Knight of Ajax, America's mod mother can
indulge her febrile imagination in a romantic conjunction with
Richard Burton and Elizabeth Taylor, who do not consider her
a crowd. Or she can, if in less heated or softer mood, commiser-
ate with Jacqueline Kennedy—poor thing—whose life had been
so radically altered by widowhood.

It follows, then, that a story about Mrs. Kennedy, or her picture on the cover of a magazine, often means the financial success of the issue. The average woman in her outer-directed
search for both real and vicarious experience demands more and
more stories about the former First Lady. Mrs. Kennedy sells
magazines, if not on street corners, certainly in the hearts of her
countrywomen. Indeed, whether the magazine is *Look, Life,
Redbook,* or *Ladies' Home Journal,* all are devoted to an inner
analysis and a Mad Hatter-Boswellian treatment of Mrs. Kennedy. The paper may be slicker than that used by the fan magazine, the story more polished, but the subject matter is the same:
what is the former First Lady doing *now;* what will she do next;
is she ever again going to know happiness?

Within Mrs. America's home and even on the telephone, these
questions may be asked; but their answers are less satisfactory
than those found through a visit to a beauty salon. A modern
salon of medium size will require a small foyer, a waiting room,
partitions that are open to a central aisle, the tools and machines
of the trade, some hundreds of pounds of beauty supplies, four
competent beauticians—preferably epicene because they are so

much more fun—one manicurist, four washbasins, eight large mirrors, four hair dryers, single copies of *Vogue, Harper's Bazaar, Mademoiselle, Seventeen*—and upward of thirty copies of movie fan magazines, preferably with "Jackie" on their covers. For example, the following letter and reply appeared in the May, 1962, issue of *Photoplay:*

> LETTER TO EDITOR: What have we now, a new political magazine? I own a beauty shop and the customers refuse to look at it if the Kennedy name is on it. Can you blame them? Mamie wasn't on *Photoplay*'s cover every month and she was a President's wife.
>
> B.J.M.
>
> ANSWER: We fully expected letters like yours. *Photoplay,* in its more than fifty years of publishing, has always been proud of its reputation for tastefulness and beauty. Mrs. Kennedy symbolizes tastefulness and beauty. Even more, she is America's newest star. Stardom is not limited to Hollywood, it transcends professions, countries, races, and creeds. As newsworthy as she is charming, Mrs. Kennedy is in every sense a beautiful, glamorous, exciting star who deserves to be on the cover of *Photoplay.*

Ladies who use the beauty salon seldom subscribe to movie fan magazines. They may be wary of revealing to their husbands, lovers, or friends their sources of inside dirt; or perhaps they prefer to visit the newsstand and personally choose the publications whose covers bear the most provocative banner headlines.

I'M GOING TO KILL YOUR BOY!—How the Secret Service Saved Jackie's Son!

HOW JACKIE KENNEDY BECAME A MOVIE STAR!

THE DAY THAT LADY BIRD HURT JACKIE KENNEDY—(and didn't mean to!)

THE MAN WHO CAME BACK INTO JACKIE'S LIFE (We have the pictures)

THE FIRST MAN JACKIE WILL DATE

Most of the movie fan magazines outside of the big three—
Photoplay, Modern Screen, and *Motion Picture*—publish from
month to month, with their margin of profit tied to the contents
of a current issue. This was not so in the late thirties, when the
Directory of Newspapers and Periodicals (January, 1939) revealed that *Hollywood, Motion Picture, Movie Mirror, Movie
Story Magazine, Photoplay, Screen Guide, Screenland,* and *Silver Screen* had an audited circulation of between a quarter and
a half million copies each month. At the same time, *Harper's* and
the *Atlantic Monthly* had a circulation of slightly more than a
hundred thousand copies a month; the *Nation* had a monthly
sale of less than forty thousand copies; the *New Republic,* less
than thirty thousand.

In the Statement of Ownership, Management and Circulation, required by law to be printed at least once annually, *Movie
TV Secrets* (August, 1964) averred that during the preceding
twelve-month period, issues averaged 286,072 copies, with a
printing of 282,791 copies for the issue nearest the filing date.
The average sales, through news dealers or otherwise, were
151,656 copies, with a sale of 134,501 copies for the single issue
nearest the filing date. Paid circulation through term subscribers, carrier delivery, or other means was—*fifty* copies.

Is it possible that a magazine with an average press run of
286,172 copies only has fifty subscribers? The statement was
sworn and published. Apparently the average return of unsold
copies was almost 150,000 per issue, which, even with "Jackie"
stories in almost every issue, and the photographs of Mrs. Kennedy on almost every cover, does not seem to be particularly
successful.

However, a significant question comes to mind: what would
be the number of returns if there were no "Jackie" stories to
stimulate the sale of movie fan magazines? In the sixties, would
their normal readership have been content with gossipy love
tales about the Hollywood personalities who were, in final analysis, portrayed as silly children in a surrealist kindergarten,
occasionally spanked in public by Louella Parsons and Hedda
Hopper? "There is great generosity among Americans"—David

Riesman wrote in his new preface to *The Lonely Crowd* (1961) —"there is also enormous meanness and mindlessness." To accept this judgment is to understand how the movie fan magazines, and even those coffee-table magazines usually purchased by women, can cast Mrs. Jacqueline Kennedy as a movie star, who, not to disappoint her "friends," must accept the role assigned to her by Yahoos, Babbitts, and magazines whose publishers, editors, and writers wear masks of decency.

CHAPTER TWO

Louella, Hedda, Sheilah, Dorothy, Rona.
Some Men in the Company
of These Ladies—and "Jackie"!

I N that not too distant past, when the thirty-fifth President was still a senator, *Redbook* (April, 1960), a magazine with an average guaranteed circulation at that time of 2,850,000 copies among young adults, was one of the first of the "respectable" periodicals to do a story about Mrs. John F. Kennedy. A caption on the cover, above the photograph of the Senator's wife, asked a probing but richly lathered question that did not irritate the mind's delicate fibers: "SENATOR KENNEDY'S WIFE: If He Wins, How Much Does She Lose?" What good, sterile housewife, who hoped some day to be asked her sudsy opinion by a pollster, could resist learning the answer? The article, by Robert J. Levin, offered a full load of cleaner-than-white but doubtful quotes, which, when pondered on, never answered the question. Mrs. Jean Smith, a sister of the Senator, observed of Mrs. Kennedy, "I don't think she's mad about politics." Charles

Spaulding agreed: "It requires a more rugged, less feminine girl than Jackie to be vitally involved in politics." Stephen Smith, husband of Jean, disagreed slightly with his wife and Mr. Spaulding: "Jackie's satisfaction is totally vicarious; it all comes to her through her husband." Finally, the article wash-cycled around to the Senator himself, who observed that he was already in the Senate when he married, and his wife "didn't think her role in [his] career would be particularly important." He continued: "I see many politicians' wives who are just as vigorous as their husbands. This may be fine for them, but not for me. I spend my days with politicians—not my nights too." However, it became immediately evident to what extent the Senator's ambition was complemented by his wife's perspicacity; thus, the Senator continued: "She realizes that I'm in a very intensive struggle—the outcome uncertain, and she plays a considerable part in it." To give women the importance the new tradition insisted they deserved, the young presidential hopeful told the homemakers how substantial a role his wife played in his future. "What she does, or does not do, really affects that struggle. Since I'm completely committed, and since she is committed to me, that commits her."

To separate the commitments into readily understood component parts is a mighty labor, but the magazine's readership reacted viscerally, to empathize with the pretty young wife of the article, especially when they learned of an early miscarriage, some three years after her marriage on September 12, 1953. They also learned other things: that her husband was a busy man, intent on a greater career, and why Jacqueline "makes no effort to imagine what life may be like if her husband should be elected President. During the past six years she has learned that a senator has limited free time to devote to his family. She can hardly expect him to have more free time should he become President. This too will call for a new adjustment on her part."

It was about time, some impatient readers probably muttered, for the lady of Mr. Levin's article to say something. At last she did; at least the article credits her with the following observation: "It's the most exciting life imaginable, always involved with the news of the moment, meeting and working with people who are enormously alive, and every day you are caught up in something you really care about. It makes a lot of other things less vital. You get used to the pressure that never lets up, and you learn to live with it as a fish lives in water."

Women sighed. They understood. And many of them worried about what life would be like for Mrs. Kennedy if her husband was elected President. Certainly, a goodly number of matrons decided that the burden would be too much for her—and they voted for Richard Nixon. It is equally safe to assume there were ladies who decided that the wearisome obligations of First Lady should not be visited on Mrs. Nixon—a nice, white, Anglo-Saxon Protestant wife, who, in 1968, would receive an honorary LL.D. degree from Finch College, a little white-glove institution for Listerine girls with everything but the ability to be admitted to Barnard, Antioch, Reed, or Smith. The degree was awarded because Mrs. Nixon "stood out from the empty-headed, over-dressed little sorority girls of that era like a good piece of litera-ture on a shelf of cheap paperbacks." Convinced, in 1960, that the Vice-President's spouse deserved better than the obligatory and irksome burdens of the White House, they voted for John F. Kennedy.

Later that year, Senator Kennedy was elected President and the nation prepared for 1961, which already gave evidence—in Hollywood too—of being twelve months of major events and de-cisions. That same year, when Debbie Reynolds married Harry Karl, *Motion Picture* informed its readers, whose open minds were deserts, of other notable events in Freakoutland: May Britt and Sammy Davis, Jr., talked to the fans about their baby and Sandra Dee *cried* the day *after* her marriage to Bobby Darin, which may have just preceded "The Night that Tony [Curtis] Broke Janet [Leigh's] Heart." Among Hollywood's chroniclers there was heated argument as to whether Debbie and Harry would have a baby by Christmas and just how the new Mrs. Karl should treat Eddie Fisher, who was—after all—the father of her two children. Problems between Elizabeth Taylor and Richard Burton overshadowed Janet Leigh's cry,

"I Need Help!"—and efforts by *Motion Picture* to sponsor a Jimmy Dean Cult. There was vapid speculation on two other fronts: would Marilyn Monroe remarry Joe Di Maggio; and Janet Leigh's children asked, "Mommy, What Church Does Santa Claus Go To?" In its emphasis on the yuletide, *Motion Picture* inquired if Sandra Dee and Bobby Darin—those two nice kids who'd had some stormy months of marriage—were going to have a "Baby for Christmas?" In a quick switch from December birthdays to junior intelligence, fans were exhorted to review and render judgment in the case of Tuesday Weld, an obstreperous teenager wholly indifferent to public opinion. Because the Christmas season of 1961 was going into high gear, Mr. and Mrs. Sammy Davis, Jr., begged mercy of the world through a fan magazine: "Please Don't Let Them Hurt Our Daughter!" This was an especially appropriate plea because in its December issue *Motion Picture* made it official: Debbie Reynolds had said, "We're Going to Have a Baby!"

Oh yes, there was some mention of Marlon Brando siring a child in Tahiti, but the fan magazines gave this only passing notice. Far more important was an article that informed the worshipful public how the stars of popular orbits were "coloring God." Frankie Avalon saw Him wearing a red robe. Ann Blythe saw Him as gold. Barbara Luna saw the Radiance as magenta, which, she explained was the color of martyrdom and suffering. Carolyn Jones revealed God as a Magnificence of purple and rose; Susan Kohner saw Him revealed as "the color of sunlight"; quite naturally, Mickey Callan saw Him as green. Pat Boone favored white buck shoes; to him God was white. It does appear that brains, reason, and theology exist to be grown out of, inasmuch as the modern world demands more, but people, especially women, and media, give the planet less.

Some months before the inaugural ceremonies of January 21, 1961, fashion-conscious America looked at the First Lady and found her pleasant to the eye. Hair stylists also approved of her "bubble," especially since it was in greatest demand. As the First Lady-elect represented the stylistic ambitions of almost every young girl, and photographs of Mrs. Kennedy proved her elegant at any distance and angle, women and the world of fashion were convinced that the simple clothes she chose to wear had some strong influence on the making of a lady. Thus, the selection of wardrobe by the young First Lady was always a newsworthy event, and young matrons oscillated between states of frustration and absolute awe because Jacqueline Kennedy's dress and accessories seemed to be exactly right for any occasion, be it the simplest informality of a family gathering or a ball governed by rigid protocol. At a sporting event or the opera, at church or the dedication of a public monument, at breakfast or supper—what the First Lady wore was mass-produced within the week in a full range of prices. In addition, Mrs. Kennedy played to perfection her role of "The Mother with Small Daughter," to the end that what *this* mother and daughter wore were also in greatest demand.

By the end of 1960, countless slim, dark-haired women made their appearance in advertisements carried by national magazines of first quality; and their resemblance to Mrs. Jacqueline Kennedy was less than accidental. Model look-alikes were at a premium, and by the spring of 1961 it was a feat indeed to open popular magazines without seeing some young women—who resembled the First Lady—modeling lingerie, serving beer, or comforting nervous travelers on airlines. The abuse was too self-evident to be ignored, which compelled the National Business Bureau to counsel its members of advisable discretions to be practiced in their advertising layouts; in addition, they were to avoid use of the Kennedy name or Mrs. Kennedy's likeness in connection with their products. The fad for dark, leggy models took hold in Europe, and in late 1962 a Scottish company made formal apologies to Mrs. Kennedy for promoting their products through a campaign that made use of her photograph. The apology was accepted, and there the matter ended.

Much of the nation was intrigued. Imagine—a young married couple now occupied the White House; this fact also captivated citizens of foreign nations, who also insisted on the fullest possible news coverage of the President and his wife. Paramount among the many virtues of the First Lady hailed by the magazines and Sunday supplement sections was her inexhaustible energy. This, as well as her beauty and style, was the envy and despair of the nation's women. The tired housewife who fell into bed after she had done the evening's dishes, put out the pets and garbage, got the children to their rooms, and left her husband—thank God—snoring before the television set, six-pack at his feet—envied the lovely woman in the White House. At that very moment, in the most beautiful gown, she was surrounded by a circle of admiring men, all handsome, all distinguished and important, all mentioned every day by pundits and columnists. And she was saying the right things in English, French, and Spanish! How wonderful. She certainly was a credit to her sex, which was more than could be said for dozens and dozens of Hollywood actresses—the tramps.

Mrs. Housewife had only to pick one of any number of magazines to learn how Mrs. Kennedy was faring in the White House and public eye. During her husband's first year in office, stories about her appeared in magazines as divergent as *America, American Home, Cosmopolitan, Horizon, Ladies' Home Journal, Life, Look, Mademoiselle, McCall's, Motion Picture, Movie TV Secrets, Nation, Newsweek, Reader's Digest, Screenland, Saturday Evening Post, Time, TV Star Parade, Show Business Illustrated, U.S. News,* and *Vogue.*

Not until the end of the Second World War did Hollywood become important as a talent pool for political candidates who perform in real life. That they are persuasive cannot be denied, for in the history of California the figure of Ronald Reagan will stand out forever as the only governor ever able to persuade most of the state's citizens that their children would be better off without education. Prior to the direct entrance of actors in politics, their contributions to the nation's civic life were limited to the sale of war bonds and charitable seals; they entertained at service centers and, once, in the case of MGM, had their talents drafted to make a short feature that helped defeat Upton Sinclair when, in the long ago, he ran for governor of California. Some actors and actresses had sufficient reputation to make meaningful endorsements of candidates for office. But in the public mind, before it was irreparably damaged by television, the stars were light-years removed from *realpolitik*. Until the advocate of New Frontier politics took office, Hollywood—capital of that popular series, *Mondo California*—was described by sociological cartographers as a state of mind beyond the boundaries of place or reality, where, as Mickey Rooney approached middle age, he observed ruefully: "I was a fourteen-year-old boy for thirty years."

The psychological insecurity of movie stars related them to Joseph's Pharaoh, for the years of top stardom and its attendant fame and fortune usually numbered seven. Lean years were unlimited, and it followed that stars had to make their professional careers large enough to last a lifetime. Before they became superannuated politicians, for whom private industry occasionally found some sinecure with far greater title than responsibility, stardom for a President of the United States could be extended a year beyond seven. After they left office, some ex-Presidents published an occasional article, even a book or two, which, like fan magazine articles attributed to stars, usually were ghosted.

In their apogee and perigee, a movie star and political star have much in common. Both require a supporting press and responsive public—or Congress—to assure them of healthy images. In the past, a star depended on a positive fan-magazine and gossip-column press, where, like a President, bad news about him was often best. If the scandalous item about a screen actor or actress in the column of a widely read gossip triggered a positive economic reaction, it was deemed good. Similarly, whatever helped elect a candidate to office was also good; whatever defeated him—be it education, wit, vocabulary range, erudition, good works, or honor—was bad. In added similarity, the political columnist, like the gossip columnist, could, through the magic of phrase and employment of wit and invective, make a hero, villain, or fool of his subject. Obviously then, columnists are important to careers.

What government figure has not been the target of a columnist? Walter Lippmann, the good gray dean of penetrating comment, was feared more than he was loved; William Allen White could make a fool of the city slicker; H. L. Mencken and a far lesser light, Westbrook Pegler, wrote with acid. The astonishing xenophobic ignorances of most Hearst editorialists did not make their opinions less weighty.

Although the importance of the printed word cannot be denied, its atomic mass has been lightened considerably by television, the literature of the illiterate, which Commissioner Lee Loevinger of the Federal Communications Commission observed was "not an expression of the elite [inasmuch as] the common man has a right to be common." Nevertheless, it is a foolish politician who makes an impromptu appearance on "Meet the Press" or the "William Buckley Show." More than one national figure has been reduced to semicoherence by May Craig or Lawrence Spivak. Weekly, the opinions of Edwin Newman and Eric Sevareid become increasingly weighty. The men who master-of-ceremony nightly talk shows—Johnny Carson, Joey Bishop, David Susskind, Merv Griffin—also make their cameras and microphones available to political figures; and politicians as divergent as President Kennedy and Senator Goldwater have appeared on the informal sessions viewed by insomniacs of all the continental states. Most of the audience tunes into these shows for entertainment, to see the great as real people, but a small segment of viewers is made up of professional politicians and representatives of public relations firms who watch the shows to discover some "celebrity" who looks as if he is speaking knowledgeably. Night after night the men who control party machines flip television dials to find an actress, novelist, playwright or athlete who rates well with the public and can, therefore, be groomed for elective office.

If the star of the political columnist is in the ascendancy, the star of the Hollywood gossipist may be at its nadir. Thousands on thousands of our nation's ladies can remember the time when they turned to the "hot news" of Hollywood columnists before they read the advice to the lovelorn, comics, recipes, and the headlines of social violence. Times have changed. Television has erased climate and most other regional differences.

Housewives throughout the nation may begin their day with Virginia Graham, hostess of "Girl Talk," a show which Miss Graham refers to privately as the "Menopausal Romper Room." She and her guests will discuss, with sodden emphasis, a limited range of topics related to free love, abortion, sexual alteration at home and abroad, and homosexuality as bent, veneer, career, and status symbol. Other topics, from topless to brainless, educate a free citizenry in the problems of a hot, shrinking world. Hands in the dishwater, then dried, Mrs. Goodwife tunes to Gypsy Rose Lee, who moves rapidly and with much laughter between recipes and advice about brassieres. Helen Gurley Brown, devoted to a clitoral interpretation of life, interrogates her guests with outrageous questions to elicit outrageous opinions, and is most poised when she asks her camera captives what birth control devices they favor and use, if they have ever practiced miscegenation, if they are willing to discuss their straight, butch, or gay experiences, what it's like to be A.C.-D.C., and why women keep their eyes shut when they are being pleasured in the dark.

Life is beautiful. The chemist's pill and television's placebo have made it so. And why should anyone read watered-down gossip columns in newspapers where ????? and ***** and ———— stand for spice, when with a flick of the wrist Mrs. Matron can get the real thing at home, in a size and color related to her credit boldness?

It is true—there was a time before television, and in that epoch the Hollywood columnists were supreme; and among the females of this specie, success was in direct ratio to their physical ability to evaginate claws. As oracles and priests interpreted for mankind the true meanings in the heroisms and miracles of ancient gods, the columnists interpreted the earth-roamings of the new gods and goddesses of the American screen. In the past, when the world's ages were golden and some of the gods were worshipped in anthropozoomorphic forms, their primary conflicts were sexual; as they loved or intrigued with mortals of their favor, the wars their human champions fought were carnal in origin. Much of extant Greek tragedy is founded in sexual conflict; even strife among allies, as in the Trojan War, had its basis in concupiscence. Contest between Hollywood's gods and goddesses is almost completely raunchy, and in the presentation of their neon myth and mythology, Louella Parsons and Hedda Hopper were as powerful and capricious as the Delphic Oracle. However, during most of the reign of these competing and vertiginous termagants, the world was a gentler place. Infantry fought with M-1 rifles, nuclear fission was imaginative blackboard exercise, lovers relied on mechanical contraceptives, and the two entertainments that truly unified all the peoples of the world were performed in the bedroom and the movie palace.

In a land where sensation is harvested every season of the year, there is no reason for any reader to get less than his fair share. The power, then, of gossip columnists was in their multimillions of readers who enjoyed the otiose prose of these highly charged females as they blessed or condemned the studios, their players, and their product. In manner they were as capricious as any of the goddesses in a mythological pantheon; their typewriters were more destructive than thunderbolts; and their mink coats, scarves, and stoles were unnecessary armor that covered hides resistant to penetration by diamondheaded drills or conscience. Courage on the screen was unable to withstand the challenge by the reigning witches of the gossip columns; and the fans loved this especially because gods and goddesses, too, must suffer agony and twilight.

In her autobiography, *Tell It to Louella* (1961), Miss Parsons is queenly in the divine style. "My house on Maple Drive in Beverly Hills is not only my home, it's my office, and sooner or later anybody who is anybody, or anybody who hopes to be anybody in Hollywood, has walked up those fifty paces to my front door." In the thirties, Miss Parsons was described as "the most consistently inaccurate reporter who ever lived to draw $600 a week"; in the decade to follow, *Time* (1947) noted that she spouted Hollywood gossip like a "ruptured water main." However, most of the American public who attended movies did not sneer at Miss Parsons, and her considerable influence was proved in the case of Orson Welles's *Citizen Kane* (1941), when she telephoned Nelson Rockefeller to advise him how displeased she would be if the picture was booked into the Radio City Music Hall. Her displeasure must have been a potent force, because the Music Hall never played this fine example of cinematic art.

Even Miss Hopper, herself a viperish lady, acknowledged how damp Louella's displeasure could be. In one of her two autobiographical volumes, Miss Hopper reported that "Ginger Rogers and Ronald Colman were both excommunicated by Louella for years for their effrontery in refusing to appear on her former radio show, Hollywood Hotel." As mistress of ceremonies, Miss Parsons received a salary of $2,500 a week; the stars appeared free, which proves that only in a society coming apart at the seams could such felonies against intellect, taste, and ethics have gone unpunished. If any star balked, the producers of this radio entertainment hastened to tell the laggards what could happen to them if they continued their insubordination to the established authority that was Miss Parsons. Most actors and actresses have spines of soft licorice, so they agreed to be introduced without payment by Miss Parsons to all the people in Radioland. A conservative estimate of the cost of talent, if it had been paid for, is about two million dollars. Because the talent came free, the show cost about twelve thousand dollars a week instead of thirty.

Deals and shenanigans were standard operating procedure for the fat little dowd with the sharp teeth, but Hearst readers, a loyal lot, were as dedicated to her as the lip-sounders gathered around Miss Hopper, who claimed political astuteness, and if pressed for proof, pointed to her friendship with Bernard Baruch. In 1964, with understandable hubris, Miss Hopper estimated that her column was as necessary as respiration to thirty-five million followers. Only Hedda could contest with Louella for the role of Hollywood's most influential chronicler, which compelled the Hollywood Foreign Press Association in 1960 to bestow Golden Globe Awards on both ladies for "journalistic achievement." Miss Hopper was cited "for news coverage and travels that have brought international prestige to Hollywood"; Mr. Hearst's Parsons was acclaimed for her "outstanding journalistic reporting throughout the world." Not quite six years later Miss Hopper died, and it is reported that Miss Parsons lamented her passing. Did she weep because death waited in an anteroom? Because the last person with whom she had shared a chokehold on the industry was gone?

Miss Parsons may have sorrowed because all teeth and bite had been removed from her column and it had become an unimportant account of what-star-wore-what-at-what-Hollywood-party. Ofttimes these bits of puff had to be embroidered to make them the least bit newsworthy, because five hundred words of sense and consequence a day were more than her staff and she could write. No indeed, these were not the good old days when Miss Parsons paid off Nunnally Johnson with a prose knife for the assistance he had given to Thomas Wood for his piece, "The First Lady of Hollywood." Published in the *Saturday Evening Post* of July 15, 1939, the article revealed that in the knowledge bank of Miss Parsons—Gabriele D'Annunzio's mistress was a famous Italian actress named Il Duce (some decades later she announced Paramount Studios' intention to film Leon Uris's biography of Arma Geddon). To prove she could have the last word in print, Miss Parsons reported: "I ran into Dorris Bowden last night. She used to be such a pretty girl before she married." Miss Bowden was, of course, Mr. Johnson's wife.

Miss Hopper could also throw a roundhouse to jar a man from testicles to teeth: "It will be ironically amusing to watch some of the scenes behind the scenes now that Dore Schary is the big noise at Metro-Goldwyn-Moscow." Only a newspaperman with a widely read column dared challenge any of the Hollywood hags who ruled the sun-blasted heath, and a memorable encounter which placed Ed Sullivan in many a private Hall of Fame is still remembered with joy and admiration. Annoyed with Miss Hopper because she was "plugging" performers to get them *without payment* on her short-lived television show (a

practice initiated by Miss Parsons when she was a radio star),
Mr. Sullivan indulged himself in some biographical sketching
that raked Miss Hopper and made her cry. "This woman used
to hang around the fringes of show business." He built rapidly
to a full head of steam: "She's no actress. She's certainly no
newspaperwoman. She's downright illiterate. She can't even
spell. She serves no higher function than playing housemother
to Conrad Hilton's junkets. And yet she's established a reign of
terror out there in Hollywood."

In their full radiance, when they wielded seemingly limitless
power in their reportage of trash, Miss Hopper had been a resident gossip and scold for *Motion Picture,* and later performed
a similar service for *Photoplay.* Louella Parsons tattled for *Cosmopolitan* (a Hearst publication) and *Photoplay* before she
rested her seat on *Modern Screen.* Sheilah Graham sniffed for
Motion Picture, which has also employed Sidney Skolsky and
Walter Winchell to prove, it seems, it is an equal-opportunity
employer. The only newcomer of promise is Rona Barrett of
Motion Picture, a pretty miss who tackles the Hollywood scene
with the breathless amazement of Louella Parsons and on some
infrequent occasions swings like Miss Hopper, whom she under-
studied at *Motion Picture.* Miss Barrett's sturdy claim to fame
has merit: on her radio spot she broke the BIG STORY—Elvis
Presley would marry his childhood sweetheart.

Gender ignored, many Hollywood columnists performed as
madams as they serviced the fan magazines with uterine tidbits
their readers could exchange without fear of intellectual infec-
tion. However, in 1968, it was no longer important that some
"famous" gossip contribute regularly to these publications; by
that late year the suggestive photograph on the cover, the
declarative confession, usually exclaimed, and the tantalizing
question, strongly suggestive of great revelation, were the circulation builders.

Although Mrs. John Kennedy had no acquaintance with
movies and had never visited the movie capital, her personality
interested the ladies of the land; thus, to improve their circulation and fortunes, the fan magazines used Mrs. Kennedy as they

might any popular star. The problem, however, was thorny: how to present her? The first clue was supplied by a number of one-shot picture-magazine concentrations on the First Lady's fashion, home, family, and past quotations on these matters. Among the first of these was *Jacqueline Kennedy,* an offering of Wykagyl Publications, which appeared on February 7, 1961, shortly after the inauguration of John F. Kennedy. There was nothing in it to offend any reader, and its good sale persuaded other publishers to rush to the presses with their interpretations of the nation's thirty-eighth First Lady.

Another publication, closer in format and vein to the fan magazines, was *Jacqueline, Beauty in the White House,* which also sold for fifty cents. This effort told "The real-life story of America's glamorous first lady," and was illustrated by "more than [a] 100 photos." Chapter headings are revealing: "First Lady and Queen of Hearts"; "Floundering!"; "The Man Nobody Talks About"; "Enter Jack Kennedy"; "Clouds on a Marriage"; "A Race for Life."

In that first year of 1961, as fan magazines dipped tentative toes in this circulation stream, they decided to pursue innocuous, inoffensive examinations of the First Family. They did not slight Mrs. Kennedy's beauty and wardrobe, to which they added frilly details of home, children, pets, and table, to assure their public that Jacqueline Kennedy really was the young matron next door, only a little more beautiful and important. *TV Star Parade and Modern Screen* (May, 1961), helped popularize the "Jackie look" by offering a benign judgment on her choice of wear. "There's no question . . . it's the look women the world over will be copying for the next four years . . . relaxed, casual and very American . . . Instead of dressing more-so than the woman in the street, she dresses less-so, and on her it looks great . . . One look at her wardrobe and you know she's a well organized shopper . . . Though she is tall and inclined to thinness Jackie Kennedy does not give the effect of having figure problems."

Does this differ too greatly from an appraisal made two years later by Françoise Sagan for *Vogue* in its July issue, wherein

Mrs. Kennedy is identified as *"the American woman,* a creature possessed of thoughtful responsibility, a healthy predilection for the good and the beautiful and the expensive, and a gift for moving through the world aware of its difficulties, its large and small joys"? Are there significant alterations of appraisal between the May, 1961, article of *TV Star Parade and Modern Screen* and that which appeared six years later in *Cosmopolitan,* after it became the most ruttish of respectable magazines for ladies? *Cosmopolitan* was still sufficiently intrigued with the stylish widow to use her photograph on its cover and allot seven of its pages to "Jackie Kennedy and Her Fabulous Clothes." The article, "The Jackie Kennedy Look," by John Weitz, and illustrated by thirty-two candid shots of Mrs. Kennedy, reduced the need for much printed copy. This enabled the magazine's readers—for the most part women who believed in the periodical's new editorial pronouncement: it was good middle-class citizenship for the American matron to do all those awful things, and, thereby, reduce the incidence of divorce—to browse among the photographs and see how even the Kennedy children were influencing the world of fashion. Indeed, John-John's coat was being copied by Bond Street and worn by Princess Margaret's son. Some lines in the article compared Caroline with her mother as a child, and the author concluded that a whole new Kennedy look might be expected in 1977, when Caroline reached her majority. Meanwhile, *Modern Screen's* June issue published a longish poem in doggerel couplets—"The Doll White House"—which, readers were told, was "A Story for Mommy to Read to Caroline on May 14."

Similar stuff is found in the September issue of *Screenland plus TV-Land,* where Dora Albert, who receives credit for "America's First Lady of Glamour," quotes Doris Fleeson, wife of Dan A. Kimball, former Secretary of the Navy and later president of Aero-Jet General: "Having Jackie Kennedy in the White House is like having your wide-eyed young daughter in a position to run things and set styles after so many years of the older generation." This sage observation gave Miss Albert pause, and she asked three significant questions: "Why has the world turned away from our film idols to copy Jackie? Why is every dress she wears hot news? Why are the fashion writers calling her the most fashionable woman in the world?" For answer, the writer turned to Ross Hunter, a movie producer whose trademark was the overdressed lady lead, and he opined that "women like to look at glamorous beautiful women in elegant surroundings."

Other magazines of this stamp hastened to establish "Jackie" as a pacesetter of style before they presented her as: The Modest but Envied First Lady; The Glamorous Political Figure Who Did Not Neglect her Children; The Withdrawn Heroine; The Shy Maid of Astolat; The Jet-Set Queen; and for a very short time, The Bereaved Widow. For a longer time she was presented as The Somebody Who Certainly Has to Get Married Again. Profitable circulation lay in these presentations, but more profits could be projected if some angle of "lifting the veil of secrecy" could be added. This was achieved by *Movie TV Secrets* (October, 1961), which, for little pocket change, told "Why Grace Kelly Was Angry at Jackie!" Princess Grace and Jacqueline Kennedy, a most natural tie-in for royal ladies, met when the President entertained Prince Rainer and Princess Grace in Washington. After some pages of coy verbiage, the reader was at last told what put Grace in a snit: she had gone to the White House for lunch—and Mrs. Kennedy had appeared in the identical dress! It was just too much, and the anonymous chronicler of this amazing bit of sewing-room history had Grace return to her hotel, where she selected another frock. Then the Princess returned to the White House; courtesy and amiability were sweeter now than the desserts offered the guests. And the President of the World Bank, the Commander in Chief of NATO, and the Security Council of the United Nations breathed more easily.

Although the July issue of *Photoplay* featured Debbie Reynolds and daughter to introduce an article of provocative title: "New Heartbreak? EDDIE'S BACK IN DEBBIE'S LIFE"— lesser typeface announced "10 ways Jack Kennedy is romantic to Jackie." In September, when Elizabeth Taylor was featured on the cover to tell women "WHAT LIZ KNOWS ABOUT LOVE—that other women don't," another article revealed "What Jack Kennedy Is Hiding from Jackie." This proved to be the pain he suffered in the lower lumbar region because of a ruptured disk. More significantly, this issue contained two letters from readers who were pleased with the magazine's July story of the "ten romantic ways."

> Your story on Jackie Kennedy was a welcome relief. I loved the picture of her and the inside story of their romance. Let's have more. I'd rather read about Jackie than Liz any day!
>
> /s/————————

> At first I was surprised that PHOTOPLAY would write about our First Lady, but after reading the story I think even Mrs. Kennedy would be pleased. I hope there will be more of the same, because I've started a scrapbook on Jackie.
>
> /s/————————

These letters certainly heartened *Photoplay*'s editors, who made history with their October cover, which again featured Jacqueline Kennedy and the proud proclamation: "JACQUELINE KENNEDY, AMERICA'S NEWEST STAR." Jim Hoffman elaborated on this in his article, whose title had some slight alteration: "ALL THE WORLD SALUTES JACQUELINE KENNEDY, America's Newest Star!" This essay, too, found favor with many readers, as attested by a letter in the November issue.

WE LOVE JACKIE!

> My friends and I are delighted to see that you're having more stories about Jackie Kennedy. We think she's just as beautiful as any star in Hollywood, and when we saw her picture on the cover of your October issue—we just flipped! Thanks, and keep the Jackie stories coming—we love her!
>
> PLEASED FANS
> Sharon, Pa.

Not to disappoint the fans, the November issue included an article by George Carpozi, whose alarum title asked the question: "Did Jackie Kennedy give the order: 'Drop Sinatra!' " This probe had an awful lot of words for the average reader to ingest, so it offered a précis to facilitate knowledge without pain. "If not Jackie . . . then who? And why? Or was such an order ever given at all? Here's the full story behind the headlines—that Frankie's in the doghouse with the White House, that the Sinatra Clan has been given the social boot." A perusal of the article reveals it to be all holes and no cheese, but the reader could look forward to the December issue of *Photoplay,* which welcomed Eddie Fisher and Liz Taylor to the cover with a neat little legend: "Behind their laughter: THE LIFE EDDIE STILL SHARES WITH DEBBIE." The cover also hailed a provocative contribution by Walter Winchell: "Adam & Evil IN HOLLYWOOD." Especially for milady, the cover hinted that within this issue was revealed "The three men in Jackie Kennedy's life." Jim Hoffman was the man to identify them as the late John Bouvier, Joseph Kennedy, and her husband. Far more revealing are some letters from readers.

> I think if I see another picture or read another story about Jackie Kennedy, I will scream.
>
> "DISGUSTED"
> Chicago, Illinois

> I was delighted to read the article on Jackie Kennedy. It was just great! I'd rather read about Mrs. Kennedy than Liz, Debbie and Eddie any day.
>
> /s/—————
> Detroit, Mich.

> When I buy a movie magazine, I want to read about films and respectable film personalities. Since PHOTO-PLAY has turned into a political propaganda sheet, I shall no longer read your Washington-oriented trash. Goodbye, goodbye, goodbye!
>
> NO NAME

Modern Screen closed the year with a censure of the movie capital, inasmuch as it published Dora Albert's instructive piece: "What Hollywood Mothers Can Learn From Jackie Kennedy About Bringing Up Children." In a matter of paragraphs, readers learned that Rita Hayworth, Joan Crawford, Lana Turner, and Elizabeth Taylor could improve themselves if they resolved to model their mother-child relationships after that of the First Lady.

What undeniable influence the First Lady had for good is related in an "Exclusive!" article in *Movie Screen Yearbook* for 1961. "HOW JACKIE KENNEDY CHANGED MY LIFE!" The entire article—which tells of "a young girl's memorable experience!"—is worthy of full recital.

I KNOW it sounds ever so dramatic to say that Jacqueline Kennedy, wife of the President of the United States, actually had something to do with changing the course of my life. I had heard that Mrs. Kennedy was rather standoffish and rarely noticed anybody outside her social circle. This is not true. Our lovely First Lady is warm, friendly, exceedingly charming. I don't think she'll ever get used to crowds, though. There is a little girl shyness about her, a reserve. Mrs. Kennedy has dignity; she is a lady—a Great Lady. Until I came face-to-face with her I didn't care if I kept house. I was tired (my mother called it lazy) all the time and much too heavy. I loathe the word fat, but that's exactly what I was. Somehow my face didn't belong to my over-sized body. I don't want to sound conceited but I am pretty—at least, I am now! Thanks to our gracious First Lady. I met Mrs. Kennedy while she was still living in Georgetown. It was a lucky day for me when she picked me out of the crowd to say a few words. She complimented me and seemed so genuinely interested in *my* thoughts. She looked so *chic,* so trim; she literally glowed, every inch of her. Right then and there I made a promise—that I, too, would be a chic lady with style, taste and grace. I would pay attention to details, important details that spell good grooming. That was six months ago. Today I weigh 110

(I used to weigh 155) and—well, my friends tell me I sort of resemble our gracious First Lady, especially when I wear my hair the "Jackie way."

So it happened. The inspiration America's misses had formerly found in movie stars for grooming and appearance had now been transferred to the First Lady. That *that* long paragraph, probably dreamed up by an anonymous free-lance writer between bites of a tunafish sandwich, would become an important blueprint for future articles about Mrs. Kennedy, was not lost on publishers and editors. There was a time, however, not too distant, when the covers and contents of fan magazines were quite different. Their appeal to the movie fan was a matter of record, their influence beyond dispute. What they were like during the golden years of silents, and the first fifteen years of sound, deserves some presentation.

CHAPTER THREE

Drugged in a Restaurant, She Barely
Escapes from an Unknown Fate;
or, "Trust Him Not,"
the Gypsy Fortune-Teller Said.

BEFORE the moving picture no more than twenty percent
of the American population had ever seen any theatrical entertainment. Now movie shows were presented in neighborhood
stores, sheds, factory lofts; throughout rural America, a traveling showman could rent the back room of a general store, part
of a barn, even the basement of the courthouse to show his
flickering images. Always, audiences were pleased. Many of the
short films were ideal for children, illiterates, and immigrants
who could follow the action through the broad gestures of stereotypical performers. They also appreciated a story as fully understood as any that was read or heard, and an actual sense of
historical participation by audiences was achieved through the
presentation of newsreels. President McKinley's inauguration,

Teddy Roosevelt and his Rough Riders, the arrival of Madame Sarah Bernhardt in New York City—these and more did much to build senses of national identity and immediacy in the United States. Movies also reduced the vast distances between the sophisticated eastern states and the cities and plains beyond the Alleghany Mountains where a true frontier still existed.

By 1910 there was a strong, insistent demand for exploitation films, and cameramen followed Theodore Roosevelt as he went on safari in Africa. At least that was what audiences believed. In fact, Colonel William N. Selig, who maintained a private animal compound in Los Angeles, merely hired an actor with some resemblance to the ex-President; makeup heightened the illusion as the look-alike stalked the wild beasts. Who could tell the difference? The public wanted such films, but even more they wanted movies about fun, about bold, adventure-some conflict between good guys and bad guys, or stories of love and affection—even about animals—to make everyone in the audience feel better.

Admissions were cheap, never more than ten cents, since nickelodeons were usually in marginal or slum neighborhoods and were patronized primarily by the poorer people, starved for entertainment. To the wonder of critics and businessmen, nickelodeons increased in number, and soon real theaters began to show movies; this created a demand for more product. Loyal audiences grew, returned to see every movie, and by 1912 the success of pictures as a popular entertainment was so well established that Adolph Zukor imported and showed with profit the French film version of *Queen Elizabeth* which featured Sarah Bernhardt. Domestically, the release of David Wark Griffith's *The Birth of a Nation* (1914) was such a financial triumph that picture companies were willing to risk substantial budgets on the production of hard-ticket attractions. By 1919 new movie theaters would have a thousand seats or more; they would also have carpeted lobbies and be redolent with intimate perfumes. More lavishly appointed in set and plot, which proved that a movie could be more than a small situation of five or ten minutes, longer feature films were assured of growing audiences.

Understandably, information about such features and the actors and actresses in the cast became increasingly important items of daily news.

Movie magazines published at the time of *The Great Train Robbery* (1903) were little more than trade catalogs. Advertising was always laudatory, and the only news the magazines carried was what new films were available to exhibitors, capsulated plot synopses, the names of distributing companies and rental prices. Mark this: the names of the cast were completely ignored. For the most part, the titles told the exhibitor all he had to know: *How Bridget Served the Salad: Undressed; The Man in the Two-Trouser Suit; A Trip to the Moon; Gertie, The Dinosaur; The Dream of a Rarebit Fiend.* Revelatory of the secret life of high society was a picture with the rare title, *How the French Nobleman Got a Wife Through the New York* Herald Tribune *Personal Columns.*

In the beginning, there were no stars, only unknown players moving across assorted feet of film hastily joined to form a situation. Pictures that told a complete story, in the manner of *Queen Elizabeth, Quo Vadis* (imported from Italy in 1913), and *The Birth of a Nation,* were still novel. Nevertheless, as they were released in greater frequency, the public insisted that it know more and more and more. Distributors and theater-owners soon sensed that moviegoers saw the shadows on the white screens as two-dimensional beings come alive in the dark. The shadows appeared to be real, they went through all the crises of real people, but—who were they? Letters sent to the studios asked for the name of the actress who made them feel so good, so anxious to see *another* picture featuring "the girl with the golden curls." Please, who is she? What is her name? Tell us about her. And who was the "Biograph Girl," the "big funny man" and the "big funny man's shrewish wife"? The studios informed the fans that the "girl with the golden curls" was Mary Pickford; Biograph's "girl" was Florence Lawrence; the big funny man and his mean wife were John Bunny and Florence Finch.

This enthusiastic interest in actors and actresses pleased yet disturbed the production companies. Quite evidently, people wanted to see their favorites again and again. But this popularity would certainly alter a profitable business practice which had established modest wages for all players—and big salaries and drawing accounts for the production executives. But there was no way to stem this interest, and soon the worst fears of company executives were realized when actors and actresses demanded as much as seventy-five dollars a week.

Among the first of the trade magazines was *Moving Picture World,* which never attempted to interest moving picture audiences, but in 1911, two magazines with such an editorial policy made their appearance. *Photoplay* and *Motion Picture* were aimed at the growing movie audiences, and their promotional brochures heralded the benefits certain to accrue to the manufacturers of articles of dress, beauty, health, and self-help who advertised in their columns. Both magazines are still on sale; along with *Modern Screen,* they represent the three most prestigious magazines that cater to the nation's voyeuristic interest in the lives and affairs of motion picture actors and actresses.

A comparison of the golden-age issues of *Photoplay* and *Motion Picture* with those on current sale readily shows the devolution of both magazines. The contemporary student will smile at the shirtwaisted ingenues who form the hearts of brightly colored flowers. He will snigger at the legend and illustration of outlandish advertisements; he may even resort to an olio leer at some of the fabrications of gesture drama or "photoplay acting," as it was called when Penrod was not yet seventeen. Contemporary standards find the contents precious, but by and large, they relate to a standard of editorial taste that, as yet, did not have to pander absolutely for commercial success.

The artistic formats of *Photoplay* and *Motion Picture* attest to the skill of A. W. Thomas of *Photoplay,* and J. Stuart Blackton, who supervised the composition of *Motion Picture.* Both magazines were printed on glossy paper and their carefully plated reproductions are better examples of popular *art nouveau.* Twenty pages or slightly more of each issue were devoted to advertisements, and it is these telltale but profitable intrusions that give age to the magazines.

In the July, 1911, issue of *Photoplay,* no less than three leading hotels in Washington, D. C., Detroit, and New York City offered welcome to readers. Along with these advertisements of distinction appeared others that attempted to sell "Real Hair Grower," "Flint's Lessons in Hypnotism," and instruction in "How to Mount Birds." Dealers were sought for Dellenbarger's Kettled Popcorn and the Uplift Press of Chicago advertised a novel well worth a dollar; its offering, *The Girl Who Disappeared,* by Clifford E. Roe, revealed how a girl was "drugged in a restaurant [and] barely escape[d] from an unknown fate."

"Little Mary," the girl of the golden curls, was twenty-two at this time, but photographs that made her look considerably younger were available in "8 characteristic poses, size $4\frac{1}{2}$ x $6\frac{1}{2}$." These could be purchased for thirty-five cents a set; a hand-colored set cost thirty cents more. "Bust developers" competed with a "new type motorcycle." One advertisement challenged the man who longed to free himself from some unrewarding work assignment in a factory:

IS HE CRAZY?

—or a man in Mississippi who is giving away a few five-acre tracts. The only condition is that figs be planted. Owner wants enough figs raised to supply a canning factory. Corporation will plant and care for your trees for $6.00 per month. Your profit should be $1,000 per year.

Mississippi had never been known as a land where figs flourished—but what had been planted there before the first seeds of cotton? Who dared say that figs could not be grown for profit in Yoknapatawpha County?

In this same issue a new film venture of Jesse L. Lasky, a former musician, was represented by a condensed version of *The Virginian* (1914), which his company had bought from Owen W. Wister. The magazine's cover featured the famous profile of Francis X. Bushman against a rainbow of pastel colors. There were 178 pages in all, the price was fifteen cents, and a sample movie title was *"Trust Him Not," the Gypsy Fortune-Teller Said.*

The historical date for the outbreak of World War I is July 28, 1914. As usual, because the medium of entertainment was reluctant to burden its customers with oppressive realities, the industry had only a limited number of war stories fit for immediate filming. Of greater concern was a limitation on the supply of cellulose nitrate, the bulk of which was diverted to the manufacture of explosives. Production of movies was cut, theatergoers had to reconcile themselves to seeing pictures twice, so they chose those in which their favorites appeared, and the industry continued to record profits. Although the best pictures about the war were made after the Allied victory, American studios made a number of features about the "men at the front" and the "women who waited for them." But slinky spies in harem garb were more the rage, and portrayals of espionage and how they vamped secrets out of good unsuspecting men were sure-fire box office.

The Battle Cry of Peace (1915) was based on Hudson Maxim's *Defenseless America.* Theodore Roosevelt recognized how strong an influence moving pictures could have on public opinion, and urged the transposition of the book to the screen. J. Stuart Blackton purchased the rights and made it into a movie that clamored for the United States to rouse itself from complacency and prepare for war. The movie heightened the public's war fever; however, in the controversy that followed, Henry Ford bought full-page newspaper advertisements to condemn the author of the book and its film version as a lackey of the munition interests and a "merchant of death."

That same year a short-lived weekly, *Moving Picture Stories,* published a unique full-page advertisement of welcome by Universal Pictures in its June 4 issue, which cordially invited anyone in the vicinity of Los Angeles to undertake a tour of education and entertainment. "Come on out to Universal City and see how movies are made. City is a great open-air studio with people and animals gathered from everywhere." The tour included a bus trip through the "back lot," lunch at the commissary and a visit to the set of pictures in production, as well as the staged enactment of stunts and other "demonstrations" of movie magic.

Carl Laemmle, the founder of Universal Pictures, had borrowed an idea from established companies which for some decades had invited tourists to visit their plants, though he would have considered charging admission at Universal City—as is now done a half century later—certain evidence of stupidity. Pictures were being made everywhere, in every park and at every beach close to Los Angeles. Mack Sennett often directed his bathing beauties at Santa Monica. The taller buildings of downtown Los Angeles were favorite locations for Harold Lloyd. In truth, Mr. Laemmle was not completely generous. His advertisements drew hundreds of tourists who later paid to see the pictures they had seen in production. Also, for the price of a box lunch, directors at Universal had hundreds of extras available at a moment's notice. Tourists were delighted to perform little bits of business so they could tell hometown friends they were in the movies. Naturally, they went to see the pictures and—if the shots were left in—they had a personal fame and immortality that a lifetime of good deeds might not match. Craft unions were then unknown, no payments were made for the shots, and more people came every week to Universal. Directly and indirectly, these tourists increased profits.

Motion Picture for February, 1915, featured photos of Lillian Russell, Beverly Bayne, and Eugene Pallette as a young, slim cowboy. Glenda Allvine had an interview with Pola Negri, and the fiery star revealed that her real surname was Chalupez. Miss Negri was despondent because so many women thought of her as a Theda Bara type who had no other purpose in life than to steal good men away from their wives. Too many untruths had been written about her, Miss Negri averred, and she wanted to set the record straight: she was an actress and not a vamp nor the mysterious "other woman."

Two months later, the advertising manager of *Motion Picture* offered a four-year summary of subscriptions to prove how

popular the magazine had become. In March, 1911, the magazine numbered 55,000 subscribers; two years later the number
was 205,000. In March, 1915, the number had grown to 275,000,
and a month later, ten thousand new subscribers had agreed
to take *Motion Picture.*

So impressive an increase in circulation was in part due to
the magazine's "Great Cast Contest," which encouraged readers
to vote for their favorite stars. "In voting," the rules read, "the
reader should have in mind an idea of forming a company
composed of the very best players in the Art. Not a question of
who is more popular, but who is best." Other magazines held
similar contests—the ideal cast for *Midsummer Night's Dream;*
the funniest thing Charlie Chaplin has ever done; should scenes
be played in a bedroom, even if the characters are married and
fully dressed?

Photoplay's circulation has increased steadily but at an arithmetic rate during the past half-century; *Standard Rate and
Data,* a publication on which advertising agencies rely, listed
the magazine's average monthly circulation in 1966 at 460,465
copies. The press run has doubled in fifty years, with strong
circulation increases in the late twenties and throughout the
thirties—when movie magazines were escapist fare for a despair-
ing nation—but with less significant increases in the next two
decades.

Motion Picture Supplement, founded in 1915, had a short
life, and its most significant contribution to the industry's history is the magazine's listing of a number of social figures who
delighted in the movies. Among these were the Duchess of
Marlborough, the Duke of Manchester, Mrs. W. K. Vanderbilt,
Jr., and Mrs. O. H. P. Belmont. Mr. and Mrs. George Gould
were so fond of movies that they had professional projection
apparatus and a screen installed in the living room of their
mansion. Why the magazine did not mention that Woodrow
Wilson was a movie buff and had ordered the installation of
motion picture equipment in the White House must remain a
small mystery.

The same month, *Motion Picture* included among its puff

pieces an article, "Inside the Camera Lens" by Alan Crosland, a respected director who would later be associated with several of John Barrymore's better pictures and make himself immortal by directing Al Jolson in *The Jazz Singer.* "My First Visit to the Movies" is a well-written article by Homer Dunne, who used the screen "spectacle" of *Judith of Bethulea* (1913), as it was directed by D. W. Griffith for Biograph, to illustrate his reactions to the medium. A reasoned, candid approach to filmmaking was also evident in Herbert Ames's article, "Analysis of a Motion Picture." Rotogravure sections toned in sepia, blue, and green, in addition to well-designed covers—often "painted from life"—made the magazines into sound examples of the printer's art. Retrospective appraisal proves that the editors of fan magazines of that-not-too-distant time sought to make their publications entertaining—but not at the full sacrifice of intelligence.

As yet, studios had not established publicity departments which rigidly supervised the activities of their stars and manufactured what they felt the press and public should know about their favorites; so interviews with movie stars were readily arranged. Writers for the fan magazines would simply drop in at the studios, the Alexandria or Hollywood Hotel, or some restaurant favored by movie people, and ask for an interview and photographs. It was that simple.

The April, 1916, issue of *Photoplay* is of particular importance to the film historian because it introduced Tom Mix to his fans. In some short span of time, this hard-riding cowboy would become the staple of Saturday afternoon kid-shows throughout the land. Long before she played Mrs. O'Leary and became involved with a cow in Old Chicago, Alice Brady told her fans how she had established a mushroom farm in the basement of her house. Less agricultural was Billie Burke, who, in the magazine's November issue, was presented as one of the leads in *Gloria's Romance,* a suspenseful serial of twenty chapters which featured gowns by Lucile, Henri Bendel, and Balcom. The serial had been written as a "motion picture novel" by Mr. and Mrs. Rupert Hughes, and relied heavily on "ro-

mance, drama, mystery [and] intrigue" as these were practiced
in Palm Beach, along New York City's Riverside Drive, and in
other enclaves of eastern wealth. Some pages later, Mary Pickford, who was now—to the surprise of many fans—a young lady
of twenty-four, endorsed Pompeian Night Cream.

December's *Photoplay* of 1918 carried an advertisement for
Fairy Soap, which asked innocently: "Have you a little Fairy in
your Home?" This issue raised its price to twenty cents, the
number of pages was reduced to 114, and Mr. James P. Quirk
took over the editor's chair. In a forceful editorial, "Let's Be
Efficient," Mr. Quirk told his readers of a government directive
that ordered all publications to reduce by ten percent the
amount of paper they used, because paper, too, was essential to
the prosecution of the war. A cover blurb gave good instruction
to the magazine's readers: "When you finish reading this magazine, place a one-cent stamp on this notice. Mail the magazine
and it will be placed in the hands of our soldiers or sailors,
destined to proceed overseas." It is forgivable to imagine a serv-
iceman standing knee-deep in mud, somewhere in a trench along
the battlefront in France; as shells burst overhead he reads a
story by Adela Rogers St. John, "Black Sheep Gish," with a subtitle that elaborated its content: "Gee, I've got a nice family—
all but me!—Says Dorothy, the Disturber!"

The serious articles still had their place, and one by John
Ten Eyck, "Making the World Safe for the Author," is enough
to make the modern writer for screen and television weep with
frustration. Mr. Ten Eyck lauded a scenario writer named Wil-
lard Mack, whom he described as a "ninety horsepower violet."
Somehow, this did not fit with the activity of a man who dared
write threatening instructions to directors on the margins of
his scripts.

> Listen, Mr. Director, this is for you. I'll murder you, as
> sure as my name is Mack, if you resort to that old trick of
> showing the girl tripping blithely up to the doctor's of-
> fice. . . . We don't give a damn about who she is, or where
> she's living, or whether she uses Jockey Club Perfume.

For Will Roger's first appearance on the screen in *Laughing Bill Hyde* (1918), Mack scribbled the following production note on the title page of the scenario:

> Show outside prison wall . . . these shots must be done at night, using an overhead arc, the same as used in prison yards. This gives us our shadows and real darkness, when the men move out of the circle of light. Please accept this as final—I will not tolerate daylight shots for these.

April, 1919, also dates a noteworthy issue of *Photoplay,* inasmuch as it carried a story about Helen Keller's appearance in her first movie, *Deliverance* (1919), based on the play of the same name. It concerned a blind nurse who triumphed over the handicaps of darkness and silence. Director George Foster instructed Miss Keller in her performance by tapping his foot against the floor to set up a vibratory code which Miss Keller understood. Less somber, hula dancer Doraldina's interview, "I'm a Wild Woman," revealed that even in the jungle she never neglected to powder her nose. Clara Kimball Young modeled the coiffure created for *Cheating Cheaters;* the hair style, which was a "combination of curl and marcelle wave," was called *Frisée la Clarayoungue.* More domestic, less sophisticated, and bucolically American, the article devoted to Bessie Love described her role in *The Enchanted Barn.*

Photoplay was the eldest, most respected of the fan magazines, and in editorial content and illustration did its best to live up to industry and community obligations. Younger magazines, such as *Motion Picture Classic,* felt less constraint, so its writers were permitted a more airy and frothy style. Therefore, Fritzi Remond—a popular writer of the time—could become rhapsodic as she exposed "The Delightful Contradictions of Gloria":

> Then, too, Gloria [Swanson] has a wonderfully imaginative mind. She loves to sit by the fire O'nights and weave a bright loom for the future. It's always interwoven with love, for the little Scandinavian wants everybody else to share her future happiness.

Occasionally, as if to persuade readers of *Photoplay* to buy another magazine, the editors of *Motion Picture Classic* offered its conception of an intellectual article. One such offering featured a philosophical interview with Henry Mestayer, a mustachioed leading man of middling reputation. Conducted by Gladys Hall, a pioneer writer of fan magazine articles, the interview with the actor was titled "The Mestayerian Theory." The opening lines bear quotation because they are a precursor of hallucinogenic Zen prose which, in some camps, passes for abstruse intellectuality:

> *The Mestayerian Theory* savors, no doubt, of Nietzsche, of Shaw—the familiar Nietzschean theory—the equally familiar Shavian theory. For the similitude is confounded at the very outset by the fact that Henry Mestayer is an absolute optimist.

Miss Hall become so enraptured with her subject and his mind that she quite forgot to mention the title of the picture Mestayer was appearing in with Grace Darling. All criticism discounted, such prose gave a periodical class. A reasonable vocabulary range also elevated the prose scoldings which James Quirk administered to actors and actresses whose conduct or judgment he faulted. This explains the impatient tone of *Photoplay*'s editorial for December, 1919, when Mr. Quirk speaks directly to the "girl with the golden curls."

> You, girl, are at the threshold of summer. We who watched you so earnestly through April flowers and May sunshine are waiting, now, to see you walk forward into the full glory of ripening June. The splendor of early womanhood awaits you. . . . Somehow, there is an anxiety in your eyes. You seem to linger, wondering if our devotion can survive the passing of the curls. . . . Sometimes, now, won't you please be a *woman* for us, depicting a woman's hopes and perils and joys? Please do not be afraid to grow up, Mary Pickford.

Miss Pickford was twenty-eight and grown up as any woman in the United States. Alas, she harkened to the advice of James Quirk, cut off her curls, and America's Sweetheart was rejected by the people who counted—the moviegoers—as an actress and *woman.*

The philosophical implications were not lost on the important men and women in the industry, to the end that Elizabeth Peltret offered the results of "An Interview in the Air," with pictures chosen to quell the doubts of the suspicious. Again, the article had a longish explanatory subtitle: "Five thousand feet up, aviator Cecil B. de Mille philosophizes at seventy miles an hour on God, the future life and womanly virtue."

The difficulty of filling the pages of fan magazines each and every month with articles related to even a smidgen of intellectual sobriety began to weigh heavily on the editors, who lightened the burdens through an increased use of trivia fillers. From a group of magazines published in 1920, one could learn that:

> Betty Blythe is no bolshevik—she just has large ambitions.
>
> King Vidor, who made "The Turn in the Road," believes in entertaining pictures, but only those entertaining pictures which carry a message to humanity.
>
> "There's a lot to this business," drawled Tom Mix, "that's nothin' but horse play."
>
> The personal epic of Count Erich Oswald Hans Carl Maria Stroheim von Nordenwall, who served his adopted country best by becoming her pictorial enemy.

Nevertheless, the ambitions of publishers and editors to make their magazines cerebral efforts persisted, and in March, 1920, Burns Mantle joined *Photoplay* to write film reviews. This particular issue also had other articles of merit: "Jubilio," by Terry Ramsaye, reviewed Will Rogers's new film; and "Clothes and Good Taste" by Elsie Ferguson made good sense. However, a discussion by Betty Shannon of "Edward of Wales as a Film

Subject" suffers more from the vapors than it does from lèse majesté.

Ten issues later, to herald the first month of 1921, *Photoplay* presented a study of Samuel Goldwyn, wherein he championed new stars and condemned the old. Octavus Roy Cohn was represented by a short story, and the first of several European travel articles was submitted by Charles Chaplin. It was the comedian's first trip abroad since he had achieved fame in Hollywood; and of his English countrymen, he asked:

> Who is it they like? That little man, or me? The mustache, the old shoes, the baggy trousers—is that what Charlie Chaplin means to them? . . . Sometimes I wonder if I am the real Charles Chaplin, or is he locked up in my dressing room in Hollywood. I feel like sending him a cable-gram:

> Charles Chaplin
> Charles Chaplin Studios
> Hollywood, California

> How are you and everything there? Everything here is all right.

> Charles Chaplin

Photoplay's first Gold Medal was presented by Quirk to Fannie Hurst after a reader's poll had favored her *Humoresque*. Significantly, this award was the only meaningful cinematic honor until the Academy of Motion Picture Arts and Sciences was founded in 1927 to publicize the industry and acknowledge its technicians and players.

However, the first great crack in the industry's public image appeared in 1922, when three scandals of national dimensions involved movie people; two of them occurred in Los Angeles, while the third was acted out in San Francisco. The newspapers had a field day, but the fan magazines, under the guidance of Quirk, cooperated with the studios through a self-imposed censorship which benefited the industry and its principals. There was a problem, Quirk admitted, and in his April, 1922, editorial, "Moral House-Cleaning," he explained the position his magazine would take in the matter of current and future scandals.

> *Photoplay* is not posing as a defender of motion pictures. It holds no brief for the purity of Hollywood. It prefers, in fact, to refrain from all discussion on the subject. But, it cannot sit by silently and behold both public and press besmirch with lies the entire rank and file of a great industry. This is why *Photoplay* has refused the recent frantic demands from newspapers for photographs of eminent actors and actresses, knowing the use to which they would be put.

So marked was Quirk's editorial discretion in such scandals that he banned mention in his magazine of the names of the director or stars involved with them. Quirk also addressed an open letter to Will H. Hayes, in which he pleaded with the industry's censorship administrator, who was critical of much in films, and especially nudity, not to judge all Hollywood by the indiscretions of less than a half dozen of its leading citizens.

Shortly thereafter, Robert Sherwood, whose plays would bring him to the attention of Franklin D. Roosevelt, became a regular contributor to the magazine. He was joined by Donald Ogden Stewart, Margaret E. Sangster, Channing Pollack, Henry Louis Mencken, and to please the ladies exclusively—Faith Baldwin. Such illustrious company certainly moved other *Photoplay* contributors to consult their dictionaries and give more attention to prose style.

But the capstone of the April, 1922, issue was the first installment of Terry Ramsaye's "The Romantic History of the Motion Picture," which would be published in 1926 as *A Million and One Nights*. This—the best journalistic history of motion pictures—traced the industry's growth through to the addition of sound to sight. How the project was conceived and put together is best told by Mr. Ramsaye:

> Late in 1920 James R. Quirk, the editor-publisher of *Photoplay Magazine,* recognizing the lack of any coherent

and authenticated record of the rise of the motion picture commissioned me to undertake the preparation of a series of twelve articles covering the subject. The preliminary survey of the field indicated so much material that the series was extended to thirty-six installments running for three years in the magazine. . . .

The enthusiastic approval of the endeavor by Mr. Quirk and access to the extensive records and files of *Photoplay* have been important to the continuance of the researches subsequent to the completion of the magazine serial version.

The publication between boards of *A Million and One Nights* was acknowledged by an overwhelming number of salutory reviews in the nation's press media; only Jim Tully of the *Saturday Review of Literature* had a petulant reaction to the book. He suggested that since the material had first been published in *Photoplay*—whose editor he had dubbed the "Mencken of the Morons"—the prose was not as polished as it might have been *if* it had appeared in a prestigious publication. Quirk devoted some of his next monthly editorial to a defense of Ramsaye and even suggested that Tully's talents might be put to better use in the preparation of fiction, where the imagination was of considerably greater importance than an ability to understand the requirements and presentation of history.

The carping reservations of Mr. Tully have been withstood by Mr. Ramsaye's book; and *Photoplay,* certain that it had made an undeniably positive contribution to American social history, relaxed and offered its readers less weighty stuff, which pleased the majority of fans who had skipped most of Ramsaye's thirty-six articles. The next crisis was whether or not the magazine was becoming "dirty." Indeed, photographs of actresses in chemise had become standard for every issue. Editors charged with the selection of such photographs were daily tested to select for reproduction stills of scantily clad chorus girls and bevies of bathing beauties, silhouette shots of a man and woman in close, intimate embrace—and even photographs of actresses willing to enhance their careers by appearing under the most transparent of veils, for ready judgment of their better points by all who cared for such work.

Daring was approved, but any photograph that might provoke more than the briefest whistle was discarded. Most of the magazine's readers were more interested in fashion than nudity, so "controversial" photographs were kept to a minimum. Popular fashion photographs, modeled by stars, were enlivened by humorous captions: "Here Is Ruth Selwyn Wearing Pants on the Outskirts of Hollywood." *Motion Picture* certainly prided itself on so clever a pun; then, in a fine display of paradigmatic ambivalence, its editors queried plantively, "Is Jackie Cooper a Midget? Skeptics cannot believe the boy wonder is eight years old!"

CHAPTER FOUR

Gossard Corsets and
"Honest and Clean Writers"

STAGGERING as this must be to snobs of American literature, the April, 1927, number of *Photoplay* offered an article by H. L. Mencken, which the Baltimore critic called "The Low-Down on Hollywood." More in keeping with the magazine's tone that year, the magazine featured a series of articles with the inclusive title, "Intimate Visits to the Homes of Famous Film Magnates." The "magnate" visited by the September, 1927, issue was Joseph P. Kennedy, father of John. Terry Ramsaye, author of the article, offered "A Picture of Joseph Kennedy," with relevant photographs of the spectacled banker, a fortune-favored man of thirty-eight, whose likeness graced the left side of the page. His wife, the young Rose, faced readers from the right. Fanned between them, as if the article was really part of a family album, were closeups of their seven children: Robert, Patricia, Eunice, Kathleen, Rosemary, John, and Joseph Patrick, Jr. Robert was almost two; John was a ten-year-old.

A successful business career in Boston had emboldened Mr. Kennedy to attempt a similar triumph in Hollywood. In a series of decisive moves he purchased two British film organizations— Film Booking Offices of America and R-C Corporation—and proved he could do more than shake hands on studio sets and view daily footage in projection rooms. Every financial detail was scrutinized by Mr. Kennedy, who pared expenses, reduced the number of employees before he reorganized shooting schedules, and arranged for the increased production of sound films. The best quote in the Ramsaye article is attributed to Marcus Loew, who was asked his opinion of Kennedy: "A banker?— Why I thought this business was only for furriers!" At the end of five years the future President's father had added five million dollars to his considerable fortune. Some ten years later, his nomination and appointment as ambassador to England rewarded a man with a record of success in every business venture to which he had given his signature.

The film magazines, flossy of appearance as befitted a form of communication devoted to fantasy's flowering, but still conservative of attitude and devoted to silent films, had at first ignored the Warner-Bell Laboratories experiments with sound. When *The Jazz Singer* was released on October 23, 1927, and made entertainment history because it was the first picture to record dialogue and musical numbers in a full-length feature, *Photoplay* was contemptuous of the movie, its star, and its sound.

THE JAZZ SINGER—Warners

Al Jolson with Vitaphone noises. . . . Jolson is no movie actor. Without his Broadway reputation, he wouldn't rate as a minor player. The only interest is his six songs.

Despite *Photoplay*'s negative notice, Al Jolson, at the age of forty-four—and by no stretch of even a fired imagination, a romantic lover or rugged frontiersman—was soon the biggest star in Hollywood. *The Singing Fool* made a profit of four million dollars, and the Warner Brothers accumulated a cash reserve that, at the proper time, would enable them to sell their films as the products of a major studio. In 1928 Warners released the first all-talking, all-sound picture, *The Lights of New York,* which destined to oblivion many millions of dollars of far better silent films completed by rival studios.

The new direction of the sound film and the calamitous demise of popular stars captured the attention of fan magazines, even when they abstained editorially from taking any hard position on the "sound controversy." Although articles to fill this demand had to be assigned to writers with some capacity for technical comprehension of the new medium, and the ability to translate the concept into simple, yet interesting prose, the magazine's problems were aggravated because Warner Brothers refused permission for relevant photographs to illustrate any articles on sound, reasoning that the opposition might learn something to help them with their technical problems. The remaining studios, technically three years behind Warners, also refused to authorize pictures, so frustrated by both sides, the magazines had to cover sound pictures in sections apart from their reviews of silent features.

Although many stars suffered, their stories were too tragic for magazines whose readers were conditioned to simple, happy endings. But what distressed the magazines was the independent attack by the recently formed Academy of Motion Picture Arts and Sciences, which, from its headquarters in the Hollywood Hotel, deplored the "scurrilous, degrading and facetious articles published about personalities in the fan magazines." As if possessed by a hematoma of rage, the Academy insisted that the magazines clean their stables, discharge all writers whose métier was scandal, and replace them with scribes sworn to truth.

These swollen demands were dismissed as unreasonable by James Quirk's editorial in the January, 1929, issue of *Photoplay.* As his vigorous prose condemned a simplistic attempt to whitewash the Hollywood scene, he emphasized the profitable cooperation that existed among the studios, their stars, and the fan magazines. Any impartial judge would agree. Quirk continued, that the magazines printed little "scurrilous, degrading and facetious" material; and the space allotted to this class of information was far, far less than could be found in the gossip columns of daily newspapers.

Four months later—in May—Quirk continued his debate in print with the Academy, which still insisted on some plan to accredit fan magazine writers. Two stars—Douglas Fairbanks, Sr., and Conrad Nagel—were prominent spokesmen for the Academy plan but Quirk attributed their hostile attitude to personal problems: Fairbanks, because several magazines had hinted that marital bliss was being dispossessed at Pickfair; Nagel, because a recent article had poked fun at him and he was also displeased with what he considered to be a tasteless layout of advertisements for Gossard Corsets.

The Academy ignored Quirk and continued with its plans to found or tie-in with some local magazine willing to print nothing but the truth about the stars. However Quirk's editorial aim seemed reasonable, everyone agreed. Even the offending magazines were willing to publish the truth—but was such publication practical? How could any magazine that printed the truth about the stars benefit either the subject of their articles or the industry? There were rounders and bounders and lechers and harpies whose public and private manners were abominable. Many of the most popular actors and actresses would have been mocked, stocked, ducked, branded, mutilated, and driven from habitat by an older Puritan society. But little of this was made public, and *Photoplay* and *Motion Picture* built their stories around the slimmest evidences of goodness and charm, for even in the worst of men and women some evidence of character—such as not robbing all blind beggars—could be exploited positively.

Pity the poor fan-magazine writer assigned to do a feature story about a star who could barely count to twelve. Truly, youth is fleeting but immaturity may have to be endured forever, so what could a writer say about a little girl from Oklahoma, who had lived all her life on a scratch-dirt farm, until by some accident she had been screen-tested and found salable? The starlet, now a star, had learned all about life from enthusiastic observance of animals, and she wanted to practice what she had seen. What hope of intelligent commentary could be expected from an alcoholic actor of tawdry private behavior who hated to be interviewed and said so in unprintable language? What noble utterances of soul might be attributed to a young, handsome leading man, who courted the most desirable women every working day but went home at night to the arms of a stunt man? What portraits of conjugal bliss could be limned when one of the most newsworthy couples in Hollywood, who had recently celebrated their silver wedding anniversary, had not even exchanged an *un*civil word for more than five years?

Many Hollywood notables, among whom were the most popular actors and actresses of the decade, reflected—in their private behavior and philosophy—the violence of daily life in America and the reckless disregard for principle which stimulated society's assault on itself. This violence and license would, in the next decade, be enlarged on by hundreds of pictures that realistically depicted the terror and destruction of an infected American social atmosphere. Certainly, these players could not be presented to the fans as they were. Business considerations decreed that reality be suppressed or altered into myths to uplift readers, which explains the practical cooperation between wise news-hens and studio publicists who had agreed to report what was innocent before they conjured up arabesque components to synthesize the stars into beings the public and its churches would buy.

Privately, the magazines cited the Academy's unrealistic demands to prove how unwise it would be for inmates to administer an asylum. Nevertheless, scurrility and burlesque in the magazines were toned down, and better fan magazines continued to maintain a considerate interest in the industry that supplied its news and most of its illustrations. In May, 1930, Quirk wrote a decent and tasteful eulogy—"Mable Normand Says Goodbye"—which made no allusion to the unhappy star's dependence on drugs and her association with the Taylor scandal; rather, he remembered her charity, generous delight in the successes of her peers, and her unfailing good humor.

When James Quirk left *Photoplay* after the September, 1932, issue and was replaced as editor by Kathryn Dougherty, the magazine still resembled sense, far more so than *Motion Picture* which—about a year later—undertook the publication of a really sappy series. "Secrets of the Stars" devoted itself to major interviews with actors and actresses as important as Joan Crawford and Clark Gable. Each article included a reproduction of a notarized affidavit made by the star, who swore the material in the article was accurate and had never before been published in a magazine or newspaper.

Fully aware how the image shaped by Quirk had placed *Photoplay* in first position among fan magazines, Miss Dougherty noted editorially (October, 1934) that the industry had responded positively to church and press criticism of sex and violence, as these were depicted and even lauded on the American screen. Individually and united, the studios publicly championed the sanitation efforts of Joe Breen, who represented the Motion Picture Producers and Distributors of America in that organization's efforts to cleanse the screen of salacity and evil. However, Miss Dougherty had cause for lamentation:

> There is another phase of the situation that is giving serious concern. A number of publications—chiefly magazines—have made it their business to print whatever they have deemed fit concerning motion pictures and motion picture players. Every pretense of a scandal, every rumor, is set forth in a manner that reeks of the scurrilous. . . . *Photoplay* has never printed an untruthful or offensive article, and I can promise that it never will.

The purpose and pledge of Miss Dougherty failed to impress Bernarr Macfadden, who in January of 1934 had added *Photoplay* to his journalistic holdings. Ruth Waterbury replaced Miss Dougherty as editor; Miss Dougherty was elevated to publisher; and by year's end she disappeared from the masthead.

Despite the efforts of responsible editors, Mr. Breen, and sermons in pulpit and press, the majority of American audi-

ences responded lickerishly to more sex, violence, and gangster-
ism in films. Editors of less responsible fan magazines capitalized
on this American liking for the keyhole by increasing their
publication of voyeuristic articles. When they were challenged
by the Academy, the MPPDA, and the studios, the magazines'
battle strategy called for an increased number of articles to
scorch the hide off the industry and its leading players. Among
the less torrid titles to articles are "How Twelve Stars Make
Love," "What's Wrecking Hollywood Marriages," "Can a Man
Love Two Women at the Same Time?" "Let's Be Civilized about
Sex," "The Sex-Jinx on Stardom," "They Name Their Next
Mates before They're Free from Ex-Mates," and "The Tragic
Story about Mary Astor's Diary."

Such articles were bad for the industry. Even the charges
against the fan magazines did the industry damage, inasmuch as
most readers of the magazines were young people who made up
the regular weekly audience at theaters. The free space given by
these magazines to future productions, pictures being shot, and
current releases made the major and minor fan magazines important to the financial health of the industry at a time when
most of the American economic plant stood idle. Nevertheless,
on August 9, 1934, the publicity directors of the major studios
issued a statement which charged "that the fan magazines have
been one of the major factors that brought about the church
attack on films."

Tension relaxed some six days later, when at a meeting of
studio publicity directors and the fan magazines' western editors, a plan was hammered out to reduce the number of accred-
ited writers for the magazines from more than three hundred
to less than sixty. The *Hollywood Reporter* revealed that the
approved correspondents on a "white list" would number only
those "writers who are established and who are noted for their
honest and clean writing." With none other would the studios
"do business"; therefore, only "honest and clean writers" would
be granted cards of admission to the studios and their sheltered
stars. At this meeting of reconciliation, representatives of the
fan magazines pledged themselves "to a policy of clean, con-

structive and honest material [and efforts] to divest our individual publications of false and otherwise salacious material, either directly stated or implied."

Photoplay's twenty-fifth anniversary was celebrated in February, 1936, which published a thin résumé of the past by Samuel Goldwyn and a perspicacious forecast of the future by Darryl F. Zanuck.

> Television is a certainty. It will come within five years. Many persons predict that the advent of television in the home will mean the end of the theater as we know it. They contend that no one will go to the theater when he can sit at home, turn a dial, and get entertainment in sound and vision.

By 1940 the depression was almost over, the American demand for anodynes was replaced by full employment and pay checks, and McFadden Publications announced on November 27, 1940, that *Movie Mirror* would merge with *Photoplay*. Good color paintings and photographs of stars were eliminated, and the issue price was reduced from a quarter to a dime. The poor color photograph which graced the cover of the "new" *Photoplay* was compensated for by the introduction of "Fearless," a dauntless writer who promised to reveal heretofore concealed sketetons he had unearthed in Hollywood's closets. Truly, no one cared. The war put many of Hollywood's heroes in uniforms, which they wore bravely on the Hal Roach lot, and screen ladies began to bake cookies and appear at the USO. In Hollywood and elsewhere in the land, it was deemed patriotic, even heroic, for young women to give themselves to brave young soldiers on their way to distant battlefields. Sex, ever a concomitant of war, became ordinary. In all candor, could anyone take issue with violence when it was used to portray how awful the Axis powers were in their uses of brutality, and how necessary it was to use violence to make their soldiers casualties or prisoners?

CHAPTER FIVE

*The Roman Spring—
and Summer, too—
of Mrs. Kennedy*

ON August 14, 1945, the Japanese Empire surrendered unconditionally; short months thereafter, Hollywood's studios
unconditionally liberated their stars. Awakened rudely into
reality, most of them were psychologically naked as infants and
far less secure. Unprotected, no longer shielded from fact by
studio publicists, without unreleased films to make news for
them, more talented actors and actresses—who had the ability to
remember lines and give sustained performances of two hours—
turned toward Broadway and signaled their willingness to take
unusual cuts in salary, adulation, and creature comforts for the
privilege of appearing on the legitimate stage. Less prestigious
stars turned to summer stock, or they attempted club and cab-
aret appearances. Only a handful of stars had any standing at
the box office or financing banks, and they formed their own
production companies or signed for independent film ventures

in Europe. Still others, who had shown financial sobriety, resigned themselves to the balms of solvency, sound investments, and large estates. The most level-headed of the lot went into analysis, which helped them adjust to losses of fame, worship, and a return to mortal state.

Meanwhile, dependent on the political sense and sympathy of its citizens, Hollywood girded itself for invasion or liberation by Congressman J. Parnell Thomas and his House Committee on Un-American Activities, whose investigation would be aided by members of the Motion Picture Alliance for the Preservation of American Ideals, the International Alliance of Theatrical Stage Employees and Motion Picture Machine Operators of the United States, the Association of Motion Picture Producers at Los Angeles, and a mixed bag of patriots whose political philosophy had been formed by reading Carroll John Daly's stories in *Black Mask* of Race Williams, for whom all Asiatics and most foreigners, especially if they originated in Eastern Europe, were compleat villains.

Although some attention was accorded actors, directors, and producers, the Committee concentrated hard on Hollywood's writers. What plots and cabals the hearings revealed have never been determined, but their lynch-atmosphere contributed markedly to a destruction of morale and to the exile—for more than a decade—of most of the men and women subpoenaed by the Committee or "named" by its cooperative witnesses. That one or more of the original group, who refused to answer the Committee's questions and were sentenced to one-year terms for contempt of Congress, did their time in the same penitentiary with J. Parnell Thomas, after he was sentenced to prison for a breach of the public trust, is an irony the industry neither sees nor comprehends.

The hearings gave movies the sort of publicity only determined lunatics bent on self-destruction would welcome; television became a reality, and the man home from the wars refused to be cooped up in a theater when he could be at home, in bed, reading a good book he had bought in India, or Japan, or under the counter at Brentano's in Paris. After four years of

C-rations, who could blame him? And women had less and less time for matinee movies because they were doing more laundry and cooking, putting in more sacktime and making their individual contributions to the population explosion.

Weekly movie admissions declined by the millions; as theater attendance shrank, popcorn became the margin of profit that kept many doors open. If popcorn sales fell, theaters closed. Meanwhile, television became a commercial reality, and the new industry created its own stars, many of whom had never received even the smallest notice from a fan magazine. The precipitous decline of movie production bore directly on the fan magazines, which also began to suffer loss of sales and related advertising revenues.

Never before, in their forty-year history, had the magazines been denied inspiration, photographs, or topical product. Interviews with stars, the mainstays of fan magazine format, were of negative value unless the subjects were active, popular, or notorious. Studios reduced their publicity and still-photograph staffs, and stars emulated this retrenchment by reducing their own expenses. Naturally enough, if a major star was appearing in a spectacular production, his studio cooperated in the placement of publicity, the distribution of new photographs and quotable witticisms attributed to the shining subject. But most of the luminaries were at liberty, and even the most tenderhearted editor would neither interview nor "quote" an actor or actress in eclipse.

Hundreds, then thousands of theaters were closed in the fifties, and this compelled eastern offices of major production companies to forbid extensive advertising in any magazine whose circulation had declined. This dictum struck hardest at the fan magazines and their reduced staffs. Then—succor came to revive the ailing magazines, and from an unexpected source. The beneficent agent was itself a magazine, whose publisher, Robert Harrison, had founded it on the simplest proposition: *Confidential* would blazon in the fullest detail possible, complete with photographs, the film capital scandals ignored or slighted by *Photoplay, Motion Picture, Modern Screen,* and its companion publications. The material had always been available; more of it was generated every week; now it was gleaned from the files of private investigators, Hollywood correspondents, even from stars, directors, producers, and cameramen who hated other stars, directors, producers, and cameramen. Other rich sources were former studio publicists, photographers, and fan magazine writers who sold—to stay alive—information they had helped suppress. More information was supplied by room clerks, bellboys, waiters, cigarette girls, call girls—even nurses and secretaries. Where more information to nail down a story was required, the magazine which housed its resident editors, Fred and Marjorie Meade, in a good Beverly Hills house north of Santa Monica Boulevard, employed private investigators to peep and pry, substantiate the bluest rumors, and trade—at times—smaller scandals for details of larger infamies.

First published in 1952, *Confidential* quickly built its circulation to about five million copies for each issue, and—to the discomfiture of Panglossian positivists—became one of the most successful ventures in publishing history. The continued, undeserved success of a magazine no one would admit buying ripened new stands of material. People who feared they were being readied for exposure sought safety by informing on their best friends, whose vices just had to be curbed before they got into serious trouble. The most purple adjectives would not do full justice to *Confidential* as it was edited by Howard Rushmore, a former newspaperman, who instructed his writers to exile their minds and abjure charity. Seemingly, every article in *Confidential* had been prepared with an attorney looking over the shoulder of the writer. Among the more "respected" contributors of leads to stories worthy of inclusion in *Confidential*'s pages were an editor for *Time*, a Hollywood correspondent for UPI, an attorney and psychologist who had worked in tandem until both men had been barred from practice in New York, and the production executives of major studios who "punished" stubborn or recalcitrant stars for scorning commands and feasances.

A time would come when *Confidential* would be a defendant in the dock, but before this came to pass no Hollywood personage seemed safe. Naturally enough, eastern executives of major motion picture companies blamed the western studio officers for making possible this offensive and dangerous magazine. No question of it, if they had exercised stricter supervision over their contract stars and free-lance players, if they had suspended or discharged stars who violated the acceptable moral code of the corn-belt states, if they had driven the deviants and prostitutes and gamblers and adventurers and panderers out of Hollywood—none of this would have ever become print.

But the damage was done. To repair this damage and prevent further destruction became the order of the day, and as studio executives ordered their messengers to buy up every copy of *Confidential* they could find, they also had to purchase copies of a spawn of magazines imitative of *Confidential* in form and format. If their stars' names were listed in the tables of content, they moaned and talked of suicide. Naturally enough, they chortled over the misdeeds of their competitors' actors and actresses, described in the closest approximation to clinical detail or pornography without any claim to redeeming social value.

So counterpointed, a combination of pain and pleasure produced nothing to inhibit the success of *Confidential*. Equally important, the current state of fan loyalty was appraised by the production companies, their stars, and the publishers of fan magazines, who concluded that former readers of these slipping magazines now bought and enjoyed *Confidential,* whose back issues commanded a larger price than those in current circulation. One story that bore rereading and amused the groundlings concerned itself with the aphrodisiac favored by a popular leading man: Cornflakes. A bartender, who serviced two stars of first magnitude with straight and mixed drinks and services, sold the story of his adventure to *Confidential* for a sum that covered his purchase of a small restaurant complete with a liquor license. Unsophisticated critics of his ethical misdeeds forecast a speedy and deserved bankruptcy. They were so wrong; both ladies thought it cute that they had set him up in business, and other ladies sought to enjoy his company. At *Confidential* he enjoyed the rank of contributing editor, unofficial but resourceful.

Because no one exposed by *Confidential* suffered in career, the fan magazines and production companies could only persuade some faded stars to undertake lawsuits against the magazine. The proceedings, fully covered by the national and international press, were a hippodrome enjoyed by everyone but the plaintiffs, who were awarded inconsequential judgments against the magazine. A settlement was negotiated between the principals, which assured the plaintiffs that in future issues *Confidential* would devote itself to the same material—but with other scenes and casts of characters at home and abroad. After all, San Francisco had as many lesbians as Hollywood, so why should tourists not be told this?

Fan magazines crowed over the major part they had played in the offensive against *Confidential*, but soon enough editors of the fan magazines were called on by their publishers to suggest *immediately* positive plans to regain the thousands on thousands of readers who had defected to *Confidential*. The problem is best put by Ezra Goodman in his study of Hollywood's decline and fall:

> When a magazine like *Confidential* ran a story about Melody Myopic, shacking up with every male in sight, the fan magazines . . . could not very well keep running articles about how sweet, snow-white, wholesome and unhappy this same Melody Myopic was, because, after all, the youngsters who read the fan magazines also saw *Confidential*. So the fan magazines countered with articles like, "Is Melody Myopic Really Shacking Up with Everybody in Town?" It was the scandal-magazine formula in reverse . . . [to] say some horrible, ugly thing to point up a peachy, darling little moral.
>
> *Confidential* also pointed another moral for the fan magazine. [The magazine] gave the lie to the story that you could not get out a book dealing with studios and person-

alities unless you played ball. Not only did they get out a book, but . . . they didn't have to go to the studios for art, for stories, for anything.

Writers who had scored successes for *Confidential* and its imitators were wooed by the fan magazines for material. All their stories now required was that they be written around a title of question, an elaborate exposition of the scandalous question, and inclusion in the closing paragraphs of some sentiments that could be construed as an attempt at social redemption by at least one of the principals. The inversion of the Horatio Alger formula, which had been used in the gangster films of the thirties—success for the anti-hero up to the middle of the picture and into the eighth reel; proper punishment in the ninth—could be applied to the "new" stories of stars in the fan magazines.

Although the new editorial formula proved successful, resistance to the *Confidential* approach kept the publishers hopping as they attempted to maintain themselves in the profit columns. Thus, the appearance of a beautiful and personable First Lady, who could have been a movie star, offered the ailing fan magazines a two-pronged editorial policy certain to keep them solvent and profitable. The fan magazines would concentrate on Mrs. Kennedy, feature her on their covers—and she would be kept company by Eddie Fisher, Elizabeth Taylor, Richard Burton, and any other lady or gentleman of the screen and television tube who misbehaved.

Ten years passed before *Confidential* could make a valid attack against this flagrant journalistic practice by all the fan magazines, and it did so with a streamer across its cover of June, 1965, that identified Miami as "The 'Fairyland' Playland." Although small photographs of Richard Burton and Elizabeth Taylor signaled an important storm warning: "LIZ IS BEGINNING TO SCARE BURTON," most of the cover was definitely indebted to the editorial inspiration of the fan magazines, for it featured a photograph of the recently widowed First Lady and a moralistic censure: "Those Indecent Attacks on Jacqueline Kennedy." A four-page article by David Conway also bore the subtitle, "How the fan mags have turned the tragedy of the century into a newsstand bonanza." To emphasize its indictment, the article featured the covers of seven issues of *Motion Picture, Modern Screen,* and *Photoplay,* complete with "Jackie pictures" and teaser headlines of "Jackie stories"—before it summarized some of the sillier stories in the rival magazines.

The fan magazines could not have cared less. Now *their* circulation was far healthier than *Confidential*'s. Stories became riper and juicier for readers who savored such flavor. Where some legal action might be taken by the principals, the stories resorted to some small disguises, which often pleased readers more, for innuendo and suggestion gave them a broader area for discussion at the beauty parlor, laundromat, or while they waited to take their children home from school or dancing class. By February, 1956, *Photoplay* featured Debbie Reynolds on its cover, but teasing streamers assured prospective purchasers there was hot stuff inside. " 'Read the Truth About Me,' Pleads Kim Novak." Susan Hayward was "Trouble Bait" and Russ Tamblyn was "Too Young to Marry." The intimate story of Stewart Granger's love for Jean Simmons would be found under the title, "A Doll for Her Guy!"

When "Jackie" first made her shy debut on the covers of better magazines, and they sold well, did anyone dare doubt that she also belonged on the covers of fan magazines? However, their editors and publishers were in a quandary. Here they had built up Elizabeth Taylor and Richard Burton, they had even helped Debbie Reynolds and Eddie Fisher; now their publicity and public images had been overshadowed by a "non-star." Pragmatists, existentialists, too—accept situations as they are and attempt to make the best of them. Thus, as practical adventurers in a free economy, publishers and editors decided to feature "Jackie covers" as long as there was a strong public demand for "Jackie stories." Successive issues enabled their editors to gauge with micrometric exactitude the enormous tolerance for screaming bad taste and insipidity characteristic of the women who bought fan magazines. Reader response was beyond their wildest optimism; circulation climbed steadily, and impressed advertisers made the proper responses.

However, circulation improved even more when Elizabeth Taylor and Richard Burton joined Mrs. Kennedy on fan magazine covers, to the end that certainty of profit demanded that even if the trio had made indifferent news, they should be regarded as sales stimuli and, therefore, cover-featured. If new photographs worthy of inclusion at deadline were not to be had, art directors arranged jigsaw cutouts for Jackie-Burton-Liz, and in very short time indeed a national conditioned response was established. Purchasers who saw a photograph of Jacqueline Kennedy would think immediately of Elizabeth Taylor and what she was doing; conversely, a photograph of Debbie Reynolds or Elizabeth Taylor would conjure up the image of Mrs. Kennedy.

The most brilliant year for Jacqueline Kennedy was 1962, when both hemispheres hailed and did homage to the First Lady of the United States. The year began with an important television special in which she was the principal docent. Taped on January 16, a "Tour of the White House" was broadcast on February 14, so the nation might see what Mrs. Kennedy and her committee had done to restore and implement the grandeur of the historic building. For the occasion, Mrs. Kennedy wore a wine-colored two-piece dress with asymmetrical button closings and the sculptured stand-away collar associated with her "look." She was a First Lady.

To say that Jacqueline Kennedy was popular in 1962 with everyone would be unreal, so it pleased some hostiles that an article in *McCall's* by Claire Boothe Luce scored the First Lady for her patronage of French couturiers, which practice—as it scorned patriotism—had the effect of placing the American garment industry in a position of secondary importance. Pamela Turnure, press secretary for Mrs. Kennedy, rebutted Mrs. Luce's charges, and announced that most of the First Lady's wardrobe was styled under the Grand Old Flag.

So significant a charge and denial was reason enough for a comprehensive review and criticism by letter and editorial of the First Lady's outer wardrobe. Evidently, her color choices ranged from white to pastels to carefully selected hot shades best suited to her complexion and chestnut hair. For travel abroad Mrs. Kennedy favored Balenciaga and Givenchy, whose particular talents had created an elegant image for Audrey Hepburn. Domestically, the First Lady favored simple suits and coats styled by Ben Zuckerman (who had dressed Princess Grace), Norman Norell—who fastidiously avoided showy designs and fabrics, Sloat, Incorporated—noted for their sportswear, and Oleg Cassini—whose creations photographed well.

The shops and designers patronized by the First Lady were favored by many middle-class women of town and suburbia. Therefore, criticism of her apparel budget, which she never revealed, startled Mrs. Kennedy; she had never spent beyond her means nor made an ambition of appearing on anyone's best-dressed list. On one occasion she had told reporters that a black silk tea dress which they admired had cost either $24.95 or $34.95—she could not remember the exact sum. When she was charged with spending at least $30,000 a year on clothing, Mrs. Kennedy dismissed this as purblind fantasy, then wondered why her clothing bill should disturb anyone? Some sensible reporters suggested that Mrs. Kennedy should not be criticized for spending what it cost to look well, but so reasonable an observation failed to impress even a single female Know-Nothing. On the other hand, American men were delighted with the appearance of the First Lady, and wished that some of her style could have been granted to their overpainted, over-dressed or underdressed wives.

Yes, in 1962, as President Kennedy submitted plans for the establishment of a cabinet-level Department of Urban Affairs; as Lieutenant-Colonel John H. Glenn, Jr., became the first American to orbit the earth, and the Atomic Energy Commission agreed that employees charged with breaches of security should be permitted to confront their accusers; and a presidential order slowed the accumulation of nuclear warheads and a "quarantine" of Cuba forced the removal of Soviet missiles—the fan magazines revealed what motivated the gossip about Natalie Wood and Warren Beatty, the heartbreak behind Dinah Shore's divorce, the truth about Sammy Davis's white sister (not really a sister, just a sympathetic young woman), the child Marlon Brando brought back from Tahiti, and Anna Kashfi's refusal to "be walked out" on, the big, BIG, *BIG!* thing Connie Stevens was hiding, and what Hollywood pitfalls Troy Donahue had warned his sister against, the intelligence that Richard Burton "always [fell] in love with [his] leading ladies," which explained the *new* crisis of "love-torn" Liz, who suffered countless fears, all of them as great or greater than Vince Edwards's secret vice.

Understanding of what passed for important in the world of fact explains why the February issue of that year's *Photoplay* attempted to fathom fantasy's version of a great mystery: "Did the Kennedys Twist?" Milt Johnson, author of this piece, didn't really know; nevertheless, he assumed that readers cared.

> No one who was at the White House denies having heard it. It was Twist music all right. Definitely! Primitive, bouncey, jouncey, it couldn't be anything else but an open invitation to swing your hips. And an invitation at the White House is like a command performance, isn't it? Yet in what may be the greatest case of mass myopia in the history of social gatherings, no one can recall actually *seeing* anyone dance the Twist!

In his Ward McCallister role, Milt Johnson speculated on what White House guests might be primitive, bouncey, or jouncey—Mr. and Mrs. L. B. Johnson, Averell W. Harriman, Peter Lawford, and Oleg Cassini? Still, he could not say who had twisted.

When Mrs. Kennedy took about forty-seven million Americans through the White House, her modesty and diction disquieted some viewers—possibly the same group, who as they criticized her choices of designers and her clothing budget, believed good English sounded as it was spoken by Lucille Ball or Minnie Pearl. Indeed, color photography showed the restored rooms at their best, and the poise and presence of their chatelaine prompted fourteen nations to request prints of the tape for their stations. To implement an opportunity to present the United States as more than its stereotypical image on both sides of the Iron Curtain, Mrs. Kennedy volunteered to make explanatory comments in French and Spanish.

While Mrs. Kennedy's taped image was on two of the three major networks that televised the tour, she was abroad on goodwill visits to India and Pakistan. And at this time, newsstands in the United States carried a full range of fan magazines filled with stories about the First Lady. March's *Photoplay* used a second "Jackie" cover and posed the First Lady with Caroline. The story, "America Falls in Love Again," made a favorable comparison of Caroline, who was four and did not wear curls, with former American sweethearts—Mary Pickford and Shirley Temple—whose curls had delighted the nation in earlier decades.

TV Star Parade posed the question, "What's Ahead for the 'Royal' Babies?" To give answer, Caroline, John Jr., Princess Grace's two children, Queen Elizabeth's three young ones, as well as Princess Margaret's new baby, were all horoscoped by the magazine's resident astrologer, Madame Valinsky, a lady much taken with sidereal time, constant logarithms, primary directions, and other mystic tools of ancient Chaldea. After Madame was transported because Caroline and John Jr. were Sagittarians (the Centaur), she hastened to venture a bold possibility: "Chances are, at least from the stars, John would make another good President of the United States." And what did the stars hold for Caroline? She "would make a brilliant partner to a man in public service, where she would have a stage to perform and act upon, to use her many talents and enthusiasms." So, at least in the cloudland of astrology, it appeared likely that the First Family's children would do reasonably well in the uncertain future.

TV Radio Mirror asked its readers if they wanted to find out something very important: "Are Peter and the Wolf Hurting the Kennedys?" Although the premise was as fanciful as a fairy tale, the questioner, Bob Lardine, made no mention of the Brothers Grimm, Hans Christian Andersen, or Prokofiev as he rehashed recent "Clan" activities. Then he insisted that "Wolf" Sinatra and his buddies raised two million dollars for the Democratic party; further hurt was being done by Peter Lawford's interpretation of "a dissolute Washington Senator in the new movie, *Advise and Consent*." That Mr. Lawford's role was *not* of a "dissolute Senator" troubled neither readers nor the article's author, who never bothered to answer the question which he alone propounded: had President Kennedy asked "Clan" members to be less noisy in their claims of friendship and not embarrass his administration?

Meanwhile, the short Roman spring of Mrs. Kennedy inspired headlines that enhanced the public image of the First Lady when she left for the Eternal City in early March, where she was met by Ambassador G. Frederick Reinhardt and thousands of Italians whose cheers were matched by the warm greetings of President and Mrs. Gronchi. After some formal diplomatic receptions and dinner at the palace of Count Pecci-Blunt, Mrs. Kennedy was received in private audience by Pope John XXIII, who accepted her gift of a book and gave her, in turn, medals of his pontificate and rosaries for all her family.

Although the *Bombay Free Press Journal* urged Mrs. Kennedy to cancel her trip to India and Pakistan, the First Lady left for New Delhi and was met at arrival by Jawaharlal Nehru, who presided at the welcoming ceremonies. After a visit with President Rajendra Prasad—Mrs. Kennedy and her party visited the site of Gandhi's cremation and the All-India Medical Sciences Institute.

All of Mrs. Kennedy's official and unofficial activities and statements charmed her Indian hosts, who regretted volubly her departure for Pakistan, where she was welcomed at Lahore by President Ayub Khan after he had barred five Indian cameramen from covering her visit for American television networks. Among the gifts she received in Pakistan were two live sheep, a dagger, a leather saddle blanket, a karakul cap, and a fine riding horse. Many people, places, and events were crowded into a month of travel filmed, from first takeoff to return, by the United States Information Agency.

An overwhelming majority of Americans agreed that their First Lady had represented her country well. Photographs of her activities ranged from kneeling gracefully before the Pope to riding an elephant in Jaipur and a camel in Karachi; and in the background of every photo could be seen crowds of approving foreigners. A minority of patriots made critical observations about "other" religions, foreigners, economic waste, and the patent absurdity of sending a woman to represent the United States in lands where women played subservient and subordinate roles. But the greater number of dissenters criticized the First Lady's wardrobe, which they considered too lavish. However, Mrs. Kennedy was quoted in the Pakistani press that—in her opinion—reactionary influences and spokesmen in the United States were best ignored.

Some headlines were devoted to a denial by Assistant White House Press Secretary Jay W. Gildner that Mrs. Kennedy was pregnant. Such denial did not suffice for Beverly Linet of *Modern Screen,* who in the August issue asked—"ANOTHER BABY FOR JACQUELINE KENNEDY?" The excuse for the article was the author's statement: "rumors spread like wildfire throughout the capitals of the world. In smart salons and at embassy functions, young matrons whispered it over their teacups." More remarkable than even the total abandonment of taste was the article's quotation of Dorothy Kilgallen, a prominent eastern asp of the dirty brassiere-strap set, who wondered petulantly, "Has the U. S. Been Scooped on Jackie?" Her query inferred that Mrs. Kennedy had been disloyal to the journalists of her country because "it would be nice to let [our] citizens in on the news if it is true."

Mrs. Kennedy returned from her Asiatic tour on March 29. After a short visit with her family and the press, she left to see her father-in-law, who had suffered a serious stroke. On her return to Washington the second week of April, she was appointed cochairman, with Mrs. Dwight D. Eisenhower, of the National Cultural Center. Mrs. Kennedy also accepted the honorary chairmanship of the Washington National Ballet Foundation. At the end of April, Mrs. Kennedy arranged for Caroline's admission to Miss Porter's School in Washington. The month of May was devoted to family visits, good works related to the Red Cross and the White House Fine Arts Committee, the christening of an atomic submarine—the USS *Lafayette,* and filmed ceremonies related to a children's charity.

On May 11, Harry S Truman, a blunt man impatient of bad manners, scolded the press for referring to the First Lady as "Jackie," which, he deplored, had become a boorish but popular term of address. The gutter echelons of the working press dismissed this censure as an evidence of dotage and continued to concentrate on the First Lady—or "Jackie" as she was known to her fans, not her friends. At this time the news services distributed a photograph of Mrs. Kennedy behind curved dark glasses; this style became so popular that the Better Business Bureau was compelled to warn manufacturers against labeling their products as "Jackie Sunglasses." On May 19, Mrs. Kennedy won a prize at the Loudon Horse Show at Leesburg, Virginia; two days later the White House denied that Sardar—the horse gifted to her by the Pakistanis—had received preferential treatment on his journey to the United States. Such minor sniping was ignored by much of the press, for the next day Mrs. Kennedy was awarded a television Emmy for her "Tour of the White House."

The fan magazines, which had left "Jackie" alone during much of April and May, compensated for their lack of attention in June, most significantly in an article by Art Buchwald for *TV Radio Mirror:* "An Insider's Guide to the White House —What You *Didn't* See on TV. . . ." What "You *Didn't* See" was never revealed; rather, the popular columnist offered the point-rating system of a fashionable game he had invented.

If you're invited for a state dinner at the White House to hear Pablo Casals, you get four points.

If you're invited to a private dinner at the White House and asked to stay for the evening, you get six points. If you're asked to come in after dinner for dancing, three points, but you get an extra point if it turns into a Twist party.

If the President dances with your wife, or if you dance with Mrs. Kennedy, you automatically get twenty points. . . .

After President Kennedy, the most sought after invitations are those given by Robert and Ethel Kennedy. You get ten points if you're invited to their house, and seven extra if you're thrown in the swimming pool. . . .

If you go to a Washington restaurant with an ambassador from one of the African countries and you get served, you get fifty points.

Arbiter elegantiarum, no matter their address, decided pushing fully clad people into swimming pools was fun, and during the summer of 1962 such activity became a popular American frivolity. Certainly, most Americans ignored the spoof's trenchant paragraph which dealt with segregation as it was still practiced in the nation's capital and too much of the United States. This was not fun, but reality; still, what was a decent man to do if he wanted to keep his neighborhood prime, his business investment secure?

Modern Screen featured "The Complete Life Story of Jacqueline Kennedy," by Florence Epstein, who fended spoken and written charges of offensive concentration on "Jackie" by her magazine with a righteous explanation that revealed in what role *Modern Screen* and similar publications had cast the First Lady: she was a star!

A country that has always been celebrity struck—while reserving the democratic right to make and break celebrities over night—has apparently found Jacqueline Kennedy the embodiment of an American dream. That is why she is front page copy every day of the week. That is why her story is not out of place in a magazine called MODERN SCREEN. Mrs. Kennedy is living a role that few actresses could play, and she brings to that role a "star quality" which has transformed the White House into the most exciting home in America.

The occupants of the White House were beautiful actors, romantic leaders, and the First Lady had "star quality." Anyone who had ever gone to an American movie was aware of the industry's practice—to pair equal stars and surround them with featured players of lesser magnitude. Therefore, it had at last come to pass that the world's longest and most exciting movie was being performed every hour of every day at the White House and in locales throughout the world related to this master set. To record this living movie and assure its proper critical place in American and international history was the contemporary historic dedication of the fan magazines. Now they knew how to deal with "Jackie," her consort, children, family and friends, and anyone else unlucky enough to fall into the compost. The fan magazines, in 1962 and throughout the President's term or terms of office, would treat the White House as a Ruritanian castle, and its occupants would act out Molnar-Strauss-Fledermaus-Chocolate Soldier-Merry Widow roles. With luck, it would be better than going to Maxim's. . . .

In a hurry to get the new editorial policy rolling, June's *Photoplay* featured their first cover of "Jackie" and "Liz." Jill Lee hailed them as "America's two queens" and as proof of homage promised "a comparison of their days and nights! How they raise their children! How they treat their men!" In an accompanying article, "What Hollywood Says about Jackie," the statements of a number of stars offer illuminating glimpses into the carapaced cerebration of performers.

JANE FONDA: "Mrs. Kennedy was never meant to be First Lady. I've met her and she is so terribly shy."

TROY DONAHUE: "If Jackie Kennedy is in public demand, then, of course her pictures should be shown. . . . Yes, she's just the kind of girl the new Troy Donahue would like to date."

ROBERT CONRAD: "Hurray for *Photoplay!* Jackie's a swinger."

EDD BYRNES: "She's a doll."

JAYNE MANSFIELD: "As a woman who is trying to get everything out of life myself, I salute Mrs. Kennedy."

CYNTHIA PEPPER: "I certainly don't approve her being in *Photoplay.* I mean next thing they'll be wanting her for a movie! She'd probably do very well—but she's the President's wife. The President's wife should be above all that."

DINA MERRILL: "I think she's terribly attractive and a wonderful First Lady. But, as a Republican, does this mean we have to run Elizabeth Taylor on our ticket in 1964? Seriously, I've known her for many years and think she's a woman of great taste and charm."

PAUL ANKA: "I've just returned from a tour of most of the major countries of the world, and I'm very pleased Jacqueline Kennedy has made a tremendous impression on young people all over. I noticed young girls, who three or four years ago dressed like Brigitte Bardot, now have the 'Jackie' look."

CONNIE STEVENS: "She has had too much of the wrong kind of publicity. I think it's all right for her to be in the news, or even in women's service magazines—but on the cover of *Photoplay!* It doesn't seem right to me at all."

That same month—June—*Motion Picture* featured Connie Stevens on their cover. Companions to revelation of what Miss Stevens was hiding were pieces on "RICHARD BURTON— THE LADYKILLER & LIZ," "SUICIDE ATTEMPT! Tony Perkins' Darkest Hour!" "VINCE EDWARDS: Marry the Girl before It's Too Late." Included in this issue was a piece by Steve Kahn, who asked: "THE KENNEDYS: Should They Pay the Star Penalty?" The article denigrated the efforts of rival magazines, and through a quantitative analysis of their contents suggested that all other magazines "call a halt to the publicity which is turning the White House and its attractive tenants into a three ring circus." The article's efforts at sobriety fell flat because the author included a number of fatuous comments on the Kennedys by show-business personalities. Among the more startling is Angie Dickinson's statement that "The President and Jackie are very alive and hip people."

The First Lady celebrated her birthday in July, and that month's *Motion Picture* atoned for the previous month's piety by the inclusion of an informative piece by Jim Williams on "How Jackie Kennedy Became a Movie Star," which treated of the film coverage given to Mrs. Kennedy's visits to India and Pakistan. A companion piece in *Movie Screen Yearbook,* sandwiched by the editors between "How Hollywood Changed Hayley Mills" and "Rock Hudson's Tender Love Story," bore a thrilling title of much promise. "Jacqueline Kennedy's Movie Career" told—without corroboration—how, after Mrs. Kennedy was seen on television, "movie offers . . . poured in by the hundreds."

More specific, and therefore of greater appeal to the fans, was an article in the *Special Year Book, Movie TV Secrets* (1962), which told of a "Ten Million Dollar Movie Contract for Jackie Kennedy." The article had first appeared in the February, 1962, issue of *Movie TV Secrets,* when Laura Jackson had reported how a "famed movie producer [had] offered 10 million dollars to Jackie Kennedy for a role in a documentary film." Naturally, she had refused and her eyes "flash[ed] dangerously. . . . Jackie Kennedy was angry. Very angry."

Certainly, some readers may have been interested in the career of the "famed movie producer." The article, however, offered no information on him, and a check of reference sources in the library of the Academy of Motion Picture Arts and Sciences was equally negative. No mention of him could be found in the library's index or biographical file; and there were no entries for him in the *Biographical Encyclopedia of Who's*

Who in the American Theater (1966), *The Film Daily Year-book of Motion Pictures* (1967), or the 1968 edition of the *International Motion Picture Almanac.*

Not content to let the fantasy fade, the magazine ended the account of the ten-million-dollar offer and rejection with a question addressed to its readers: "How do you feel about the issue? Should Jackie Kennedy accept a ten-million-dollar contract from Hollywood? Send your opinion to MOVIE TV SECRETS, 2 West 45th Street, New York City, New York."

The year wasn't over. The *papparazzi* had managed to annoy Mrs. Kennedy and her daughter when they had returned to Ravello for an August holiday at the villa of her sister, Princess Lee Radziwill. But their efforts were amateurish, even kind, compared with what that portion of the American press devoted to movie fans had in store for Mrs. Kennedy during the autumn and winter months of 1962.

CHAPTER SIX

Photoplay's *Jackie Kennedy Poll.*
Has Jackie Gone Too Far—
or Has Reverend Ray?
Be the Judge!

I F we accept fan magazines as social sensors of the movies and their players—as the fans want them to be—the peer group at which these magazines is aimed is united by a fervor religious faith has never achieved in this century. Age, class, condition of life, opportunity for achievement, tradition, propriety—all these are eliminated by the group's unswerving dedication to ignorance, fantasy, and an ambivalent interest in sex and its practice. In a projection which is no more startling than the disordered world around us, it is not inconceivable that the United States of the future will be a country governed by a president elected to office because everyone in his family has "star quality." The nation's media would keep the electorate stupefied by presenting the President and his family as the principal players of a

91

continuing melodrama. Meanwhile, the affairs of government, for good or bad, progress or decline, peace or war, enoblement or subjugation of the human condition, would be the concern of an anonymous, self-perpetuating group who—in moments of crisis—would order an increase in the melodramatic complexity of human relationships in the President's family. This would keep the electorate blind and contented.

An example of such drama was presented by *Modern Screen* (September, 1962) in Bethel Every's offering, "Exposed! The Threat to Jacqueline Kennedy and Her Family." Manufactured from the fact that all public figures receive crank mail, much of it obscene and threatening, Miss Every drew the conclusion that if some disgruntled, anonymous malcontent should fail in his attempt to destroy the President, he might succeed in destroying the President and First Lady by committing a violence against their children. That such an article might trigger criminal activity against the Kennedy children may not have occurred to the editor and publisher of *Modern Screen*. But the article left its readers unfulfilled; it only *suggested* what might happen; but nothing had happened, and in the established course of melodrama—something *should* happen. Readers waited impatiently. Not that they sanctioned the illegal irrationality—but in terms of drama its commission made for real excitement.

There is hope, however. During the autumn months of 1962, as thousands of leaves fell from the trees on the White House grounds, several hundreds of angry letters, prompted by the appearance of "Jackie" articles and photographs in the pulp magazines devoted to movie-fanism and olio romance, were received at 1600 Pennsylvania Avenue. Equally significant and heartening, the letters proved that a sane sector of the American public was disturbed by the exploitation of the First Family in the cheapest of magazines.

Movie Stars ran a fall piece that also titillated its readers. "Is Jackie in Danger?" was an obstetrical alarm to warn the uninformed how serious were the matters of pregnancy and birth; indeed, they were ofttimes dangerous, and both mother and infant were subjected to many, many perils. Not to be left unsold at the newsstands or neglected in the beauty parlors, *Modern Screen* featured two such pieces for late summer and autumn. For August, Beverly Linet rehashed maturative rumors in "Another Baby for Jacqueline Kennedy?" The September issue dealt with the continuing possibility of physical danger to Jacqueline Kennedy and her family.

But drama of a different sort was generated in an October offering by Bethel Every, dramatically titled—"Jacqueline Kennedy's Sacrifice for Her Husband!" Imagine, Mrs. Kennedy went to Ravello *alone* because affairs of state precluded their going on vacation together. This lonesome vacation in turn inspired the November article—"Jackie's Daring Photos that Started Talk!"—which prompted *Modern Screen* to discuss again the photograph of the First Lady in *that* bikini.

Motion Picture only granted two fall stories to Mrs. Kennedy: "The Love Story of the Year—The Behind-the-Scenes Story of Jackie Kennedy's Courtship," as it was chronicled by Ed De Blasio, and a December piece by Jim Hoffman, which put Caroline Kennedy on the front cover. Hands clasped prayerfully, Caroline drew attention to a question that pleaded for answer: "How Long Can They Hide the Truth from Caroline Kennedy?" "No matter how much the Kennedys may regret it, Caroline cannot be shielded from the facts forever. Though she's too young to read, she has ears that hear the whispers . . . eyes to see the telltale expressions all around her! . . . How long can her parents hide the truth from Caroline Kennedy—that she is a celebrity, a star in her own right, and that father and mother aren't just like the family next door or the folks down the street?" This adjunctive inquiry was rhetorical. Certainly, Caroline's parents were "not the family next door." Would the "family next door" be linked to an exposure of "Vince Edwards's Secret Vice?"

The fair number of letters addressed to the White House to protest the commercial use made of the First Family by a blatantly uninhibited breed of magazines that seemingly had abandoned Hollywood keyholes for a tree perch in Lafayette Park, demanded some reply. Although there were occasions

when John Kennedy used printed cards or form letters to acknowledge mass mailings—such as family birthdays or national
holidays, as a matter of personal policy the President was un-
usually scrupulous about answering all mail addressed to him.
He employed secretaries to prepare appropriate replies and if
time permitted, he signed these letters; otherwise, they bore a
facsimile of his signature. But such routine responses could not
be sent to people who protested the bad manners of the fan
magazines, apologized for their publication, and demanded that
some censorial action be taken against them.

It became a matter of public knowledge that the President's
staff had composed a reply to letters that called attention to the
deliberately unflattering commercial use made of his wife and
family by the fan magazines. Therefore, to test the tone, temper,
and any possible action the Kennedys might take, a number of
fan magazines assigned staff members to write letters from their
home addresses to decry the treatment received by the First
Family in these very magazines. In due time the replies to these
letters were evaluated in the offices of fan magazines. In tone
and temper the White House form letter was mild: Mrs. Kennedy was a public figure; she had, therefore, no control over
articles, photographs, and capriciously eccentric interpretations
of events with which she had been associated, or would be associated in the future. The White House neither approved nor
sanctioned the use and likeness of the First Lady by publications
of a sensational nature. But in a country where an unfettered
press was guaranteed by the Constitution, use and abuse of public figures was one of freedom's penalties.

The editors and publishers rejoiced, for even the bleakest
interpretation of this form letter by their attorneys suggested
no punitive action by the President or Mrs. Kennedy. They
could safely continue to use everyone in the First Family, particularly "Jackie," for as long a time as it seemed profitable.
Quotes from the President's form letter were published in domestic and foreign newspapers, but they made no impression on
the devotees of fan magazines, for they never read anything that
demanded an inner-directed concentration. Thus, by the ego-

adjustive process which enables the emotionally unhinged to justify the most outrageous behavior or event, the readers of fan magazines became increasingly convinced that the articles were knowledgeable pieces and that the First Family welcomed the attention shown it by the segment of the public caring about romance and pregnancy and children as well as about what people in Hollywood did and why.

Some critics favorable to the administration disapproved of the form letter's tolerance and pointed out how its content and tone—polite and aloof—could only encourage fan magazines to make greater use of "Jackie." The putative unwillingness of the White House family to do something about the offensive periodicals encouraged them to spread the base of Kennedy interest. Understandably then, *Photoplay* (September, 1962) featured Jim Hoffman's unfunny piece about "Bobby," wherein the Attorney General of the United States was introduced as "the little brother that Jack built." Hoffman then compared him to the ninety-seven-pound weakling who was no match for any man who had taken a body-building course. Relevant information to delight readers was how Bobby had met Ethel, and that the President—his own brother!—had scolded him for wearing shirts with button-down collars.

Fortunately for the occupants of the White House, there were more pressing affairs of state and obligation to demand their attention. For Mrs. Kennedy the closing months of the year had to be divided between those public appearances demanded of a First Lady and her preparations for national and private Christmas observances. In September she had attended the America's Cup Race and the formal opening of the Lincoln Art Center's Philharmonic Hall in Manhattan, where she thanked her former classmates at Miss Porter's School for their endowment of a seat in her name at the music center. At Middleburg, Virginia, she entertained President Mohammed Ayub Khan of Pakistan and showed him how well Sardar, the horse he had given her, had adjusted to a new environment. When *Mr. President* opened in Washington on September 25, Mrs. Kennedy—in the audience—received more attention than the play's principals, Nanette Fabray and Robert Ryan. Several weeks later, in October, the First Lady attended a benefit for the Red Cross; later in the week she was honored in New York by the Fine Arts Institute. This short visit enabled her to endow a seat at Lincoln Center in her father's honor. The Bolshoi Ballet Company was scheduled to perform at the White House in November, and Caroline was permitted to attend an afternoon rehearsal; in the evening the President, his wife, and invited guests saw the company in repertoire. During this time, while the First Lady entertained members of Chancellor Konrad Adenauer's party at the Executive Mansion, some fogbound members of the House and Senate attempted to make hometown capital of the United States Information Agency's plan to release domestically the film of her visit to India and Pakistan. Surprisingly enough, good sense prevailed, and plans were made to distribute the film to commercial theaters some time before Christmas.

A special project of Mrs. Kennedy was music to arouse the interest of young people, so she was pleased to announce that such a concert would be held at the White House on November 19. The entertainment was another first for the historic mansion and led an increasing number of young men and women of both political parties to identify and empathize with the handsome Chief Executive and his First Lady, who appreciated art, music, and literature.

Mrs. Kennedy spent much of December in short trips to New York City where she combined visits to her father-in-law with theater attendance. Shopping for the holidays also accounted for much of her time, and she planned to do as little as possible between Christmas and New Year's week because the year's required activities had tired her. In addition, Mrs. Kennedy had to endure *Photoplay*'s November and December issues. The first featured "Jackie and Caroline" by Cal York—with photographs of Mrs. Kennedy and her daughter at Ravello. The second was Ed De Blasio's piece, "Happy Anniversary," which informed readers that at "exactly 4:30 P.M. on Wednesday, September 12th, the President of the United States and his Jacqueline began the tenth year of their marriage." In lieu of gifts, Mr. De Blasio offered several hundred words of wilted nosegay prose to immortalize "this yearly account of their first incredibly beautiful and heartwarming nine years together." Every avenue of those years was decorated with clinquant, nothing meretricious or in poor taste was neglected, which explains why the author emphasized the "ordeal" of Mrs. Kennedy's pregnancy in 1955 and its sad conclusion.

> One gray morning, alone, she went walking along the beach. Suddenly she stumbled and fell. Normally she would have gotten up, brushed off the sand and continued walking.
>
> But she couldn't get up this time—there was something wrong, she knew; something wrong with her baby, something terribly wrong.
>
> She dug her nails deep into the sand. She screamed for help. . . .
>
> A little while later, Jackie lay in the hospital. An emergency Caesarean was performed. Her baby was removed from its mother's womb—dead. . . .
>
> The following night . . . Jack arrived at his desperately sick wife's bedside. . . .
>
> The tears—it is said—came to their eyes at exactly the same time. . . .
>
> And they wept softly together.
>
> And as their tears touched and melted into one another that night *something,* at least, was born to them: a strength and understanding that would never, could never, be taken away from them.

Strange, indeed, that after so love-story-confession-magazine a tale, the piece ended on a note of speculation about the Kennedys' *tenth* anniversary, which would be the "critical, the most challenging of all." Stranger still was the sudden alteration of tone in the article as it concluded on a series of critical indictments and boorish charges against Mrs. Kennedy. These—Mr.

De Blasio wanted everyone to believe—were made not by him but by the people behind "the whispering campaign."

> She's criticized for allowing too much publicity to be centered around herself—and her children. . . . She's criticized suddenly for the "egghead" parties she's been giving at the White House. . . . She's criticized for not having attended her husband's birthday gala . . . last spring . . . She's criticized for having spent this past summer in Newport, Hyannis Port—not to mention that stay in Italy! "Most of it," as the whisperers whisper, "without him!"

Unidentified "whisperers" are subject to something less than full credence by readers. When, however, it is possible to quote fully the source of such information, a story bears added weight. And in two stories carried by *Photoplay* in their December issue, the "whisperers" were fully identified.

The first story by Michael Joya—"Minister Attacks Jackie! Has She Gone Too Far—or Has *He*?"—was related to a good man of the cloth, the Reverend Willis J. Ray, executive secretary of the Colorado Baptist General Convention. Reverend Ray's censure took place in August, 1962, and was reported by one or more news-starved papers that circulated in Colorado and the parched Southwest. By and large, the piece had been ignored by more respected journals, but *Photoplay* took pains to reprint in entirety the August 25 interview with Reverend Ray, who had sent a letter to Senator Wayne Morse of Oregon, sharply critical of the President for his "improper" appearance on a California beach in swim trunks, while his wife, in pedal pushers, was taking the sun in Italy.

Even the papers that had cared to notice Reverend Ray, only gave him four short paragraphs. But *Photoplay* assayed the paragraphs and confirmed them as bearing a rich lode of sensation. In all goodwill the magazine decided to lengthen the holiday season and be first to give the President's wife a journalistic gift bigots and fanatics would cherish and remember; and to do so, Joya telephoned the Baptist minister, a "don't-get-me-wrong-some-of-my-best-friends-are" gentleman, who was white, Anglo-Saxon, and Protestant.

An average crypto-Christian resistant to the apostasy of tolerance, the minister was in a chatty mood as he repeated his disapproval. He had written Senator Morse, he avowed, because he was a senior statesman, "old and wise enough to talk to the President and his wife." The minister insisted that Senator Morse had answered his letter, but the reply was "private and confidential. . . . However, he did not exactly defend the Kennedys, nor did he criticize *me* for taking *my* stand."

Queried about politics, the minister's reply is interesting and worthy of full quotation.

"Are you a Democrat, Reverend Ray?"

"No, I'm a Republican," he answered. "I did not vote for Mr. Kennedy. But this is not because I am opposed to his or his wife's particular religion—we all have good friends who are Catholics. I am, of course, opposed to the hierarchy in Rome. But I must say that I admire the President's stand on separation between Church and State, very much."

"While we're on the phone with you, sir, is there anything else you'd like to say on the subject of President or Mrs. Kennedy?" we asked.

There was another pause now.

Then: "Yes, I am retiring from my present position on October 15th. And I am accepting a public relations position—for a new development near Tucson. It is a lovely place, and we were naming all of the recreation places there recently. It was quite easy to name them—for a while. For instance, we decided to call our golf course the Ike Course. We are working on a two-mile walk which we decided to call the Truman Walk. Our bicycle path will be named for Dr. Dudley White. But there was one problem. We had not been able to think of a name for our swimming pool. Until recently, that is. When certain news was made by certain *other* Kennedys. So now we are calling it just that—the Kennedy Pool." He laughed a little here.

"Swimming, I think, is very good recreation," he said. "It's just that it should be made a more private affair."

Then not laughing, he added: "And one thing more you may find interesting. I have been getting quite a bit of mail since those portions of my letters to Senator Morse concerning the First Lady and the President were printed. I guess I've received letters from every state in the Union. Some opposed me. I've been called various names. But others praised me. And these letters had one thing in common—they all agreed with me that the First Lady, especially, should not behave like a pin-up girl. After all, we just don't like to think of this as an image of the United States . . . do we?"

To conclude the article on a Gallup note, *Photoplay* decided to poll its readers. This page is an interesting example of format, inasmuch as it featured a photograph of the Reverend Willis J. Ray, who bears a striking resemblance to Lyndon Baines Johnson.

HAS JACKIE GONE TOO FAR—OR HAS REVEREND RAY? BE THE JUDGE!

VOTE NOW!

I HAVE READ REV. WILLIS RAY'S CRITICISM OF JACKIE. HERE IS MY VERDICT: (check one)

| ☐ | The criticism of Jackie is FAIR | ☐ | The criticism of Jackie is UNFAIR |

COMMENT (if you wish) _____

_____

_____

Clip and mail to:
PHOTOPLAY'S JACKIE KENNEDY POLL,
P.O. BOX 3517, Grand Central Station
New York 17, New York

Photoplay's second gift of the season rehashed the old and hallucinated statement of Louis L. Blauvelt of East Orange, New Jersey, who, in his privately printed *The Blauvelt Family Genealogy* (published in 1957, a year after his death), stated that President John F. Kennedy had been married to a twice-divorced member of his family. Whether Louis L. Blauvelt was senile or merely an indifferent genealogist is a matter of opinion, but his statement was unsupported by fact and was even termed untrue by all other Blauvelts. When the rumor was picked up by the racist-reactionary-anti-Catholic press, whose editors were firmly convinced that Christ had been born a Baptist, and south of the Mason-Dixon line, they gave prominent headlines and space to the story.

In April, somewhat tardily for the event, Pierre Salinger informed the press that Mrs. Kennedy was expecting her third child at the end of August; therefore, her state visit to Italy would be postponed until 1964. On the day following Salinger's announcement, this was page-one news in London, whose citizens have had a long and substantial history of interest in every human activity of its royal families. International interest in the anticipated birth was heightened because for the first time since 1895, a child would be born to an American president while he was in office.

In the aggregate, the reaction of fan magazines was mixed, for the announcement came at a time when they could not rush an issue onto the newsstands the very next day and they were scooped by all the newspapers and columnists. This seemed most unfair since the fan magazines had been rebuffed months before when they started rumors about the First Lady's pregnancy. However, editors of the fan magazines were somewhat consoled because now they had an opportunity to order *new* articles about the First Lady's delicate condition. This new development also presented a bright, golden opportunity to compose modern gospels about an American Mother and Child. Everyone loved a mother; if not, they should. So the magazines ordered their writers to lactate generously because the summer accouchement could be milked for many, many, many issues. Meanwhile, a survey of the first few issues in 1963 revealed that *Photoplay* (January, 1963) credited Michael Joya with giving the Ravello vacation another assessment. "Jackie and the Church—How the Trouble Started," suggested that Mrs. Kennedy had visited the Pope to get his sanction for an annulment of her sister's first marriage, which would confer validity on her present union to Prince Stanislas Radziwill.

That same month *Motion Picture* attempted to gooseflesh its readers with a scare-piece, "Jackie Kennedy's Life Is in Danger!" Why? "Because she seems unwilling to take simple precautions to protect herself. At times, in fact, it appears that the First Lady actually goes out of her way to risk injury and invite disaster!" It was now the melodramatic time to quote "a veteran observer" from a dream factory, and not to disappoint her readers, Charlotte Dinter did: "Mrs. Kennedy's actions, in my opinion, are the kind that would make a studio break its contract with her—if she had a contract in the first place, that is. . . ." Quickly disengaged from the labyrinthian rhetoric of the "veteran observer," Miss Dinter proceeded to apply her own prose switch to the First Lady for giving the slip in Ravello—that she might shop incognito—to seventy-five policemen, *carabinieri*, and American security agents. Some paragraphs later Mrs. Kennedy was again scolded for "engaging in dangerous sports," such as water-skiing: "The official count had it that she fell into the choppy water twice. Eyewitnesses, however, claim she capsized twelve times that day."

The mood established by Charlotte Dinter in January was reaffirmed in February's *Motion Picture* piece by Jim Hoffman, "A Great Lady's Last Words to Jackie Kennedy." His article was founded on the proposition that readers of any fan magazine are bereft of all intelligence and require little more than headlines and exclamatory type face to give them uterine contractions. The "last words" of Eleanor Roosevelt had not been delivered from her deathbed, but were excerpted from an NBC-TV telecast, "The World of Jacqueline Kennedy" (November 30, 1962), wherein Mrs. Roosevelt advised the young First Lady "to be herself" and treat unpleasant situations with calm dignity.

More cosmetic in theme, February's *TV Star Parade* asked rhetorically, "What's the source of Jackie's charm?" This query was answered by an anonymous writer in "How to Be Your Town's Jacqueline Kennedy." Neither money, wardrobe, position, nor beauty were required. The secret was to "be yourself."

Photoplay aced its competitors by associating a matter of gravest international importance with Joe Lyle's story in its February issue. "The Three Days Jackie Hid from the World— Her Biggest Crisis as a Wife and Mother," related to the Cuban missile crisis of October, 1962, at which time, Mr. Lyle insisted, the First Lady canceled all formal White House functions for at least three days. More domestic in theme, the magazine's March issue featured Charlotte Dinter's intimate piece, "Jackie Kennedy's Biggest Problem with Caroline"; this did not prove to be discipline, school, sharing her toys, her diet, or going to bed on time—but shielding the youngster from publicity, none of which, it seemed, was provided by the fan magazines.

A prolific and creative interpreter of banal domesticity in high places, Bethel Avery provided three articles for *Modern Screen* in the first quarter of 1963. "The Hidden Life of Jackie Kennedy" revealed how, like any other American housewife, she longed for an anonymity that would have enabled her to go to the supermarket without exciting anyone. "The Night Jackie Almost Lost Her Husband," was tied to the by-now-familiar Cuban crisis, when night after night, the President stayed up late. Cattiness best describes the March offering, "Jackie's New Rival." She was Virginia Joan Bennett, wife of Edward Kennedy, and *so* popular!

TV Radio Mirror, not so prestigious as its older relatives, but equally as sloppy, also honored Mrs. Kennedy by featuring her in its first three issues of the new year. Chrys Haranis described a daughter-in-law's "sorrow and anxiety" for Joseph P. Kennedy, whose stroke was "The Illness That's Breaking Jackie's Heart." In February, Irene Storm interpreted the Gallup poll to summarize what women liked or resented in the character, conduct, and appearance of the First Lady. The following month Leslie Valentine compared first ladies in "Eleanor Roosevelt: Her Legacy to Jackie Kennedy." Once again, substantive and qualitative analysis reveal how these three articles seemed to be culled from material that first filled the pages of better known magazines.

In the genre of magazines devoted to popular entertainment and entertainers, *Show*'s avowed editorial purpose was to be fit company on the coffee table for the *American Scholar,* the *Saturday Review, Ballet Today, Bühne, Dance, Drama Critique, Filmkritik, Modern Drama, Paris Theater, Theater Heute, Gambit, Sight and Sound,* and *Cahiers du Cinéma.* Although its ambitions were noble, *Show* did poorly in sales and circulation, so it is not surprising that in an effort to attract more readers, the editors apparently decided that whatever had increased the circulation of the fan magazines might be good for an ailing *Show.* It is no great astonishment, then, to find *Show* featuring in April, 1963, a family devoid of theatrical performers. Photographs of the President, Mrs. Kennedy, Caroline, and the nation's flag were grouped in patriotic collage. In the corner devoted to "Among the Contributors" we find a defensive paragraph to explain why *Show* had followed the example of the fan magazines and starred the First Family.

> Probably never before in American history could the residents of 1600 Pennsylvania Avenue, Washington, D. C., be so comfortably included in an issue devoted to the unreal realities of Hollywood. Today, they fit nicely, according to *Alistair Cooke,* a confirmed Kennedy-watcher (see "JFK: Author?"—October, 1962) as well as an all-American watcher for Manchester's *Guardian.* Cooke, who once dispensed his cool brand of culture via the television show, *Omnibus,* and, more lately, on the United Nations' program, *International Zone* (NBC-TV), examines the problem of Presidential privacy on page 69 with clarity, wit and historical precedent.

In Cooke's discussion of this "currently thriving form of public entertainment," he ranged between the theatrical appeal of the President's press conferences to the wild invasions of cameramen with telephoto lenses, who attempted to capture any member of the First Family in some act certain to make viewers whistle, cluck, or shake their heads. In the body of the article, Cooke noted that "The President's wife is publicly embraced on television by Leonard Bernstein, and while there were plenty of oldsters who recoiled at the sight, I know youngsters of impeccable upbringing who thought the whole vignette 'kind of cute.' "

The principal value of Mr. Cooke's survey of the show business interest in the First Family lay in its discussion of other aspects of this phenomenon than those that were the staked claims of the fan magazines. Kennedy coloring books were enormously profitable. *The First Family* album, with entertainer Vaughn Meader as the sound-alike President, sold so quickly that dime stores in Manhattan were able to sell every reject they could buy from the manufacturer. Truly, the tenants of the White House were astonished at the popularity of the album, and when the President was asked in a news conference what he thought about it, the Chief Executive forced himself to laugh and remark that Meader sounded more like Teddy. Mr. Meader began to cut his hair like the President and even to emulate his dress. On television he was a big draw. No advertiser could ask for better ratings.

CHAPTER SEVEN

The Beat of the Drums and the Sound of Distant Music

PROOF of the Kennedy administration's liberal approach to domestic affairs was evidenced by a significant announcement on April 5, 1963: Dr. Robert J. Oppenheimer, whose security clearances had been revoked in 1954 after hearings held by the Atomic Energy Commission at the request of President Eisenhower, would now receive the Enrico Fermi Prize, the Atomic Energy Commission's highest award. Plans were made for Dr. Oppenheimer to receive the award on December 2 at the White House. Other bright summer and fall nebulae involved the President's plan for a high-level conference to seek international agreement on a nuclear test ban as well as other rational steps to assure a "strategy of peace." One of the more important of these included the establishment of a "hot line" communications link between Washington and Moscow to avert "accidental war." Domestically, the President responded to the bluster of Governor George E. Wallace by federalizing the Alabama

National Guard, an action which insured the enrollment of two Negro students at the University of Alabama and the desegregation of public schools in three major cities of that state. To minimize the necessity for future shows of force, the President asked Congress to enact comprehensive civil rights legislation which would bar discrimination in all privately owned public facilities.

Social functions at the White House were reduced in number so that Mrs. Kennedy's strength might not be taxed unnecessarily. The prospects of another child and the success of the President's leadership in domestic and foreign affairs delighted leaders of his party. Unquestionably, John F. Kennedy would be renominated by the Democratic party and, in sweeping victory, carry with him all candidates of his party for office.

Yes, the time was happy, the year certainly one of promise, and old Washington hands could report to their media that life in the Executive Mansion was active and cheerful and far different from that observed during the Eisenhower administration. The President and his wife were rare tributes to youth, to taste, to American family life as it should be—with children, games, much laughter, and a variety of well-mannered and personable pets. The stock market decline of 1962 had only been a temporary matter, the gross national product was climbing steadily, and "Jackie" was still the biggest single plus-commodity on American newsstands. No Hollywood story, even if it revealed what it was like to be Marlon Brando's love slave, why Carol Burnett had eloped with another woman's husband, the reasons Liz had to give Burton a baby, how Sophia Loren was dragged into a call-girl scandal, why Debbie couldn't stop thinking of Eddie, or how Mrs. Burton planned to ruin Liz—none of these could compete with stories about the First Family. If a Martian in a spaceship had been able to beam up a number of fan magazines and had computerized the names of the persons photographed on the covers, he would have learned that Jacqueline Kennedy was the nation's greatest luminary and far more important, it seemed, than the ten top stars who brought the most money into box offices.

The popularity accorded the First Lady raises a logical question: do the persons who buy and therefore read fan magazines go to their neighborhood theaters to see their favorite stars perform? Or is it morbid curiosity about the private lives of actors and actresses rather than an interest in their performances that intrigues the fans? Barbara Stanwyck, in Hollywood since 1927, won *Photoplay*'s Gold Medal award as the most *popular* actress of 1966. No doubt this award was welcomed by Miss Stanwyck, who had not made a picture since 1965, when she appeared in a small budget affair, *The Night Walker*. However, Miss Stanwyck is the leading star of a television series, "The Big Valley." Did her exposure on thousands of family TV sets have anything to do with the write-in vote?

The choices made by fans have always puzzled dispassionate men. For example, in 1940 Bette Davis was crowned "Queen of the Movies" by Ed Sullivan. Was her "King" Clark Gable, Gary Cooper, Cary Grant, or Humphrey Bogart? No, Miss Davis reigned all year with Mickey Rooney as her consort. True to form and precedent, when readers of *Photoplay* in 1962 voted her another of the magazines Gold Medals for "Star of the Year" for her characterization in *Whatever Happened to Baby Jane?*, she reigned with television's Richard Chamberlain who, as yet, had never starred in a movie.

But neither had Mrs. Kennedy. . . . So why was she so popular with movie magazines, their writers, and readers?

On April 18, 1963, Mrs. Kennedy was named honorary chairman of a committee formed to restore Blair House. Located across from the White House, the old and historic landmark had been used most often to accommodate visiting dignitaries, though the Truman family had used it as their official residence during the 1948–1952 restoration of the White House. Mrs. Kennedy had worked such wonders with the White House that the Committee to Save Blair House realized the value and influence of her sponsorship.

Meanwhile, *Photoplay* rewarded Mrs. Kennedy by having

Charlotte Dinter cook up an old hash, "Jackie Kennedy's Biggest Problem with Caroline." This was just another warmed-over helping of the difficulties attendant on rearing a child in the White House. But there was a more somber future to consider, as Miss Dinter saw it in her crystal ball:

> Caroline Kennedy will awaken one morning and find herself in a new, indifferent world—for which she may be badly prepared. The shock of that awakening is something Jacqueline Kennedy dreads, and with good reason. Another resounding failure has been Jackie's attempt to keep Caroline out of the limelight. It is a serious failure, because so much effort and heartbreak has gone into the attempt.

The interest in child stars taken by the audiences of the sixties, whether they read or just looked, could never approximate the enthusiasm generated by the moviegoers of the twenties and thirties. But readers who passed for mothers might be interested in comparing their successes with the failures of the First Lady. However, for the most part, the adult Kennedys, and adults whose names could be linked to them, were the major concentrations of interest. Anyone who had once stood close to a young Kennedy, who had exchanged even a word (or might at some time) became a major concern of the fan magazines. Indeed, the very next month *Photoplay* reported a journey undertaken by Doug Brewer, who had visited Point Saint Esprit in France, the birthplace of Mrs. Kennedy's forebears. His purpose? Read on.

> Fortunately, right off, I ran into a fellow named Aristide, who would soon lead me to them. . . .
> "Why do you want to see the Bouviers?" he asked, quite directly.
> "To find out," I said, "if Jacqueline ever visited them— or if not, would they like her to visit them."
> "No," said the young man. "Jacqueline has never visited them or this village. . . ."

Mr. Brewer, it appeared, had run into the village town crier, a willing guide with an encyclopedic knowledge of rumors old and new, and as they strolled through the village he gave the *Photoplay* writer a history of the community and speculated volubly on why "Jackie" had not visited her relatives during her recent tour of Italy. Not all the Smiths or Thompsons or Goldbergs or Kellys are related to all the other Smiths, Thompsons, Goldbergs, or Kellys. Therefore, because two families bore the same patronymic did not mean they were related. *C'est entendu!* Proof would be forthcoming shortly. Meanwhile, Aristide insisted that the writer meet his fiancée, Marie.

At this point many readers began to wonder if Mr. Brewer would ever meet the Bouviers. *Patience, patience, s'il vous plaît.* After a chat with sprightly Marie, Aristide launched into an even more extended account of local color, historic and picturesque, and concluded with a Baedeker description of the Bridge of the Holy Ghost. At last the footsore Brewer was led to the door of Number 6 Quai de Lynes, where he was welcomed by Madame Paulette Bouvier-Souquet. At last, the writer could rest. During the visit two rather impersonal letters were shown to Mr. Brewer: one had been written by Mrs. Kennedy's secretary, Tish Baldridge; the other, from the First Lady herself, was a note of condolence to the bereaved family of "cousin Danielle [*sic!*]," who had set out for Paris to see Mrs. Kennedy and crashed his car into a tree.

At last it was time to go, and at the railroad station the scribe asked the loquacious Aristide if there was anything that he—personally—would like to say to the First Lady of the United States? The young Frenchman waxed more lyrical than a budget-tour travel folder:

> . . . "Yes—yes—I would tell her, 'To really know this village, Mme. Kennedy, slip away from me and all the rest of the crowd for a moment, if you can. And go for a while down by the river. Alone. And stand there and gaze at the Rhone. And breathe its particular scent. Its lovely scent. Plus the scents of the *mistral*—the wind from the north—

and the *platane* trees all around you, and the sun above
you and the vineyards to the south. Breathe in deeply,
Mme. Kennedy, these scents. For these are the scents of
your past. . . .' "

Fortunate indeed are readers that Mr. Brewer had met the
well-informed Aristide. Fortunate indeed are historians for the
inclusion in the article of photographs of the Bouvier family,
whose names are romantic enough to suit the needs of even the
most preposterous of domestic novelists: great great-aunt Pélagie
Bouvier, Mlle. Baudichon, and Raymond, Paulette, Mireille,
and Jacques Souquet.

That same May, *TV Radio Mirror* ignored foreign relatives
and brought its readers a heartwarming American story by Jim
Hoffman—"Jack Kennedy Found My Husband for Me"—an
account of a tearful Bronx maiden's problem:

> In front of her on the table were symbols of her grief,
> the reason for her misery, the cause of her tears. A photo-
> graph of a soldier, a newly printed wedding invitation, a
> tearstained letter, a calendar with the date December 22nd
> circled in red lipstick. . . . She looked at the photo for the
> millioneth time, but it didn't help. Instead, her tears
> flowed faster. [He] might be a billion miles away—or a
> couple of thousand. If she knew exactly where he was sta-
> tioned, it might make things more bearable. She could get
> a book out of the library and read up on the place.

After many more tears and anguished reflections on her
marine, which brought on new freshets of tears, the hopeful
bride-to-be realized what she had to do:

> From her purse, she took a pen. She went quickly to her
> own room and got a few sheets of her best stationery and
> an envelope. . . . She daubed [*sic!*] at her eyes with tissue—
> it wouldn't do to have tear-streaks on *this* letter. Then
> she began to write:
> "My dear Mr. President," . . .

Press notice of the letter helped the cause of love! Secretary of the Navy Paul B. Fay, Jr., wrote the anxious bride-to-be that her groom, a stripling of nineteen, would be transferred from Guantanamo, Cuba, to Camp Lejeune in time for the wedding. For the overjoyed lass "the reception before the wedding . . . the ceremony itself and the celebration afterwards . . . fuse into one wonderful blur of happiness."

Who could doubt that the President of the United States was not the active servant of his people? Had he not brought happiness to a girl and her fighting man? Should so good a man and his family be neglected by the press interested only in so-called important matters which plain, simple people could never understand? Thank God that there were writers like Jim Hoffman, who told Kennedy fans in the July issue of *TV Radio Mirror* about "Jackie's Danger—What She and Her Baby Doctor Are Doing to Fight It." The piece dealt intimately with past problems experienced by Mrs. Kennedy—four caesarean sections and other complications. Then, as the magazine's editors looked over the Hoffman article, they wondered if their readers knew what a caesarean section was? To make up for this lack of knowledge, a supplementary article—"Pregnancy: A Medical Report"—was included; a series of questions, addressed to Dr. W. Tennoff Reich, were answered so simply that anyone with even an average aptitude for mechanics could have become a *locum tenens* for Richard Chamberlain.

Q. WHAT IS A CAESAREAN SECTION?
A. It is a major surgical procedure for removing a baby from the uterus of the mother. The surgeon cuts through the woman's abdominal wall and through the peritoneum, opens the uterus, takes out the child, snips and clamps the umbilical cord, removes the placenta, and then, reversing the process, closes each of these openings. . . .

Among the questions asked and answered were: Was it more difficult for a woman in "her thirties" to have children? Was it more dangerous? Were "public appearances involving strain" dangerous? Were "things like that" dangerous? Every question was answered in medical journalese, which prompts but one more question: Is it too bold to suggest that after the magazine's readers had finished the Hoffman article, which made them spectators at an imaginary medical amphitheater as it dealt specifically with Mrs. John F. Kennedy's pregnancies, Dr. Reich's answers to questions about caesarean birth would enable concerned readers to picture the First Lady in every step of delivery?

And the year was only a little more than half over. . . .

After the sex that could bear children had vicariously experienced the mystery, danger, and anguish of a caesarean section, which they now understood would again be "Jackie's" lot, they were no doubt happy over a related story in the next month's *TV Radio Mirror*. With a bunny-pablum focus that could only have delighted the cute side of the American character, Chrys Haranis, whom we have already met, told her readers "How Jackie Is Telling Her Children About the New Baby." Because the writer had no *personal* knowledge of Mrs. Kennedy's approach to the subject, her piece dealt with the way Caroline *might* have been told by her father about the coming of John-John. As usual, without protest, readers were left unfulfilled because the title had promised to tell them how "Jackie" was preparing Caroline for the blessed event.

More worldly in aspect, *Motion Picture* for August included Ed De Blasio's fanciful piece—"Jackie Kennedy's Bohemian Year in Paris!" Oh, she was a wild, headstrong one, indeed, and Mr. De Blasio was just the man to tell how "Jackie" had turned up her nose at Reid Hall, the shelter for most "wealthy American girls" when she had matriculated at the Sorbonne in 1949. Rather, because she was independent of mind, the post-debutante who had graduated from Miss Porter's School and spent a year at Vassar College, decided to live in the tiny apartment of the Comtesse Robert de Renty.

This is the story of an unforgettable year in Jackie Kennedy's life, a year of delicious memories, a year whose details she has managed—until now—to keep very, very private. It was the year she turned nineteen. She had left home, sailed to Paris—carefree, sophisticated Paris where anything goes—and made a silent vow to herself, to do everything the Parisians do. She kept her promise!

Volutes flared, breathing hard, fingers tightly clutching the pages of *Motion Picture,* readers bent forward to learn all the nuances of bohemianism as they are practiced by Parisians, and that the then-future First Lady had emulated with abandoned enthusiasm. The fans were ready: *what had she done?* Plenty! Mrs. Kennedy had lived with the Countess and attended the Sorbonne. That was her "unforgettable year."

August's *Photoplay* neither speculated on Mrs. Kennedy's past nor dipped into the baby's bath for a story. Rather, with his editor's permission, James Gregory probed for a new low in public lack of taste with an account of the sleeping-pill suicide of Charlene, former wife of Igor Cassini, whose social gadabout column was written under the pseudonym of Cholly Knickerbocker. In "The Suicide that Broke Jackie's Heart" the author believed the following took place at 1600 Pennsylvania Avenue:

> In the White House flower garden, on the day of Charlene's death, Jackie Kennedy did remember—she remembered, and tried to hold back the tears. Tears of heartbreak for a friend who had died too young. . . . No, she mustn't cry anymore. There were too many people watching, and it was an important occasion of state. Tears were a luxury that no First Lady could afford in public.
>
> It was important to think of other things. Surely, even today, there must be something to be happy about. . . . And, of course, there was. Stirring within her was a wonderful secret of her own, a secret the whole world would soon come to share—the secret of a new life, with all the hope that new life brings.
>
> Yes, better to think of that, and to look to the future. For the recent past was too sad to bear.

Here again, the readers of *Photoplay* were duped. They had every right to expect something juicy from Mr. Gregory, but he had done no more than talk about the anticipated birth at Walter Reed Army Hospital. However, Mrs. Kennedy had decided to celebrate her thirty-fourth birthday at Squaw Island, Hyannis Port and since she had a troublesome medical history, emergency quarters were readied at Otis Air Force Base on Cape Cod.

Mrs. Kennedy and both children flew to Newport on June 27, where she accepted the gift of a ceramic crib fashioned by the artisans of Caltagirone, Sicily. On July 28, Mrs. Kennedy's birthday, the Marine Corps recorded and performed a song written by Rudolf Friml to commemorate the First Lady's birthday, which she spent quietly with the President and family. Outside the Kennedy enclave the wildest, most inflated rumors circulated about the luxurious alterations and decorations which had been ordered for the rooms reserved for Mrs. Kennedy at Otis Air Force Base. These rumors were given such credence that Pierre Salinger made a strong and only partially successful effort to persuade the public of their total lack of substance. By this time, speculation about the sex of the unborn child had so unnerved all members of the Kennedy family that the President, impatient with the citizens he represented, barred further preoccupation with the subject.

On Wednesday, August 7, some minutes after noon, Dr. Walsh announced the birth of Patrick Bouvier Kennedy, who weighed four pounds, ten and a half ounces, and was the first child born to a president in office in sixty-eight years. After delivery, Mrs. Kennedy received a transfusion of two pints of blood. The infant, born almost six weeks prematurely and afflicted with idiopathic respiratory distress syndrome, was rushed for intensive medical care to Boston Children's Hospital. When the President was informed of the serious condition of his younger son, he joined Mrs. Hugh Auchincloss, the First Lady's mother, at the bedside of his wife. Assured that her condition was satisfactory, the President flew to Boston to consult with staff doctors about his gravely ill son, who succumbed the next day to prematurity and hyaline membrane disease. With heavy heart the President returned to the Air Force base to be with his wife.

Understandably, but to the annoyance of some segments of public media, the President, members of his family, and close associates raised a wall of privacy around the First Lady. Although members of the press and photographers were barred, one enterprising fellow with a camera used a telephoto lens to take a photograph of Mrs. Kennedy being wheeled from the delivery room. Expressions of condolence were received from a majority of world leaders; among them Premier Khrushchev.

On August 13, Mrs. Kennedy returned to Squaw Island with her husband. Dr. Walsh issued a medical bulletin that the First Lady had made a "very satisfactory recovery"; nevertheless, she was advised to relinquish her official duties for the rest of the year. In an unsuccessful effort to squash the persistent rumor of extensive redecoration at taxpayers' expense of the quarters reserved at the base hospital for Mrs. Kennedy, UPI reported that the President had sent a personal check for $174.25 to the finance officer at Otis to pay for his wife's seven-day stay at the base hospital. This check included subsistence payments of $1.75 a day for Mrs. Kennedy, Dr. Walsh, and the Secret Service agents assigned to her staff.

Meanwhile, the fan magazines were busy, and proof of their industry is evidenced through their prodigious efforts to record the most recent dramatic events in the life of the First Lady. In *Motion Picture*'s September issue, Ed De Blasio was credited with a piece that hinted at scandal. "Jackie Kennedy: What Her Personal Maid Could Tell You!" was introduced by a sideshow-barker's screamer: "ONE WOMAN, AND ONLY *ONE*, KNOWS WHAT JACKIE IS LIKE WHEN NOBODY'S LOOKING. HERE'S EVERY INTIMATE, REVEALING DETAIL OF JACKIE'S HIDDEN LIFE!"

Three of the more revelatory tidbits divulged by the maid—Providencia ("Provy") Pardes—were: (1) "what Jackie calls the President when no one else is listening . . . Bunny": (2) "the secret passion of JFK himself . . . a noodle casserole for dinner";

and (3) "Jackie's shortcomings as a housewife . . . she's not the greatest cook in the world."

By this time, good sense should have prevailed even among the foolish types who bought fan magazines. Like rats in the laboratory of a psychologist, they should have been conditioned through frustration to realize that the banner headlines of sensation were as fradulent as the cotton candy bought at carnivals—reduced to nothing once it was mouthed by the purchaser. But the fans seemed incapable of learning, or perhaps preferred not to learn, in order to help the fan magazines pursue the fast buck. This prompted *Playboy* (June, 1967), after an editorial condemnation of the established fan-magazine practice, to note how this inconstant publishing practice succeeded best when it carried "the disparity between the cover headline and the story to its illogical extreme and [made] a grand guess-what-the-piece-is-really-about game out of the whole business."

> Human curiosity being what it is, we believe we're offering, gratis, a circulation builder that can't miss. And now let's run some examples on the projector and see how they focus:
>
> **TONY CURTIS: "I KICKED KIM NOVAK OUT OF MY BED!"**
> (Tony finds neighbor Kim tromping all over his begonias: asks her to leave his garden.)
>
> **SAL MINEO AND HAYLEY MILLS: "WE WENT TOO FAR!"**
> (Hayley and Sal, out on a date, overshoot their mark on the Pasadena Freeway.)
>
> **SIDNEY POITIER: "I STARTED A RACE RIOT!"**
> (Poitier, due to indecision, is very slow placing his bet at Santa Anita pari-mutuel window, infuriating bettors waiting in line behind him.)
>
> **ANN-MARGRET: "MY MOTHER RUINED MY LIFE!"**
> (In which she reveals how her mother inadvertently used the copy of *Life* Ann-Margret was reading to line her garbage pail.)

LIZ TAYLOR: "I DESPISE RICHARD!"
(Now a student of English history and a Shakespearean actress, Liz becomes incensed over the actions of crookback Richard III.)

DEBBIE REYNOLDS: "AM I AN UNNATURAL MOTHER?"
(How Debbie bottle-fed a kitten she found on her doorstep.)

ROCK HUDSON: "HOW I BROKE ALL TEN COMMANDMENTS!"
(When Rock was a child he appeared as Moses in a Sunday school play and dropped the Tablets onstage.)

SANDRA DEE: "FROM CALL GIRL TO MOVIE STAR!"
(Sandra reveals how a producer discovered her working as a switchboard operator.)

The headline technique burlesqued by *Playboy* had also come to the attention of *Mad,* which devoted itself to an analysis of how the big-promise-small-payoff had been employed by the true confession magazines, which might feature a lady writer who revealed that SHE HAD LIVED IN SHAME!—Shame, Mississippi.

If these pieces ever came to the attention of fan magazine editors, they were ignored; if they came to the attention of readers, they were, most likely, beyond their interpretation. So the editors continued in their efforts to widen the credibility gap. Such a course required practice, even vision, but to make the most of the premature birth and death of the President's second son required nothing more than hardshell callousness. An article by Scott Stuart in November's *Motion Picture*—"Doctors Debate: Should Jackie Have Another Baby?"—is a "good" example. Readers were ordered to conjure up the scene of "Jackie's" farewell to the officers and men at Otis Air Force Base—and what might, or should have been said.

> . . . Jackie stood motionless for a moment in her pink dress, her dark eyes still clouded with grief, and she looked around for the last time at the room in which she had

known so much hope, joy, fear, pain, despair. Then her eyes cleared. She turned to the nurse standing nearby and held out her hand with the same grace she would have shown to a reigning queen. "Thank you for all your kindness to me," she said in her soft, steady voice. "I hope that I will be back next year—to have another baby!"

It was only a word of farewell. Yet it rang around the world like a bell on Christmas Day.

The First Lady was willing to try again!

Jackie Kennedy believed she *could* have another baby. And, despite the heartbreak and the pain she had suffered, despite the fact that after five difficult pregnancies and four emergency Caesareans she had only two living children—Jackie Kennedy wanted to have another baby!

In another serving up of dross, *TV Radio Mirror* offered George Carpozi in its November special: "What the Baby's Death Is Doing to Jackie."

The White House was a-buzz with the gaiety, laughter and noise of little children. Their voices rang through the Presidental home and echoed faintly out over the spacious tree-covered lawn now laden with fallen rust-colored leaves of autumn.

Here and there the bubbly voice of a little boy can be heard drifting in the wind. It may be some incongruous or childish phrase, but he can be forgiven for not making sense, because you don't expect too much out of a not-quite-three-year-old, though he is John J. Kennedy, Jr.

Listen again and perhaps you might catch the girlish ripple of laughter, perhaps a squeal of delight, or a yelp of annoyance. Certainly even Caroline Kennedy has a right, like all little girls, to an oratorical outburst. Especially if her little brother pulls her hair. . . .

Amid this cacophony of chatter swirling out of the Presidental home, one voice is missing. A missing voice that adds inherently a painful note to the scene. It is the voice of Patrick Bouvier Kennedy—a voice never heard and never to be heard and yet, strangely missed.

When Emperor Haile Selassie visited Washington on October 1, Mrs. Kennedy interrupted her mourning to greet the Ethiopian monarch. Caroline and John particularly liked Selassie who, despite a full schedule of state functions, found time to play with both children. While Caroline sat on the Emperor's lap, John found delight in Selassie's beard.

The visiting chief-of-state departed and Mrs. Kennedy flew to New York on the first leg of a trip to Greece. At Athens she was met by her sister, Lee Radziwill, the appropriate number of American and Greek officials, and a Greek girl with a heart ailment who had been befriended by the First Lady. Mrs. Kennedy and her sister were guests at a tea given by King Paul and Queen Frederika, and they then boarded the yacht of Aristotle Socrates Onassis for a tour of the Aegean and some of the Greek islands. Among the guests were Prince Radziwill, Undersecretary of Commerce Franklin D. Roosevelt, Jr., and his wife.

A photographer snapped the First Lady as she stumbled without injury into a hole at the Temple of Apollo in Delphi. From Greece, she and her sister toured Morocco as guests of King Hassan, and a visit to the market of Marrakesh ended their holiday. Homeward bound, Mrs. Kennedy stopped in Paris, where she bought several neckties for her husband and received a bouquet of orchids from President de Gaulle.

On November 13, Mrs. Kennedy was hostess to 1,700 children serviced by the agencies sponsored by the United States Givers Fund as the Royal Highlanders Regiment, Black Watch, performed on the White House lawn. Photographs of the First Lady corroborated printed dispatches about her return to good health.

Less complimentary news was revealed through the office of Representative Glenard P. Lipscomb (R., Cal.), who condemned the USIA-United Artists' plan to make the documentary of Mrs. Kennedy's trip to India and Pakistan into a commercial feature to be shown in American theaters. With evident delight the California congressman reported Comptroller General Joseph Campbell's ruling that the USIA had neither the legal right to make the film available to United Artists nor could it enter into a distribution contract with any company.

Only the clinically anile delighted in Representative Lipscomb's churlishness, for most people were bored with the entire
matter. More took pleasure in the photographs published in
Look of the President and John-John romping in the Executive
Office. Although there was fanatic criticism by those determined
citizens who saw nothing good in starring a young, attractive,
liberal, Democratic, Catholic President in an office that should
have been held by a sound character actor who could convinc-
ingly portray an elderly, imposing, conservative, Republican,
Protestant gentleman, good mothers were pleased that the office
of President of the United States could look like their own
living rooms—when, during Spock-time, their husbands played
with the children.

The President seemed in a bitter frame of mind as he prepared to leave Washington for political fence-mending in Texas.
At his last press conference he had expressed his displeasure
over the failure of the Congress to act on a tax cut and, more
importantly for the future, the civil rights bill. He put his signature to the last documents and letters on his desk in the oval-
shaped office and shook hands with his staff and children. As he
had done so often before, John-John broke into tears because
he was being left behind. President and Mrs. Kennedy boarded
a helicopter and flew to the airport. *Air Force One* cleared the
field at 11:05 in the morning and headed south-southwest for
Texas. Not quite two full days later, at 4:34 in the morning, a
coffin containing the President's body was carried into the
White House.

For the President's family and grieved people everywhere,
1963 was reminiscent of the year 1666—when England suffered
a war with Spain, a drained exchequer, national riots provoked
by unemployment and high taxes, the plague and the Great Fire
of London—that had prompted Samuel Pepys to note in his
entry for December 31, "Thus ends this year of publick wonder
and mischief to this nation, and, therefore, generally wished by
all people to have an end."

CHAPTER EIGHT

"Lace" Mourns the Death of "Lancer" and the Fall of "Camelot."

THE Reverend William H. Dickinson, Jr., a Dallas Methodist minister, recalls that on November 20, 1963, he was a guest at a "nice, respectable dinner party [where] a personable [and] bright young couple [told everyone that they] hated the President of the United States—and that they would not care one bit if somebody did take a shot at him." Two days after the assassination, Reverend William A. Holmes delivered a sermon at the Northaven Methodist Church, in Dallas, where he scored "the hatemongers in [their] midst." Dismayed that "the spirit of assassination has been with us for some time," Reverend Holmes charged that in a Dallas elementary school "fourth grade children . . . clapped and cheered when their teacher told them of the assassination of the President."

"In the name of God," the minister asked, "what kind of city have we become?"

It is either a saintly charity or oversight that Reverend Holmes did not indict other national regions, for there was considerable jubilation and celebration of the President's murder in Plaquemines Parish, the feudal fief of Leander Perez. In Sun Valley, a suburb of Los Angeles, the right-wing peddlers of their own brand of fundamentalist patriotism were joined in *Gemütlichkeit* by former members of the German-American Bund, who preferred a better Hitler to anything democracy could offer. This disreputable lot gathered in a restaurant on Sunland Boulevard and toasted the marksmanship of Lee Harvey Oswald. Meanwhile, in Montgomery, Alabama, an attorney who was one of George C. Wallace's advisers in the fields of racism and minority repression, left his law offices to dance a jig down Dexter Street when he learned that the President had succumbed.

On the emotional level, that such shocking conduct could be evidenced in the United States stunned and frightened many citizens and even more foreign observers, who sought an immediate, all-purpose explanation of this shocking ambivalence in the American character. The average citizen was devoted to the American myths of patriotism, the Declaration of Independence and the Preamble to the Constitution; his eyes would fill with tears at the raising of the nation's flag and merely to say "the spirit of 1776" induced an objective correlative of embattled farmers at Concord Bridge, valiant drummers and fifers preceding gallant Minutemen. And the same was true of every American engagement fought by its troops, sailors, and marines in almost two centuries of national history. Knowing this, feeling this, honoring this—how could Americans be so rabid in their hatred, so vindictive, so contemptuous of people they considered their inferiors, so callous in flinging their paranoia in the face of the world? Might not Adolf Hitler's misfortune have been that he had come to power in Germany rather than the United States?

On November 25, as the body of President Kennedy, now a symbol of a thousand days, lay in state under the great rotunda of the Capitol, one aspect of the nation's normlessness—or anomie—could be found at thousands of magazine stands where fan magazines were sold. As the body of the martyred President was carried to Arlington Cemetery, what did these magazines proffer their readers? For its contribution to the December children's hour, *TV and Movie Screen* offered an anonymous contribution, "Jackie–John Kennedy: The Two Little Words that Broke Their Hearts." This proved to be another insipid account of the death of little Patrick; and the words that broke the heart of the recently murdered President and his widow were "He's gone."

Equally as concerned with the education of Caroline Kennedy as *Motion Picture* and other sponsors of the jejune, *Photoplay* assigned Betty Cullen to defend Caroline in its December issue. "Caroline Kennedy . . . We Answer the Critics WHO Say: [She] Is Being Spoiled!" No, Miss Cullen insisted, Caroline was not being raised improperly; rather, she was subjected to discipline by her father, mother, uncles, aunts, her nurse, her kindergarten teacher, and the Secret Service men assigned to protect her "against jumping over the side of [a] boat [for a swim] in the middle of the ocean."

None of these articles had any bearing on the recent national tragedy which had stunned good people everywhere, but major revulsion at fan magazine callousness first made itself felt when *Photoplay*'s issue for January, 1964, carried an article, "Christmas in the White House." This incredible piece was written by Jim Hoffman, a standard contributor to fan magazines, and in elaborate detail, omitting nothing, it told how "Jackie" was steeling herself for the traditional jollity of the holiday season. True, she was saddened by the death of little Patrick, but in her determination to set a good example for the nation, her husband, and her family, the First Lady had done her own Christmas shopping in Palm Beach, where the Kennedy family always celebrated Christmas.

Only in the last paragraph did the author reveal that his story was conjecture, but even this was no worse than Ed De Blasio's contribution to January's *Modern Screen*—"The Past Loves of Jacqueline Kennedy." Below the standard provocative title was the legend of an even more provocative tagline: "THREE

MEN PLAYED IMPORTANT ROLES IN THE FIRST
LADY'S LIFE BEFORE SHE MARRIED JOHN F. KEN-
NEDY. THE MEN WERE HER FATHER, HER GRAND-
FATHER, AND HER FIRST FIANCE. HERE IS THE
EXCLUSIVE STORY OF JACKIE AND THESE MEN."

Movieland and TV Time contributed to the New Year by
posing the query of an anonymous contributor—"Are the Kennedys Out to Get Sinatra?"—a ghoulish yarn that hinted at
plans set in motion by the President before his death to send
federal investigators after Mr. Sinatra because the popular
singer had gaming interests in Las Vegas, and it was Frank's
habit to reply to "any criminal accusations tossed his way with
a shrug and a side-of-the mouth comment such as: 'The man's
a friend of mine. That's all I know.'"

> Friendship is a wonderful thing, and loyalty is a most ad-
> mirable trait, but when it is a direct slap in Jack Kennedy's
> face, then Frank is unwittingly looking for trouble. Re-
> cently, the President said, when Frank's name came into the
> conversation, "He's Peter's friend, not mine."

> The Peter in this case was Peter Lawford, married to
> Jack Kennedy's sister, Pat, and a Sinatra buddy. . . .

Innuendo nudged innuendo for space on every page, but
nothing of substance or merit was reported. More importantly,
the President taken to task by De Blasio was already dead.

In early December, the President's widow and children
moved from the White House to a house in Georgetown which
belonged to Averell Harriman, where she lived until about a
week later when she bought her own fourteen-room house in
that district. But fan magazines continued to provide wet-
tongued gossip for their readers to mull over at length. In
January *TV and Movie Reporter* was a piece guaranteed to
stimulate its readers' salivation. "Jacqueline Kennedy—Can She
Have Another Baby?" suggested that Mrs. Kennedy might not
have told Caroline and John of their infant brother's death.
"Did she, perhaps, tell them that there was a delay, but that

someday soon, the baby would be brought home to them? It is possible. . . . And as soon as God is willing, there will be a happy, smiling infant brightening up the new nursery, which now is so cold and silent and so very empty."

In January, 1964, of course, the father of Caroline and John lay at rest in Arlington Cemetery. . . .

That same month *Movie Stars'* James Gregory propounded a rhetorical question, "Is America Losing Jackie Kennedy?" Before answer was made, the author demanded that his article record again the premature birth and subsequent death of Patrick Bouvier Kennedy.

At that time—January, 1964—the fan-magazine articles devoted to Mrs. Kennedy and members of her family were, it seems, wholly unaware of an absence of Christmas joy for the Kennedy family, and the same could be said for the decent people of the nation. The President's assassination, the murder the next day of Lee Harvey Oswald by Jack Ruby (in full view of everyone with a television set) had stunned the nation. Important concepts of democracy, ethics, morality, and religious precepts were challenged and debated, but during this time of national shame and sorrow the fan magazines, it must be concluded, were unaware of recent tragic history, and their activities during the tragic months of December and January shocked and depressed any person capable of decency. Understandably, fan magazines, like most other periodicals published on a monthly basis, assemble their material three months prior to publication. President Kennedy died on November 22, which gave all magazines a month to stop the presses or withhold from distribution dated or inappropriate material.

To emphasize that the fan magazines could have removed some of the articles from their January issues before they went to press, attention need merely be called to the appearance in January, 1964—no more than eight weeks after the assassination in Dallas—of fan books with "Jackie" stories replete with her reactions to the murder of her husband. The removal or recall of the December issues of fan magazines placed on sale before the first of November was probably impossible, but certainly it was possible to have altered or removed from sale the *January* issues with their offensive material about the slain President, his wife, and children. In June, 1968, after the assassination of Robert Kennedy, *Look* took advertisements in the major newspapers of the United States to call attention to its current issue which featured a portfolio of portraits of Robert Kennedy and his family. This issue had been distributed just prior to his murder, so *Look*'s publishers could neither destroy nor recall the issue. Their advertisements were public notices of frustration and apology. At the very least, couldn't the fan magazines have taken similar advertisements? That they did not do so is an unhappy matter of record.

An office in the Old State Department Building had been assigned to Mrs. Kennedy and her staff to answer mail and business left over from her residence in the White House. The press noted quietly Mrs. Kennedy's placement of a plaque in the White House bedroom she had occupied with her husband. Some days later she attended a mass for her husband in Boston, and by January 19 she returned to Washington for her first encounter, some eight days later, with that portion of the media devoted to innuendo, enlargement, and venomous extrapolation. The occasion was a dinner attended by Mrs. Kennedy to discuss plans for a charity affair scheduled by the Kennedy Foundation months before her husband's assassination. The foundation's major concerns were the better understanding and care of mentally retarded children. The dinner meeting would have received attention in any event, but not as much if Marlon Brando, George Englund, the producer who would stage a benefit show on February 15, and Princess Lee Radziwill had not been present. Mr. Brando had volunteered to assist Mr. Englund, but gossip columnists of all degrees of spitefulness hinted that the evening was actually a "date"—that Mrs. Kennedy's sister and Englund were the "covers."

February's *Photoplay*—which appeared on newsstands in earliest January—featured "Jackie" on its cover and an exposision by Ella Ormandy called "Daddy Is Gone." The descant was intended as a "Tribute to Jackie, to Her Children . . . to Their

Love that Will Keep Him Alive Forever." Miss Ormandy revealed how Mrs. Kennedy "thought of him that first terrible moment—when the shots rang out and his head went limp and fell into her lap and his precious blood began to cover her skirt."

> She thought only of him during the vigil at the hospital, when they placed those long amber tubes into his chest and lungs, as she stared down at the beautiful and violated and waning body of her husband—as the old and sad-eyed priest, alongside her, intoned his prayer of absolution. She thought only of him as the doctor snapped for someone to bring him a stool, and sat, and began to rub his long fingers over her husband's chest, trying to get a heartbeat again, because the heart, incredibly, had ceased to function. She thought of him . . . and then, when the doctor stopped, finally . . . and slowly shook his head, she thought of the children.

Elsewhere in the issue was another example of brass offered as a "TRIBUTE TO JOHN F. KENNEDY" by Gerald A. Bartell, chairman of the board, MacFadden-Bartell Corporation. Mr. Bartell averred that "deep in the heart of our late President was a desire to live life decently and productively." Evidently, this desire for productive decency was not the editorial policy of *Photoplay,* which would be expressed fulsomely and too often in successive issues of the magazine.

That same month, *Movieland and TV Time* proved how easily it adapted to whatever specific nuance of interest was important to the insensitive Americans who read their offerings. "Will Jackie Kennedy Leave America?" quickly stated its proposition: "No one knows what goes on in the heart and mind of another person . . . but based on recent tragic events, Americans are afraid that Jackie Kennedy will want to get away!" Warmed to this theme, the anonymous writer observed: "There is no question that Jacqueline Kennedy more than deserves a long, long stretch of privacy and time to gather her strength. Can she find it here where everyone knows and loves her? Or would she be more apt to find it abroad? Of course even there she is well known and loved and a public figure." Speculation followed speculation to spin a story where none existed and—more significantly—to signal the intention of fan magazines to deny Mrs. Kennedy hope of relief from their unwelcome concentration.

Of similar substance is the February offering of *Motion Picture*, which showcased Aljean Harmetz's "How JFK Gave Jackie the Courage to Go On." Dramatically, the weaver of this tale made significant revelations: "The swings have been removed from the White House lawn. The rocking chairs have been placed in storage. Lyndon Baines Johnson is already shaping the Presidency to his own image—and is himself being shaped by the sea of change that the Presidency forces each new occupant to suffer." Caught up in a light-headed analysis of tragedy, television, patriotism, and how, because of a rifle shot, we were for a time "one nation indivisible," the writer never got around to any revelation of how Mr. Kennedy had given "Jackie" the courage to go on.

The March, 1964, issue of *Movie Stars* had been prepared only two months after the President's assassination, but was placed on sale some three months later. Seven months of self-imposed mourning still remained to the President's widow, but as the magazine's editors saw the morrow, the time for speculation about her future personal plans was now. Calloused, unfeeling speculation about the widow's plans for 1965 deserved some immediate mention, and Emily Lewis was chosen to ask and answer the question: "Can Jackie Marry Again? Her Problem: The Past, the Church, Her Children . . ."

> From that terrible moment when bullets struck on a street in Dallas, Jackie Kennedy felt that she could not leave Jack . . . ever . . .
> A split second before, she had been sitting close beside him, smiling and waving so proudly. Holding the big bouquet of red roses they had presented her at the airport.
> "Red Roses for Me" . . . it was strange, the way the title

of Sean O'Casey's tragic play had struck her at that moment. Nonsense, she must have thought, as she brushed it
from her mind. Probably the people of Dallas wanted to
be different—until then, all the roses given her had been
yellow—the Yellow Rose of Texas. Or perhaps they'd complimented her pink suit . . .

Then, in that split second, it was all mixed together, in
a horrible nightmare. Pink suit, red roses. Red Blood . . .
Jack's blood. And she was crying, "Jack! Jack! Oh, no, no,
no, NO!"

She held him in her arms as they sped to Parkland Hospital.

This tragedy in narrative and stream-of-consciousness exposition had been limned; now Miss Lewis, in a Freudian hop-
scotch in and out of the young widow's mind, observed primly
that "Jackie" certainly knew her children needed a father—"all
children do. But . . . could they *accept* one?" A second marriage
—possibility, probability, adjustment of personalities, the scrutiny and approval or rejection her second husband would experience—were all touched on with agility. But somehow the
writer never got around to the "Problem [of] the Church,"
before she wrote a conclusion of energetic piety: "Everyone
prays that she will find the happiness she deserves—and for any
woman, that happiness includes marriage."

During those first months of 1964, when fan magazine editors
and publishers reflected on how far they dared go now in featuring the former First Lady and how close to impudent marriage
brokering their future exploration of the "happiness [that]
includes marriage" might become, Mrs. Kennedy remained in
Georgetown. Unhappily for the street, the community, the
District of Columbia, and all the nation—as soon as Mrs. Kennedy's new address was published, sightseers jammed the street
to the embarrassment, despair, and outrage of anyone with even
a jot of sensibility. Tourists rang the doorbell, climbed over
gates and fences, stood on boxes and ladders to peer into win-
dows. Bolder barbarians climbed trees and even managed to

get onto the roof of Mrs. Kennedy's house. Photographers braved the worst weather to get their shots. Every guest was photographed twice—once on entering and again on leaving—with the time elapsed duly noted by zealous reporters who, with the photographers, exercised their freeborn right to be inglorious.

Even the most case-hardened observers agreed that Mrs. Kennedy would have to seek privacy elsewhere, and in the middle of February she flew to New York City to look at a large, vacant apartment at 810 Fifth Avenue. After she returned to Georgetown, the young widow was appointed to the White House Preservation Committee by President Johnson, who commended her efforts at restoration and preservation of the nation's historic past.

Mrs. Kennedy spent Easter at Stowe, Vermont, where there was still good skiing. Accompanied by Caroline and John, and the families of Robert and Ted Kennedy, and Sargent and Eunice Shriver, she did not lack for company of her choice. Not of her choosing, however, were the swarms of photographers who had decided to observe Holy Week and Easter with the Kennedys. Their diligence, their religious observance and practice were proved by the number and variety of pictures they took of the young widow and her children at the White Mountains' resort. Quite successfully, they transmogrified Mrs. Kennedy's short vacation into a "wild, fun weekend."

Some months later, in July, *Movie Stars'* cover featured the Beatles and a bold tagline—"DID JACKIE BREAK HER VOW? The Pictures, Her Critics, The Proof." The story by James Gregory was based on the criticism by readers of the New York *Daily News,* a unique tabloid with one of the largest circulations of any newspaper. Most of the *Daily News* is a composition of comic strips and columns, which please its low-income, uneducated, suspicious, and reactionary readers.

Movie Stars published several photos of Mrs. Kennedy and her children in ski garb, and the magazine also reprinted a letter from a distaff reader of the *Daily News,* who scored Mrs. Kennedy for not wearing a skirt when she attended church on

Easter Day. "Why should women want to look like men?" she demanded. To relate this churlish letter to the article, Gregory took it on himself to inquire rhetorically as to what was "proper behavior for a widow during her period of mourning. It's a question which, unfortunately, will affect many of the readers of this magazine some day." In absolute denial of the hopes of the scruffy, Mr. Gregory concluded his article with an observation that Mrs. Kennedy should be spared from criticism, for "in her heart of hearts, she must know that she is doing exactly what Jack would have wanted her to do."

Photoplay again pilloried Elizabeth Taylor and Richard Burton on their April cover. The feature by Ed De Blasio—"The Last Promise Jackie Made to Jack"—is notable for its stickiness and the attempted suggestion to readers that Mrs. Kennedy had granted De Blasio an interview.

In May, *Movieland and TV Time* oyezed "The Secret of Jackie's New Glow," which was inspired by "her cultural pursuits and helping us all to live in a better place, rather than a suitor." In its shrewd assault on mind and pocket change, *Movie Life* combined three of the most prominent makers of headlines into one story: "Jackie Kennedy, President Johnson's Family and the Beatles." Taglines to arouse interest asked—"Why Didn't LBJ Invite the Beatles to the White House?" and "Would Jackie Kennedy Have Snubbed Them?" Quantitatively, the article was a bald excuse for the magazine to conduct a poll among its readers, who were invited to mark their preference for one or two courses of action: "YES! The Beatles SHOULD have been invited to the White House," or "NO! The Beatles SHOULD NOT have been invited to the White House."

On May 2, the occasion of her husband's birthday, Mrs. Kennedy, Caroline, and other members of her family attended a memorial mass at St. Matthew's Cathedral in Washington. Afterward she visited the President's simple gravesite in Arlington Cemetery. Some weeks later, from Hyannis Port, she joined Willy Brandt of West Germany, Harold Macmillan of Great Britain, and Sean Lemas of Ireland in a trans-Atlantic broadcast dedicated to her husband. Memorial Day was spent in seclusion.

At this time, renewed efforts were made by concerned friends to put an end to the unnatural attention given to the First Lady and her children by the fan magazines. Some years later, William Manchester, in *The Death of a President* (1967), remarked how in May, 1965, Mrs. Kennedy "couldn't even take her daughter into a drug store, because every issue of every movie magazine carried her photograph outside." Manchester reported that Pierre Salinger "begged the pulps to stop, but they kept on, knowing she would never sue because that would merely bring more detested publicity. Even the slick periodicals behaved questionably."

Proof that Salinger's appeal was ignored is offered by *Photoplay* for June, when it presented Jae Lyle's lachrymal: "Jackie Kennedy . . . Why She Tells Her Children 'Daddy Is Not Dead!' " But by some unexplained reversal of roles, in the article it was Caroline and John-John who convinced their mother "that [Daddy] was not dead." And that same month's *Motion Picture* featured another Florence Epstein menses: "Jackie Kennedy's First Mother's Day Alone . . . The Love That Keeps Her Going." "When she got married, at 23," Miss Epstein informed her readers, "she didn't want a President, she wanted children. If it were all up to her, her name would have appeared in the newspapers three times—at her birth, at her marriage, at her death. But she had a destiny. . . . At 34, half of what might have been is gone. Jacqueline Kennedy no longer broods about it. Only once, on the day of her husband's funeral, she turned to his brother, Robert Kennedy, and asked if providence would now take her other children, too."

Leslie Valentine, in *TV Radio Mirror* for June, gave her readers a damp paper handkerchief embroidered with the legend "How Jackie Finds a Father's Love for Her Children." This is accomplished, the writer claimed, by taking John-John with her when she visits the Executive Office Building. The next month the busy Valentine was back again with a piece reminiscent of a defunct soap opera about Helen Trent ("can a woman of thirty-five or over find romance?"). "Jackie's Newest Heartbreak . . . What It Means to Be a Woman Alone at 35" is revealed as a series of "long, hot days [that] drag on." But Ed De Blasio (*Photoplay,* July) revealed "The Miracle that Made Jackie Laugh Again" was wrought through the books in her Georgetown house. Among the poets, philosophers, and historians favored by the former First Lady, she had found the wisdom to return "to life, and even laughter."

Movie Life for July suggested how in the former First Lady's return "to life, and even laughter," she had undertaken the role of matchmaker to the now-First Family. "The White House Wedding Jackie Wants NOW!" revealed that "Great bouquets of freshly cut flowers—a Jacqueline Kennedy touch—enliven the elegant white and gold East Room of the White House where Lynda Bird Johnson will become the wife [*sic!*] of her handsome Naval Lieutenant, Bernard Rosenbach." When a writer—like a politician or theologian—is in error, it is best to make the boner a majestic one, which may explain how Dixie Dean Harris could assure her readers that, "No matter what painful memories Lynda Bird's wedding may stir in Jacqueline Kennedy, you can be sure that because she wants others to know the joy she herself has had, that this is truly the White House wedding that Jackie wants now."

July, which would mark Mrs. Kennedy's birthday, was a busy month of concentrated conjecture on her past, present, and future by writers who had made up their minds about Mrs. Kennedy and refused, therefore, to be confused by facts. In an action possibly designed to plant some charity in the minds and hearts of its readers, *Movie Mirror* for that month solicited funds for the John Fitzgerald Memorial Library through a plea it chose to title "Help Pay Tribute to President Kennedy's Dream." Not so public-spirited or philanthropic of mood was *Modern Screen,* which published Leslie Valentine's "The Men Who Love Jacqueline Kennedy," who were belatedly identified as Pierre Salinger, President Johnson, Robert and Ted Kennedy, Dean Rusk, and Adlai Stevenson. By this time, however, there were readers who thought the list incomplete. Certainly,

Marlon Brando *and* Richard Burton should have been added. Why not?

Convinced by now that their readers would accept anything sufficiently boorish or inane, *TV and Movie Screen* believed there was one marriage Jacqueline Kennedy preferred even to that of Lynda Bird Johnson and Bernard Rosenbach—her own. To this good end the July cover was composed of two profile photographs of Mrs. Kennedy and Elizabeth Taylor; and bold type urged concerned citizens to buy the issue and find out why—

JACKIE	LIZ
WILL	WILL
MARRY!	DIVORCE!

Because Mrs. Kennedy made a television address to thank everyone who had sent her an expression of sympathy, and "the Jackie on that show was a smiling one, one who obviously hoped to create a new and happy life . . . obviously, from what we know of Jackie, there would have to be a new husband in it." Conversely, a "bright future is not in the picture at all for Liz Taylor. . . . Liz and Burton seem too different to ever fit together on a permanent basis." Made heady by rhetoric, the anonymous haruspex concluded that the screen pair would "live together, love, fight, make up . . . but never find the harmony of a lasting marriage."

Some months later, in October, *Movie Mirror* also used a split cover divided between Jacqueline Kennedy and Elizabeth Taylor. But originality was shown by the addition of the daughters of both ladies. "Jackie's Hopes for Caroline" were contrasted with "Liz's Fear for Liza." Miss Taylor had to be assured by her friends and family "that she [would] not fail at the most important thing in a woman's life . . . motherhood"—so the writer believed. The anonymous but agile memorialist quoted an unidentified "middle-aged lady who lives in Washington, D. C.," to express her concern for the young widow and her daughter: " 'Now, when I pray, I always say a special prayer for Jacqueline Kennedy and for the children. . . . I ask that

Jackie be given the strength to raise them with all the obstacles that face her . . . the publicity wherever she and the children go. . . . And, most of all, I pray that Caroline will not be unduly affected by what she still has to face as she grows up.' "

In July, Mrs. Kennedy bought a cooperative apartment on upper Fifth Avenue from Mr. and Mrs. Lowell Palmer Weicker. Once the purchase had been approved by the cooperative's board of directors, Mayor Robert F. Wagner pledged the resources of his city to assure Mrs. Kennedy and her children the deserved privacy they had been unable to enjoy in Georgetown. While the apartment was being readied, she would live at the Carlyle Hotel, whose site the mayor and the city's police department chose not to turn into a popular tourist attraction. Before the first of August the former First Lady arranged for Caroline and John to visit her mother, because she planned to leave for London, where she would join Princess Lee Radziwill, Lord and Lady Harlech, and other guests on the yacht of Mr. and Mrs. Charles Bierer Wrightsman for a cruise of the Adriatic.

Somewhere, everywhere in the land there was a morose, dissatisfied, unfulfilled American housewife who sat at the kitchen table, coffee cooling in the cup, cigarette in hand, and dreamed of seeing the world through the dark glasses of the rich. Husband at work, she could relax at last, thank God, because this had been one of those strike-me-dead mornings. Feeling better now, she opened her August copy of *Movie Stars* and read about Mrs. Kennedy, who wasn't a movie star, not really, although she certainly moved around in the kind of places movie stars could afford to go to—the lucky tramps—and she became all steamed up—really hot—over the cover of the magazine which promised to tell everything about the man who'd come back into "Jackie's" life. The cover had even promised "Pictures," but these proved to be no more than paste-ups of Mrs. Kennedy with her sister and the former President—and Regis de Cachard, a portraitist. Not once were the painter and the former First Lady in the same picture, although once Mrs. Kennedy—in a swimsuit—had been placed between two photos of the fashion designer-painter-possible-relative-and-happily-married-man. Damn—the housewife had been taken again. Still, the magazine seemed to promise other goodies and among them she might find something really juicy. Which should she choose first? Let us see what she was offered.

4 BIG BEATLE SPECIALS

KEEPING UP WITH THE BEATLES
BEATLES IN-LAW
THE FEUD THEY MUST HIDE
THIS IS SHAKESPEARE?

Tyrone Power's Forgotten Children
How to Make a Sophia (Loren, that is)
The Terrible, Tangled, Tormented Lives of Hollywood
(Liz is just the beginning)
The October 5th Threat Against Patty Duke's Life
"I Like the Way Elvis Kisses": Is Joan Freeman the Girl
who's Taken Ann-Margret's Place in Elvis's Arms?
"I Was a Girl for Four Days" (a male star confesses)

Poor housewife—every story proved colder than her breakfast coffee, flatter than the cigarette that should have had that other blend of fine tobaccos. Still, she continued to hope for something, even tears. So she really really wept as she read September's *Modern Screen* with Charles Worth's "Jackie's Own Story of Her Life Today," which hinted that Mrs. Kennedy had given the author a personal interview before her press conference to open an exhibit of Kennedy memorabilia in New York City. Thus she had bared her secret soul and told the writer how difficult it had become to look at photographs of her husband— especially the one taken "only nine days before [he] was killed."

The same magazine tried harder in October with James Gregory's "The Man Who Made Jackie Leave Washington"— who proved to be "the persistent, ever-present ghost of her beloved husband . . . a ghost she would not exorcise if she could." In similar vein, October's *Motion Picture* used Carla

Turner to tell her readers about "The Day Caroline Kennedy
Went Looking for Her Daddy":

> She slipped away and flew to that special place hoping
> he would be there, waiting, smiling. He would sweep her
> up into his arms and she would say, "Daddy, please don't
> go away again . . ."
> No heart is too young to break and no one would ever
> know how much she missed him . . . missed his funny jokes,
> holding his warm hand, going to church with him, playing
> in his office, his goodnight kiss . . .

Stream-of-consciousness also served Jim Hoffman in the October issue of *TV Radio Mirror*. "Must She Say Goodbye to
Everyone She Loves?" revealed that the First Lady had lacked
the courage to visit her brother-in-law Ted as he lay in the
hospital after his near-fatal plane crash of June 19 because she
might weaken and recall "her newborn son's death . . . her
beloved husband's death."

Such pleonastic employment of rumination, as it was supposed to be practiced by Jacqueline Kennedy, her children, and
her family, the interpretation of these secret thoughts and silent
soliloquies, became a favorite device of fan magazine writers
called on to fill an assignment and unable to find in the activities of the former First Lady as reported by the responsible
media anything to interest urban and rural rustics. Mawkishly
they invaded the mind of Jacqueline Kennedy and furnished it
with banalities of the poorest quality and taste.

None of this disturbed the average reader of fan magazines,
as she settled herself quite comfortably to read the October *TV
and Movie Screen* where Jan Darby delivered herself of a febrile
sweat that prompted a title and tagline combination to delude
the reader more fully than anything previously offered by any
other magazine. "JACKIE KENNEDY's FIRST PROPOSAL!
Must She Say 'NO' for the Sake of Her Children?" was another
rehash of the courtship and marriage of Jacqueline Bouvier to
John F. Kennedy, which led the author to conclude that

"Jackie" would never remarry "just for the sake of providing another father for her children. She will have to be madly in love again."

If readers were disappointed, they would also be let down hard by the other articles, which included "HOLLYWOOD'S NEW NEGRO LOVE CODE!" and "PRESIDENT JOHNSON'S HOLLYWOOD SECRETS!" When would the rubes learn that suggestive, exclamatory questions and statements in fan magazines did not guarantee a story to match the lurid, dramatic type?

Never, the editors and publishers hoped.

The Adriatic cruise of Mrs. Kennedy was only as eventful as an energetic, inventive press could make it. Ship and shore excursions were covered by reporters and photographers as doggedly persistent as the Italian *papparazzi;* but despite their unwelcome surveillance, Mrs. Kennedy went water-skiing off the shores of Yugoslavia, had a short, pleasant chat with an aide to President Tito aboard the Wrightsman yacht at Zadar, and inspected the *Borac,* a Yugoslavian patrol boat assigned to escort the yacht in Adriatic waters. Rain interrupted a tour of Dubrovnik and led Mrs. Kennedy and her sister to leave the yacht and go instead to Venice and Porto Ercole; before she returned to Newport on August 20, Mrs. Kennedy and her sister dined with Queen Juliana and Princess Beatrix of the Netherlands.

Late in August, Mrs. Kennedy informed officers of the Democratic party that she would not attend the memorial session dedicated to her late husband scheduled for the last day of activities at the National Convention in Atlantic City. She also declined President Johnson's invitation to sit in his official box. However, Mrs. Kennedy changed her mind and joined other members of the family in Atlantic City, where she was greeted with affection by the crowd.

The only affair she attended was a reception given by Averell

Harriman for almost six thousand Democrats. Guests admired her dress of white silk brocade, which she wore without benefit of jewelry, and they joined her in the hotel auditorium where Frederic March and his wife, Florence Eldridge, read poetry the late President had enjoyed. Excerpts from some of the President's more memorable speeches were also read with feeling, and many delegates wept openly. In conclusion, Mrs. Kennedy addressed the guests in a low voice and thanked them for their help to her husband in 1960. "May his lights always shine in all parts of the world," she concluded.

In the administration's determination to honor Mrs. Kennedy, a new White House garden was dedicated to her on September 8, the first time the wife of a former President had been so honored. That same month Mrs. Kennedy supervised the transfer of three van-loads of furniture to her duplex apartment on upper Fifth Avenue. However, until the apartment was fully decorated, Mrs. Kennedy remained at the Carlyle Hotel. On September 17, she took possession of her apartment, and on the first day of the fall term she took Caroline to meet her teachers at the Ninety-first Street Academy of the Convent of the Sacred Heart. Ten days later, her name was dropped from the *Washington Society List,* but in November she was included in the *New York Society Register.* Of greater concern to most New Yorkers were two telephone calls made to the local telephone company warning of time bombs in Mrs. Kennedy's apartment. A search of the premises proved the calls a cruel hoax.

Although Mrs. Kennedy occupied herself with family and civic affairs, the fan magazines continued to prove how busy they were with the former First Lady. In *Modern Screen*'s November number, commemorating the first anniversary of the former President's death, Jack Madison admitted responsibility for "Jackie Kennedy and the Negroes—The Story That's Never Been Told." This proved to be a clever piece of self-servicing for the genre of publications that kept Mr. Madison and his peers in provisions.

The middle-aged Negro woman studied the newsstand rack very carefully. She went down the line and each time she came to a magazine that bore Jacqueline Kennedy's picture on the cover, the woman would take a copy and cradle it in her arms. When she finished, she gave the clerk eight magazines. . . . A passerby, watching the woman and the magazines she selected, was overcome with curiosity. . . .

"Pardon me, madam," he said, "but I cannot resist asking why you have bought so many magazines with covers on Mrs. Kennedy. Would you tell me?"

The woman stared at the man for a moment and then said: "Because I admire and believe in Mrs. Kennedy. I know what she's been through."

The man said, "I understand."

The woman turned and walked away.

In commercial enterprise there can never be too much profit. If Jacqueline Kennedy could motivate a poor woman to spend $2.40 on eight magazines, might not the inclusion of other public figures in these same magazines inspire *their* "admirers and believers" to purchase periodicals which they had heretofore neglected? Some attempts had been made to make the daughters of President Johnson "star quality" personalities, but their appeal with "fan mag" readers seemed to be in direct proportion to their connection with Mrs. Kennedy. If she played the role of elder sister or young sister-in-law or aunt, they were popular, but such stories taxed the ingenuity of the reliable contributors whose names were familiar to the fans. More meaningful, an election campaign was in progress, and if pollsters agreed that President Johnson was the stronger candidate, there were people who remembered how Harry Truman, an underdog, had bested front-runner Thomas E. Dewey. And if Barry Goldwater defeated Lyndon Baines Johnson, *his* family might become more important to the fan magazines. So a hedged bet seemed the wisest course, which led the November

Photoplay to insure itself against charges of favoritism by a cover-line of promise:

LYNDON & LADY BIRD
BARRY & PEGGY
Two Marriages They Said Wouldn't Last

And if there were readers who wished to learn more about Barry Goldwater than just an account of his marriage, the Mac-fadden-Bartell Corporation, the publishers accountable for *Photoplay,* ran a full page to advertise six of its paperbacks, "GOLDWATER: Learn About the Man Who May Be Our Next President!"

Meanwhile, romance: first the President, then his challenger, and of course—their ladies. If Paul Anthony, the author of the Johnson piece, is to be believed, although Mrs. Johnson's mother "died when Lady Bird was only five, the little girl inherited a romantic dream—a dream of romance that would one day be hers. 'She would read to me,' Lady Bird says, 'and I remember so many things. All of the Greek and Roman myths and many of the German myths. *Siegfried* was the first person I was in love with.' As the shy, reticent girl grew older, in her secret heart she was *Brunhilde*—and somewhere, someday, some-how, her own *Siegfried,* light-hearted, heroic and handsome, would come to claim her." And so he did and from of all places —Texas—but he forgot to bring the wedding ring to the cere-mony, which was why someone had said, "I *hope* that marriage lasts."

Jae Lyle bears the responsibility for recreating the courting historiette of Margaret Johnson and Barry Goldwater. Peggy admitted that Barry *"was* attractive," but he was one of the "rambunctious Goldwaters [so] irrepressible . . . attractive . . . handsome as any movie star." When classmates learned of Peggy's love of fun and music, they referred to her as the "vo-do-de-o-do girl," which Lyle hastens to explain was the twenties' equivalent of a "real swinging chick." But Barry was too "vo-do-de-o-do" for comfort. After he was dropped from college at the end of his first semester and put to labor in the family department store, he enlivened the workday by "slipping live mice into the pneumatic tubes." They were also "incompatible," because Barry loved Arizona and Peggy couldn't stand the place, and hated flying. Although all her friends warned Peggy *"that marriage also wouldn't last,"* she consented to be his bride. And even on the day of the wedding "they smiled at the ecstatic bride and groom [and whispered,] 'It will never last.' "

It is a matter of record that President Johnson was reelected to his office and Senator Barry Goldwater was retired to private life until 1969. Now the former President is a man of enormous ego and little patience with any attempt to diminish his personal dignity; and the same can be said of the former presidential candidate. So it is possible that some pressure was put on *Photoplay* to cease and desist in their attempts to make Brunhildes and Siegfrieds and Elaines and Red Barons of the Johnsons and Goldwaters, but probably of more import to the publishers, neither couple projected the images readers demanded of famous people granted pages in the magazines devoted to "stars." Leslie Fiedler, in *Waiting for the End* (1964), observed that "John F. Kennedy [was] not only our first sexually viable president in a century, after a depressing series of uncle, grandfather, and grandmother figures, but the very embodiment of middlebrow culture climbing." What Fiedler said of the assassinated President could also be said—and more—of his widow: Therein lay her magic; therein was her exponential value to the fan magazines.

On safer, more satisfactory ground, was the semi-solipsistic effort in the November *TV Radio Movie Guide,* which devoted its cover once more to Jacqueline Kennedy and Elizabeth Taylor. This was sound ecumenism and business. And the coverlines promised much: "LOVE . . . The Jinx That Haunts LIZ!" and "TRAGEDY . . . The Jinx That Threatens JACKIE." If these disappointed readers, possibly some visceral stimulation might be found in "EXPOSED! THE PLOT TO KILL THE BEATLES!"

But of all the fan magazines that November, the tarnished

Grail must be awarded to *Movie Mirror,* which managed to obtain an interview with Monsignor Francis X. Duffy of the Catholic Information Office at St. Patrick's Cathedral in Manhattan. In "A Priest Talks about Jackie Kennedy's Next Marriage," the good father was told by the writer, who was never identified, that *Movie Mirror* had "received so many letters about Jacqueline Kennedy asking about the possibility of her remarriage and where the Church stood in relation to . . . her future [that] we thought we had best discuss these questions with someone [of] authority [like] Monsignor Duffy."

> We told him that these letters came from every state in the Union and from just about every country in the world.
>
> "Please be clear about one thing," he told us. "I do not necessarily speak for the Church. However, I will be very happy to give you any information I can and shall tell you what, if anything, the Church has already taken a position on, if your particular question refers to it."

The anonymous spokesman for *Movie Mirror* then told Monsignor Duffy of the many communications received from "good people" who preferred that "Mrs. Kennedy *not* remarry and that, as Catholics, they felt they were reflecting their religion's attitude toward this." Was this correct, the writer asked? The Monsignor smiled as he shook his head and explained that "should Mrs. Kennedy remain a widow, there might be a very special virtue attached to that . . . but there was definitely no obligation on the part of a widowed Catholic woman to either remarry or not." Because the writer asked readers to believe that all questions, no matter what their intimacy, were answered with tolerance, he—or she—made reference to the intermarriages and divorces in the Bouvier and Kennedy families, before the Monsignor was asked what would happen if the widow under discussion were to marry outside her faith.

> "Mrs. Kennedy . . . would still be a Catholic and could receive all the sacraments if she married in a Catholic

ceremony. That is a priest would have to officiate . . . there would have to be two witnesses, and the couple would have to sign certain documents."

From the moment the writer had entered the Monsignor's office and begun to sprinkle moral confetti, he—or she—had stayed too long. Now, on departure, he or she felt called on to conclude the article on pietistic notes appropriate to oratorio and religious exhortation.

If you do visit St. Patrick's some day, and you should see Mrs. Jacqueline Kennedy there, please remember that you are more than welcome to move into a pew nearby, join her in quiet prayer, and whatever your religion may be, pray that this brave woman may be given the strength to raise her family and find the future.

Movie Mirror's concern for "Jackie" and her single status, now that her year of mourning had ended, was evidenced again in December. Using a format of dialogue and commentary— "The Kennedys Want Jackie to Marry Again," is another exercise in speculation that did nicely without the clutter attendant to interviewing its subjects. The anonymous historian (who may also have interviewed Monsignor Duffy) reflected pensively on the former First Lady, who was "young . . . too young, most people say, to remain a widow. . . . Marriage, for Jackie, will be something she will not consider easily until she can feel free to find another husband."

The November *TV Picture Life* asked readers to mull over an article that must qualify as the lowest, most vulgar excess taken by any fan magazine in 1964. "A Doctor's Report on Jackie" was introduced by an editorial note that could only bring dismay and consternation to those persons who oppose any censorship of the press. "The opinions in this report are those of a well-qualified New York doctor. Although he has not met Jacqueline Kennedy, he has carefully studied her medical and personal history and watched her on TV. Because the medical associations do not permit doctors to give medical opinions in non-medical cases, the doctor's name is not revealed. For convenience sake, we'll call him Dr. John Jones."

Two flavorsome examples are sufficient to give us a taste of the report: "Every time her children effusively greet a friendly male, Jackie will be reminded that they crave having a daddy. It will be difficult for her to shut her eyes to the possibility of loving another man." A little later readers are given more evidence of diagnostic optimism: "She seems to be in full possession of her situation, is making good decisions, and can be counted on to continue being a perfect lady for the rest of her life."

In that broad area of life unknown to the fan magazines and their readers, Mrs. Kennedy had a full schedule of sane activities to round out the year's autumn and winter months. In October she sent two deer gifted to her by President Eamon de Valera of Ireland to the Children's Zoo in Central Park. Later, she declined an invitation to attend a Liberal party campaign rally for President Johnson. Whether this action prompted a visit the next day by the President and her brother-in-law, Robert Kennedy, is unknown, but she entertained them in her apartment. Later in the month she rented a house in Glen Cove, about an hour's drive from Manhattan, where she worked on the article she had agreed to contribute to *Look* for their memorial issue, honoring her husband's achievements. Featured contributors to this issue were Laura Berquist, Fletcher Knebel, T. George Harris, Bela Kornitzer, Richard Wilson, and Joseph Roddy.

Mrs. Kennedy's contribution, "A Memoir," was introduced by a reproduction of Mrs. Kennedy's handwriting: "I should have known that it was asking too much to dream that I might have grown old with him." In her moving tribute, which might have been written by any wife who had lost her husband before his time, she observed: "His high noon kept all the freshness of morning—and he died then, never knowing disillusionment."

The same issue of *Look* also carried memorable photographs of John F. Kennedy at home, work, and play. Some critics quibbled at the photographs of Mrs. Kennedy with her children, which they believed to be too candid, as if they were convinced that all pictures must look better than their subjects. The cover photograph by Stanley Tretrick of Jacqueline Kennedy and young John suggested that Mrs. Kennedy was well on the way to full emotional recovery. All in all, the issue was a popular and tasteful tribute to the late President. Devoid of morbidity or conjecture about Mrs. Kennedy's personal plans, it was well received in most homes.

Shortly thereafter, the National Broadcasting Company aired the first of its "Profiles in Courage" (November 8, 1964). These were based on President Kennedy's book, first published in 1956, and on fourteen additional profiles chosen by Robert Saudek, the show's producer, and approved by the President. Although the series received good critical notices it could not compete with weekly situation comedies of a domestic and fatuous nature, or with the *Lawrence Welk Show,* which had just begun its tenth lobotomous year on the boob-tube. The renewal of the *Lawrence Welk Show* was of particular importance to *TV Radio Mirror,* which through its concentration on the careers and related activities of younger television and recording stars, had attempted to establish itself as a fan magazine of special interest. Among the more favored performers to receive the magazine's prose and pictorial attentions were the Lennon Sisters, a sweet, wholesome quartet who were featured on Maestro Welk's weekly hour. Welk presented a detergent-clean image of the American way of life which, next to football, was rated first in the affections of Vice-President-to-be Spiro Agnew and his good wife. All the songs and instrumental numbers were chosen to please the "golden age" set and their offspring, who gathered as happy family groups around their television sets to see oldsters in the studio glide and jig their way around the dance floor to the bubbly rhythm of "Champagne Music"— the worldliest activity of the show. And for those who were advantaged and had colored television sets, the Lennon Sisters —who had grown up with the show—paraded around in their pastel gowns with high necklines, for décolletage was unknown on *this* entertainment.

TV Radio Mirror featured the Dimpled Darlings on no less than four covers a year. This editorial practice enabled fans of Welk and the Lennon Sisters to keep scrapbooks of how from year to year the girls had grown from children into young ladies, and finally mothers. Suddenly the songbirds faced unusual competition for covers, and the new rival was "Jackie," who first appeared in January of 1963. Later, in the months of June and September, the magazine featured "Jackie" again, which helped her match the appearances of the Lennons in February, May, and July. Another rival—Elizabeth Taylor—was chosen to grace the covers of the August, October, and November issues, although it must be noted that Miss Taylor had to share the October cover with Carol Burnett. A quick count proves that, for the editors of *TV Radio Mirror,* the most popular "stars" of 1963 were "Jackie," the Lennon Sisters and "Liz"; but by 1967, "Jackie" held a slight edge.

Movieland and TV Time for December—put on sale at the end of October—decided that a more subdued use of "Jackie" was called for, and featured "It shows on her face . . . it's evident in her actions . . . there's ONLY ONE PLACE JACKIE KENNEDY FINDS PEACE"—in Europe. *Motion Picture* for that month preferred the gaiety of Rose Wolfe, who is responsible for "Fifth Avenue, New York City . . . Where Jackie Kennedy Is Finding a Fabulous New Life." Bait was supplied by a provocative tagline that promised healthy exercise to readers who were invited "To practice the fine art of Kennedy watching, please turn the page and come along as we take a wonderful walking tour of Jackie-land."

An aerial view of Manhattan's East Side was incorporated into the four-page spread; Central Park and Fifth Avenue were in the foreground and the East River, Governor's Island, and Queens could be identified in the background. For readers who wished to visit "Jackie-land," cerise ink was used to mark significant landmarks with appropriate captions:

> 1040 Fifth Avenue where Jackie, Caroline and John-John live in a 15-room co-op apartment on the fifteenth floor.

995 Fifth Avenue, Hotel Stanhope, where Pat and Peter Lawford have taken a $3,200 suite until their next-door apartment is ready.

Church of St. Ignatius Loyola, Park Avenue at 84th Street, where Jackie and the children attend church each Sunday morning.

990 Fifth Avenue, where the Lawfords bought a 14th floor, 14-room duplex for $140,000 after being refused entry at another building.

969 Fifth Avenue, where Jackie's sister, Lee, her husband, Prince Radziwill, and their two children have a 12-room duplex.

950 Fifth Ave., where Jean and Stephen Smith and their two children have an apartment. He manages all finances for the Kennedy Clan.

Carlyle Hotel, 35 East 76th Street, 11th floor suite, is home for the Bobby Kennedys when they're not at their 30-room mansion on Long Island Sound.

For readers who might think twice before setting out on their own for so exclusive an area as Fifth Avenue above East Fifty-ninth Street, Miss Wolfe assured them of security and welcome. "At most it takes a couple of hours—it's only two miles in all—to visit Kennedy-Land (New York City's answer to Disneyland) and, unless you lunch at the Carlyle, the trip is free." In the course of her role as tour guide, Miss Wolfe interviewed a cab driver who worked in the area, asked directions of a policeman, and was refused admission to the apartment building where the elderly Kennedys lived when in New York.

The success of this invitation to a fun pilgrimage was proved some two and a half years later when the *Saturday Evening Post* (March 11, 1967) published an almost identical piece by Alan Levy. In "Jackie Kennedy: A View from the Crowd," only the colored photographs are better. Instead of a "Kennedy Area" in Manhattan—as it had been presented by *Motion Picture*—the

Post reproduced a full-page portion of a map of the city—"Jackie Kennedy's Manhattan," which featured line drawings of Mrs. Kennedy in a résumé of her daily and special activities. The former First Lady and her children were sketched on horseback along a Central Park bridle path; buying ice cream from a wagon; exercising on the rings in a gymnasium; at Lincoln Center; at Kennedy Airport; having her hair styled; stores patronized in daily shopping; the route taken by both children as they walked or were driven to school. Thirty locations where Mrs. Kennedy and her children might be seen were indicated on the map—as if in imitation of *Motion Picture*'s cerise-ink—and addresses were also supplied.

Taking readers into his confidence, Alan Levy revealed how early one Friday afternoon he had set up shop on a park bench opposite 1040 Fifth Avenue and devoted four hours to listening to conversations within his hearing. This material was later organized to make the most of four chance meetings with Mrs. Kennedy; and he had even managed to get into the background of several photographs of the glamorous widow. But how had he known where to be, and when? A fair question deserved a fair reply, and the author generously acknowledged his source: *Women's Wear Daily,* a specialized newspaper which caters to the garment trade. It also keeps a sharp eye on Mrs. Kennedy and her family.

Anyone, Levy concluded, could spend a good deal of time in the presence of Mrs. Kennedy; all the determined fan need do was follow reports of her activities or just set up an observation post outside her Fifth Avenue address. "By staying *behind* Jacqueline Kennedy, I was photographed with her numerous times. A photo of her and of me had gone out on the Associated Press wire that slow Sunday, and now a long forgotten boyhood dream of mine came true: in Monday morning's photographic captions, I was identified as a Secret Service man."

The use made of such an article by the *Post* became understandable to anyone acquainted with the precarious financial balance of the magazine. Efforts to regain lost readers impelled the publisher and editors to commission a series of sensational muckraking exposés; but unfortunately these had resulted in lawsuits at considerable cost to the magazine. In efforts to remain solvent and viable, the magazine had become a biweekly, and in an attempt to woo new readers, Levy's article had been advertised extensively through radio spot announcements. What truly saddens a journalistic historian was the application of an economic law first propounded by Sir Thomas Gresham, to the effect that bad money drove good from the marketplace. That the *Post* might become another *Motion Picture* was not the primary concern of the *Post*'s editors. Who asks to know the intelligence quotient of a blood donor?

On November 22, 1964, Jacqueline Kennedy remained in seclusion while her mother placed a floral tribute on the grave of the former President. He had been dead for a year and his widow had approved the model for the monument to mark the grave. Condolences were sent by Willie Brandt, Charles de Gaulle, and other state figures. Two days later, the press published the testimony Mrs. Kennedy had given the Warren Commission. Whether the re-publication of the photographs of Mrs. Kennedy in her bloodstained suit was a current necessity is moot. What is known is that the publicity related to the anniversary of death had caused the widow such strain that she canceled all scheduled appointments for at least several weeks.

On December 10, Mrs. Kennedy resumed her social activities, when she was escorted by United Nations Ambassador Adlai Stevenson to a concert at the United Nations to commemorate the sixteenth anniversary of the adoption of the Human Rights Declaration. After a quiet Christmas she joined other members of the Kennedy family at Aspen, Colorado, and photographers devoted themselves to the former First Lady and her adventures on the ski slopes. On December 29, she declined President Johnson's personal invitation to attend his inauguration on January 30, 1965.

The calendar year of mourning was ended.

CHAPTER NINE

> "... *I've Just Become a Piece*
> *of Public Property.*"

IS it already five years since the dark, demonic side of the American spirit agreed that Mrs. Jacqueline Lee Bouvier Kennedy had observed an official year of mourning, therefore she could wear a white frock rather than black and would be forgiven for an occasional smile in public? A full year had passed for Mrs. Kennedy; another—1965—was begun; and if she longed for the gift of privacy, should she be chided for anti-sociality or—as fan magazine readers would have said—for not wanting other people to mind her business?

For months now, fan magazines had been tooling up. The formal dictates of society had been met. "Jackie" had completed a year of mourning; now—at last!—editors could instruct their reliable hacks to come up with a romance-angle worthy of Elizabeth Taylor or—if they had any memory span—Ingrid Bergman, and to make it fit the President's widow. Who would court "Jackie"? What suitors would vie for her affection and hand?

Might an Englishman or some less acceptable foreigner win the former First Lady? Would such a marriage be unpatriotic? Would she, could she, choose a movie star? Who were the most available Benedicks in the world? How many of them were American? Would Lochinvar be a bachelor, a widower, or a divorced man? There were so many marvelous angles!

"Jackie" deserved the best. Therefore, fan magazine writers would not be guilty of prolepsis if they hailed 1965 as the "year of romance." So publishers instructed editors to exhort their contributors to charge their imaginations and really swing, because —at the very least—the mythogenic capacity of fan magazine readers was far greater than their taste. Romance was good, the motives of the fan magazines were impeccant, the sky could be looked to for inspiration and the sky was the limit. The challenge was there, the standard fixed; successful articles would give women prolapsus.

Fan books, in the year just past, had been able to capitalize on a number of approaches. Even in mourning, Mrs. Kennedy had private and public obligations that demanded her presence, and she traveled enough to delight the photographers. Some material about *her* was always available. Had Jacqueline Kennedy sought refuge in a stone tower on a rocky crag prowled night and day by the wildest beasts, the reasonless community of fan magazines would have been able to use positively this isolation. Some of the articles might have borne titles such as these:

Is Jackie REALLY in the Stone Tower?

Is JACKIE in the Stone Tower ALONE?

Lonely Thoughts of the Lady in the Stone Tower.

WHO Put JACKIE in the STONE TOWER?

RESCUE JACKIE FROM HER STONE TOWER!

WE POLL OUR READERS! SHOULD HOLLYWOOD
SEND JOHN WAYNE OR BURT LANCASTER TO
RESCUE JACKIE FROM THE STONE TOWER?

WE EXPOSE THE PLOT! *WHY* Jackie is in the
STONE TOWER!

In the Stone Tower . . . Jackie Looks Down on Those
She Knows and Loves.

Is It True That the Ghost of JACK KENNEDY Visits
Jackie in the Stone Tower?

How Jackie Spent—
    St. Valentine's Day
    The Ides of March
    Easter
    Mother's Day
    Bastille Day
    Thanksgiving
    Christmas
    New Year's Eve
    Guy Fawkes Day
      —in the Stone Tower.

We Take You to a Party! How JACKIE Could Make a
Stone Tower SWING!

Movie Mirror, as it hailed the New Year, diverted its January
readers with "Jackie's Dates in New York," and added a petty tagline: "Jackie began her new social life before her announced year
of mourning was up . . . and everyone's glad she did." In elabora-
tion, the nameless spinner of innuendo told of her appearance
at Shepheard's with "Mr. Earl E. T. Smith, a friend of her late
husband. . . . Then, as the music swelled, and as the dancers
twirled, Jackie stood up with a beautiful smile for Mr. Smith.
The next thing that happened was that Jackie was out there on
the dance floor, delighting everyone who watched her as she
picked up the beat of the music and twirled for almost two
hours."

Because fan magazines deal in vertiginous unrealities their
editorial activities often become eccentric; proof of this is Jim
Hoffman's *Photoplay* piece: "We Say: End the Indecent Attacks
on Jackie . . ." For his first-of-the-year, unseasonal calenture,

Hoffman lashed out unprofessionally at his peers and described *their* orations as "etched in acid and venom, framed in envy and spite," before he scorned them for "recent indecent attacks on her [that] could be entitled, 'Grieving Widow—A Pitiless Caricature.'" But readers of the magazines quickly recognized how Hoffman had only feinted at the enormity that was other writers, inasmuch as he then proceeded to charge Mrs. Kennedy with a full bill of particulars prepared by all the *other* writers:

> . . . a woman who enshrouded her dead husband in the mantle of Lincoln and mourned him excessively and for too long a time—and encouraged others to do so; who promised to bring up her children in Washington, where her husband had achieved his glory, where the Eternal Flame now blazes above his grave, but who broke her word and ran off to New York; who pushes her children into the limelight while pretending to "protect" them; who favors civil rights and integration, but shields Caroline and John-John from contact with minority groups; who seeks special favors and privileges for herself and her youngsters; who took a two-week vacation from her children—and away from the United States—and who plans to live abroad permanently; who allegedly wanted "privacy" but who exposed herself to publicity by involving herself in brother-in-law Bobby's campaign for U. S. Senator from New York; who pledged to spend a year in mourning but who began dating again before the first anniversary of her husband's death, and even plans to marry again.

Now that *others* had flayed *his* subject unmercifully, Hoffman may have clasped his hands in some semblance of piety before he typed—"What can we do—you and I—to end the indecent attacks on Jackie now?" Confronted by a problem as difficult as straining at a gnat and swallowing a camel, *Photoplay* could not —*Photoplay* did not know the answer. . . .

It happened: in January of 1965 Ben Hultz of *Movie TV Secrets* contributed "Must Bobby Die Like JFK?"—which he introduced with an ominous observation: "Somewhere in this country, a man is waiting for Bobby. . . . Waiting to do the same thing to him that Lee Oswald did to his brother!" However, "Jackie" was still the real circulation-builder, and in the same issue the ladies were offered a conversation piece with sufficient insincerity to please the most finicky. "Jackie Adopts Lynda Bird" established the President's older daughter as a rebel, and if voiced a year earlier might have given Barry Goldwater many more votes in November.

> "I bet you think I'm a beatnik. I guess I am. What difference does it make whether I comb my hair or not? We're all going up in an atomic explosion anyway," Lynda Bird Johnson said to this reporter in 1960 to jokingly explain her bare feet and messy hair.

But why would Mrs. Kennedy want to "adopt" anyone with "bare feet and messy hair"? Because "Jackie" understood "the difficulties of White House life" and she loved Lynda Bird. Bowed and "beset with tragedies in her own life, and with a family of her own to raise, Jackie has found the time to take Lynda under her wing. . . . Jackie has faced many of the problems confronting Lynda. She, too, once lived with a broken engagement."

If the fan magazines were made insensate by a world whose violence and organized evil led them to believe that they would not be challenged by rational press protest in 1965, they were wrong. *Time* (January 22, 1965) reproduced five fan magazine covers of Jacqueline Kennedy and evaluated what the magazine chose to identify as a "journalistic conspiracy" against their subject. In particular, *Time* called attention to Charlotte Dinter's article in the February issue of *Photoplay*, which discussed whether—for Mrs. Kennedy—it was ". . . TOO SOON FOR LOVE?" Possibly to chart Jim Hoffman on the richest course—*Photoplay* again decided to poll its quixotic readers:

I have read "Too Soon for Love?" and I think Jackie Kennedy should:

(Check one)

☐   Devote her life exclusively to her children and the memory of her husband.

☐   Begin to date—privately or publicly—and eventually remarry.

☐   Marry right away.

Clip and mail to: The Jackie Kennedy Poll, Box 2809 Grand Central Station, N.Y., N.Y. 10017

To conclude its censure, *Time* observed that "Mrs. Kennedy has been treated to this sort of gratuitous attention before. Two years ago, a rash of equally meretricious cover stories popped up on the newsstands. One of the articles ruefully confessed that Jackie Kennedy hated Hollywood. If she didn't then, she has every reason to now."

In *Time*'s next issue three letters to the editor congratulated the magazine for "put[ting] those money-hungry bums in their place." Fairness suggested that the editors of fan magazines would welcome an opportunity to prove they were not "money-hungry bums," so I wrote identical letters to the officers of *Photoplay, Motion Picture, Modern Screen, Movieland and TV Time, Movie Life, Movie Mirror, Movie Stars, Movie TV Secrets,* and *TV Radio Mirror.* My letter called attention to *Time*'s recent article and the published responses of its readers to the article. "There must be some reasonable explanation for your unusual interest in Mrs. Kennedy," I wrote, "and I would appreciate knowledge of it. In addition, there are four questions to which I would welcome answers: (1) What entertainment and intellectual inspirations do your articles about Mrs. Kennedy serve or fill? (2) Would you say that Mrs. Kennedy ap-

preciates these articles; and how do you arrive at your positive
or negative conclusions? (3) What is the average educational
level of your readers? (4) What contribution does your publication make to the shaping of minds toward socially acceptable
ends?"

None of my letters was acknowledged, but through another
source my third question was answered. In *Forbes·* (June 1,
1968), the magazine's publisher incorporated the findings of a
study completed for him by W. R. Simmons and Associates Research (an organization that studies media circulation, commercial markets, and related subjects) to prove that *Forbes* was
read by more "adults who attended or graduated college [and
were] employed as professional or managerial [personnel]."
Fifty-six magazines are listed, and although *Photoplay* ranks
fifty-third and *Modern Screen* is fifty-fifth (in both lists *Modern
Romances* is last), 15.8 percent of *Photoplay*'s readers and 10.7
percent of *Modern Screen*'s have a partial or full college education. Among adults who held professional positions or managerial posts, 6.7 percent read *Photoplay* (fifty-third in this
ranking) and 5.1 percent read *Modern Screen* (which stood fifty-
fifth).

By February the grist millers who supply the fan magazines
with "Jackie" stories had ground out a variety of trivia that
ranged from the melodramatic in *TV Radio Mirror* (" 'Tonight
You're Going to Die!'—How Jacqueline Kennedy Faced a Mad-
man's [Bomb] Threat") to a "sincere" piece authored by "A
Friend" for *Movie Mirror*—which informed palpitating readers
that "Jackie Is in Love Again." With whom? Well, not exactly
anyone, "A Friend" wrote; rather, "She is in love with life . . .
with people . . . with her new surroundings [and] the sounds
of her children's laughter."

Judith Perry was gossipy in that same month's *Movie TV
Secrets,* which featured her piece, "Jackie's New Neighbors Tell
All . . . WHERE SHE GOES, WHO SHE SEES, WHAT SHE
DOES!" But neighbors were slighted by Miss Perry for the

doorman at 1040 Fifth Avenue—and if readers were let down, they could turn to a companion piece in the same number by Sara Bowles, "How Jackie Saved Teddy's Marriage." It tells of a visit "Jackie" made to Ted after his plane crash, and stream-of-consciousness was employed to ready the fans as they roller-coasted into the injured man's mind: "How long will it really be before I'm out of here? Am I going to be permanently para-lyzed? They tell me I'm not, but what if I am? What about my campaign? And what about Joan and the children? I've been away from them so long. Joan is lonely, and I'm afraid Kara and Ted Jr., will forget how much fun we had together." But *what* did "Jackie" *do* to save Ted's marriage? There is vague refer-ence to the hospital visit and sitting at Ted's bedside to give Joan confidence. In truth, it isn't quite clear, but clarity was never a virtue in a fan magazine.

The theme of illness was further explored in March by re-liable Jim Hoffman, and once again in *Photoplay,* which de-voted almost the entire cover to a photograph of Mrs. Kennedy and a streamer: "WHY THE DOCTORS ARE *WORRIED* ABOUT JACKIE." Space was also devoted to Caroline Ken-nedy's supposed statement—"I know a lady who cries all the time—my *mommy* . . ." For substantive weight, Hoffman first quotes Marion F. Langer, Ph.D., identified as executive secretary of the American Orthopsychiatric Association, who says that "Mrs. Kennedy's mourning would differ only slightly from that of most of the 8,250,000 other widows throughout the United States," which gives Hoffman leave to snipe at the former First Lady for having had a personal interest in her husband's funeral and her subsequent activities on behalf of the National Cul-tural Center and the Kennedy Memorial Library. These, the author believed, were "abnormal manifestation[s] of grief."

And *Modern Screen*'s Kate Christiansen that March offered glimmerings of hope for the widow in "Jackie Kennedy Changes —Her New Life, Her New Look, Her New Love . . ." It was the second spring since the death of John Kennedy, but for his widow—who was "beginning to see [and] smile" again, it cer-tainly "seem[ed] the first." Shoddy reasoning conveyed by foggy verbiage befuddled any explanation, if any had been made, of how Mrs. Kennedy now chose to face life through a new look and a new love.

Of course the fan magazines wanted "Jackie" to know love again, they could hardly wait, but when Mr. Right came along, things would not be easy for her. Indeed, Leslie Valentine confided to readers of March's *TV Radio Mirror* that "The Hardest Words Jacqueline Kennedy Will Ever Have to Say: [are] 'You're Going to Have a New Daddy.'" Could *Movie Mirror* have had a publishing spy in the offices of *TV Radio Mirror?* If not, it is strong coincidence that a March offering by Hal Alfred should bear the title "Mommy—Why Do We Need Another Daddy?"

Elastic coincidence was employed that month by *TV Star Parade* when an anonymous contributor wrote "Dorothy Malone—Jackie Kennedy: The Secret Heartbreak and Happiness They Share." In explanation, "Dorothy's past life, like Jackie's, has been tempered by heartbreak. Jackie saw death reach for and take two children at childbirth. Her husband was torn from her in their hour of great triumph. And Dorothy felt pain at the death of her younger brother, who was struck and killed by lightning when he was only 16."

It certainly heartened some people that the real-life Mrs. Kennedy had enjoyed three months of comparative personal peace in 1965—but this could not have been the conclusion of anyone who read of her activities as presented by the fan magazines. There are, however, other agencies of media, and the daily press, radio, and television reported that Mrs. Kennedy was at Aspen, Colorado, for New Year's Eve, which she observed quietly after a pact was struck with photographers who agreed to accept a ten-minute session with Mrs. Kennedy and her children; thereafter they would be free of cameras. Other Kennedys joined her on the ski slopes for the first family holiday since the assassination, and Caroline and John joined Robert Kennedy's children at church and for play in the snow.

On January 4, 1965, Mrs. Kennedy and her children returned by air to New York where their plane circled Kennedy Airport for about an hour before it could land. Ten days later she protested the sale at auction of a letter she had written to Oleg Cassini, Incorporated, which disapproved the production of a fashion show to raise funds for a hospital to be built and named after her husband. The letter was withdrawn from auction. Later that month she declined a second invitation to attend President Johnson's inauguration, but she was present at the baptismal ceremonies for Robert Kennedy's son Matthew. At the end of the month she was one of a group of notables who greeted Mrs. Indira Gandhi at the opening in New York of an official photographic exhibition by the Indian government and dedicated to the "Life and Times" of former Prime Minister Jawaharlal Nehru.

Before Mrs. Kennedy and her sister, Lee Radziwill, left for a week's vacation at Acapulco, she was a guest at a luncheon given by the United Nations Secretary-General U Thant, in honor of Edgar Faure of France.

About a week after her return from Acapulco, Mrs. Kennedy took her children to Lake Placid; this weekend would have excited little attention if the press had not reported her refusal to stay at the Lake Placid Club because of its alleged discrimination against Jews. For much of March the daily press could report nothing of interest about Mrs. Kennedy until the 19th, when she was in the audience at the Metropolitan Opera House. Some six days later she wired congratulations to Robert Kennedy after he had reached the summit of Mount Kennedy in the Yukon.

During the month of April, Mrs. Kennedy gave a dinner party for twenty dignitaries and was honored by the dedication of the Jacqueline Kennedy Garden at the White House. The fan magazines continued to hammer hard at love and marriage for "Jackie," and in *Modern Screen* Kenneth Seller added his link to the nebulous chain of connection that makes this world so small in "The Untold Story about the Kennedys and Burtons," who—the author insisted—shared common memories. How? Long ago, when John Kennedy had been a bachelor in his early thirties, he had dated Elizabeth Taylor, just seventeen.

" 'I never met him again,' " the author reports Miss Taylor's wistful observation. " 'I don't even know if he remembered it.' " Burton, too, had met John Kennedy at a party given by Merle Oberon. But of greater importance, Mr. Seller insisted, was the fondness Mr. Kennedy had shown for *Camelot,* and particularly one of Mr. Burton's songs.

Even *Lady's Circle,* which identified itself as "The Friendship Club for Homemakers" and appeared to be a publication devoted to matters hearthside, published "The Love That Healed Jackie Kennedy's Heart" by Mary Andrews. It followed established fan-magazine literary practice by so thorough a rehashing of old "Jackie" events that the author never got around to revealing who or what was "the love that healed."

Of more interest to the housewife, *Inside Movie* for April employed the services of an anonymous quidnunc to pose a question fraught with international implications: "Now That Grace Asks, Will Jackie Forgive Her?" He reported a recent invitation to visit Monaco in which the hand of friendship had been extended to Mrs. Kennedy and her children by Princess Grace, who hoped to heal the breach between the ladies when "Jackie" became "miffed at Grace for failing to attend the late President's funeral." It was all the fault of Charles de Gaulle, the writer insisted, who would have also been "miffed" if the Monagasque rulers had attended the funeral. In retaliation, "Jackie may have returned the compliment when she snubbed Grace's picture book kingdom on her Mediterranean cruise last summer."

If March had been a slow month for the daily press in its coverage of Jacqueline Kennedy, May revealed a similar drought of "Jackie" articles in the fan magazines. *Photoplay* pulled Charlotte Dinter's "Jackie's Memory Book of Jack" out of its editorial trunk and published several photographs "never seen before." *Movie TV Secrets,* which had enjoyed a good response from its scare piece in January—"Must Bobby Die Like Jack?"—probably used the same anonymous writer for "Jackie and John-John Threatened." The article's inspiration lay in events of the previous year, when a young, deranged Canadian without employment had sent two letters to Mrs. Kennedy which threatened her and John with death unless she sent him a large sum of money. *Movie TV Secrets* seemingly did not care that their article might trigger another latent psychopath into dangerous and irrational activity.

Page 10 of the same issue offered another story without a by-line: "Teddy vs. Bobby." It speculated about a *possible* feud and "Senate-split" between the brothers. Eleven pages later, yet another unidentified writer presented "Jackie to Be First Lady Again?" This master of simulation included some torchy lyrics sung at an unnamed nightclub where Mrs. Kennedy might have been a guest. Touched by the sentiments contained in the song, "Jackie's [eyes] were lost somewhere in an eternity of pain and memory." After some more lines of bathos, the writer slipped in the zinger: Adlai E. Stevenson might wish to "take Jackie with him to the White House as his First Lady."

How nice indeed for the editors of *TV Radio Mirror* to give to readers of their June number reproductions of a painting they had commissioned of "Jackie" and her children. It went along with a piece entitled "A Mother's Day Gift from Jackie to You."

> This portrait . . . painted by artist Rosa Silverman especially for TV RADIO MIRROR readers, cannot be purchased anywhere, at any price. That is as it should be. For it is a gift, a Mother's Day gift offered in the hope that you will find . . . inspiration in it . . . and comfort.

Certainly it is evident that the portrait had not been presented to the magazine's readers by Mrs. Kennedy. Yet an unfamiliar reader who glanced through the pages of this particular issue would have assumed that Mrs. Kennedy had commissioned a family portrait, had presented it to the magazine, and was grateful to the publishers for their distribution of *her* gift to *their* readers.

"The Man Bobby Kennedy Protects Jackie From—And Why!" by Jae Lyle in the July *Photoplay* used a mystery-story approach. The piece put Bobby on the summit of Mount Kennedy in the Yukon (which the author lauded him for climbing) just as he placed JFK's personal flag on a snowbound rock. Then Lyle had "Bobby remember" a remark made by Jack about his "being strong and protecting the family if anything ever happened." Thus "Bobby" was portrayed as the stalwart brother-in-law who protected "Jackie from a man who threatened her present hard-won equilibrium and the prospect of future happiness." The plot thickens! The mystery deepens! Who is this man? Who can be he? After much speculation and a seasoning of red herrings, this prose bouillabaisse reveals the man as a purely mythical "fortune-hunter!" Of such whimsical nonsense is fashioned yet another episode in the fan magazine countdown, as "Jackie" is reported to have observed shortly after her husband was elected President: "I feel as though I've just become a piece of public property."

Not to be denied its fair share of this "public property," *Motion Picture* printed Jim Hoffman's inspiration, "Day by Day—Jackie Begins to Live Again." It employed another old device much favored in the Ruth Chatterton-Kay Francis-Irene Dunne vehicles of the thirties: The-Lonely-Woman-with-Tragedy-behind-Her-Building-a-New-Life. The Hoffman setting is Aspen, Colorado; the time is the ski outing during New Year's Week; the action is "Jackie's" shy speculation about the possibility of relinquishing her widowhood. Then in soap-opera style, the most effective dramatic device, came the wrap-up: "Today, Jackie smiles; today, Jackie laughs; today, Jackie warms the world with her own warmth. But her eyes are still a mirror of her soul, and those sad beautiful eyes continue to say (in an echo of the words of one of her favorite poets, Edna St. Vincent Millay), 'Pity me that the heart is slow to learn.' " This points up yet another axiom of fan-magism writing: when you can't think of an ending for a story, for God's sake, quote a little poetry—it adds such tone to the piece!

From time to time, *The New York Times* offers some of the most prescient psychological summations of the nation's emotional state. Thus, concern for mental health prompted Russell

Baker to discuss the merits of fan magazines. Datelined June 14, 1965, and filed from Washington, "Observer: The 'Burton-Liz' Bromide, Please," suggested in part:

> The cheap way to restore a failing superiority complex is to stop at the drugstore and buy an armful of movie magazines. Talk about misery! Nobody knows what misery is until he has had three hours on the couch with movie magazines.
>   . . . chewing through a sheaf of these lotus leaves convinces the reader that while his own life may be bad, it is a thundering success compared to the lives of the Gods.
>   . . . Take "Burton-Liz" which is movie-mag shorthand for Mr. and Mrs. Richard Burton. . . . The editors use two basic techniques for making the reader feel superior to "Burton-Liz." One is sympathetic recitation of their problems. The other technique is outright "abuse." Sensitive people may feel tempted to sympathize with the Burtons. Surely, nobody should have to sit still for all this peep-hole gossip. . . . Such sympathy would probably be misplaced. "Burton-Liz" probably seem even more fantastic to them than to us.

This is a revealing aside. Many of the "famous" people in fan magazines cannot recognize themselves on the printed page. And their quotations—when they are used—are rearranged to create contexts that become the envy of the most devious writers of Chinese contracts.

While fan magazine editors assigned staff clerks to comb the newspapers for inspirational material that could be used for future "Jackie" articles, Mrs. Kennedy made very little news. In May, she and her children flew to England aboard a USAF plane for the dedication of a memorial to her husband at Runnymead. The family was honored by the Crown on their arrival on May 13th, and John particularly enjoyed the changing of the guard at Buckingham Palace. The next day, at the ceremony of dedication, Mrs. Kennedy issued a statement of appreciation to the people of Great Britain. Later she had tea with Queen

Elizabeth at Windsor Castle, went sightseeing with the children, and shopped with her sister Lee. Unfortunately, British reticence was not in evidence; they were mobbed everywhere and the former First Lady was compelled to make a public appeal to permit her to enjoy the last days of her visit.

After she returned home, Mrs. Kennedy declined yet another invitation to the White House, although the occasion was an arts fête to be held in June. In the middle of the month she hired a new English nursemaid; on the 29th she attended the off-Broadway production of Leonard Bernstein's *Theatre Songs*. Her thirty-sixth birthday was spent at Hyannis Port with other Kennedys.

Immediately after President Kennedy was assassinated, his autograph and letters began to bring substantial sums of money from collectors. Later, a number of inconsequential letters written by Mrs. Kennedy turned up at auction. In one lot, a letter to Mrs. Johnson from Mrs. Kennedy was offered for sale by a campaign worker who had found it when she cleaned out some old files. When Lady Bird learned that Charles Hamilton of New York was offering this item for sale, she demanded its return. Hamilton obliged. However, various other letters written by the former First Lady were sold for substantial sums.

To cash in on this matter of legitimate interest, *Modern Screen* for July printed a James Albert Smith, Jr., article, "The Letters of Jacqueline Kennedy," which went flat out in its use of letters dating from 1953. Among the people with whom Mrs. Kennedy had corresponded were dressmaker Minnie Rhea, who had worked for "Jackie" during her "Inquiring Photographer" days in Washington; a member of the working press who was refused permission to photograph the Georgetown house where she and the Senator lived; and a little girl scheduled for open-heart surgery. But the most interesting letter concerned a Mr. Millard A. Dorsey, who had once loaned the Kennedys fifteen cents in 1954. In this instance, Mrs. Kennedy wrote in part: "I do hope we shall meet again soon. I wish it would be when you were trying to get into the movies and had forgotten to bring enough money so we could help you have a pleasant evening, the way you helped us." Along with the letter, was Scotch-taped three nickels.

In another treatment of the end of the mourning period Joyce Gilbert offered, "Friends Beg Jackie—Give Your Children a Father . . . The Decision She Had to Make!" in the July *TV Picture Life*. The story speculated on every conceivable romantic problem that might beset "Jackie," then neatly packaged all the speculations in a wrapper of homespun philosophy: "Jackie will open her heart. She won't rush into anything, because that is not her nature, but, in time, she will allow herself to think of loving again, marrying again, giving her children a father to love."

Two August stories gave fan magazine readers a taste of the sticky flavor of the month. *Photoplay* offered "Why Her Nurse Left the Children" by Jay Richards; and Christopher Kane in *Modern Screen* made good use of quotations from newspaper columnists to puff out "Why Jackie's Famous New Friends Are Hurting Her." Among these fascinating choices is included Walter Winchell's—"Jackie Kennedy made such a hit in Acapulco with a 3-inch-above-the-knee dress that fashionists hope she will wear it here"; and Joseph X. Dever's—"Ondine, the most 'in' of the current discothèques, added another chapter in its brief but action-filled annals when Jackie Kennedy came by with Rudolph Nureyev and Dame Margot Fonteyn."

August, 1965, was also a month when Mrs. Kennedy, through no fault of her own, was cast in a *chronique scandaleuse* which deserves presentation as a playlet.

WHO WAS THAT LADY I SAW?
(melodrama-comedy)

SCENE: Luxurious yacht, the *Southern Breeze,* afloat in the waters off Massachusetts.

TIME: August 7, 1965.

CAST OF MAJOR CHARACTERS:

Middle-Aged Singer: Frank Sinatra
Lovely Young Maiden: Mia Farrow

Two Middle-aged Duennas:
Claudette Colbert and Rosalind Russell
Mysterious Lady (wife of former juvenile
movie star): Pat Kennedy Lawford
Bystanders and Chorus; Boatload of Working Press
and Photographers; Assorted Groundlings

PLOT

Under the vigilance of two Middle-Aged Duennas, Middle-Aged Singer has been courting Lovely Young Maiden aboard yacht.

Mysterious Lady in dark glasses and bandana leaves motorboat for evening aboard yacht!

Photographers match pictures and after conference with Working Press conclude that Mysterious Lady who has boarded yacht is Widow of former President.

Widow's Secretary and Robert K. deny visit of Widow to yacht.

Press and Photographers pooh-pooh denials. Pictures and conclusions widely published in many many newspapers.

Several days later: denouement! Mysterious Lady *not* Widow of esteemed President, but sister-in-law of Widow and Wife of former juvenile movie star!

FAST CURTAIN

This particular episode was sparked by a continuing public interest in Mrs. Kennedy, as it was coupled with a visit by Mr. Sinatra and Miss Farrow to the Kennedy patriarch. Then, when the mystery lady appeared, wish became father to the deed, and the press agreed that the singer and his g.f. had invited Mrs. Kennedy to dinner. Fustian gossips on both coasts had it straight from the bilge: the yachting trip was either a wedding trip or a honeymoon for Sinatra; however, it was sometime later that the actual marriage took place—and then in the full glare of kleig lights.

Although the Sinatra-Farrow-Jackie affair kept the fan magazines in a hot simmer of creativity for months, Mrs. Kennedy lived quietly at Hyannis Port for some of August. Letters of Mrs.

Kennedy again became news in September, when Basil Rathbone, who had read at the White House in 1963, placed three letters sent him relative to his appearance, for sale with Charles Hamilton. The dealer advertised that the letters would be auctioned off on October 1 at the Gotham Hotel, and that he also intended to offer some letters and mementos of Lee Harvey Oswald. Mrs. Kennedy was reported to be "resentful" over the sale of her letters, but much to the despair of the hotel, which publicly deplored the transaction, Rathbone and the autograph dealer refused to cancel the auction. The packet of letters written by Mrs. Kennedy only brought $1,600, which disappointed the consignor and his agent. About two months later, Hamilton offered collectors an opportunity to buy a letter written by Mrs. Kennedy to Mr. and Mrs. A. Plagnard, a couple she had once considered employing.

When Pope Paul VI made his historic journey to address the United Nations Assembly in New York on October 14, Mrs. Kennedy heard him speak and later met His Holiness in private audience. Later in the month she leased a home in Bernardsville, New Jersey, a community well known among fox-hunting enthusiasts. At first, the permanent residents were pleased to have the former First Lady among them, but pilgrimages of sightseers and droves of newsmen and photographers made life so unpleasant and unsightly that the householders soon wished Mrs. Kennedy had leased elsewhere.

October marked Mrs. Kennedy's full return to social life. After the self-imposed year of mourning, the former First Lady had seldom appeared at large parties, and for nine months of the following year she had limited her entertainment to small groups at her home. The first real dinner party she gave was to honor John Kenneth Galbraith; after the dinner at her apartment, guests went to a sophisticated restaurant for late dancing. Several days later, in Boston, Mrs. Kennedy presided as honorary chairman at a ball to benefit the Boston Symphony Orchestra.

Pleasant events for November included the call Mrs. Kennedy made on Princess Margaret after her arrival in New York.

She also accepted the chairmanship of the Committee for the Whitney Museum. Less to her liking, certainly, was her failure to keep the *Ladies' Home Journal* from publishing in December an excerpt from the memoirs of Maud Shaw, the children's former nurse, soon to be published as *White House Nannie: My Years With Caroline and John Kennedy, Jr.* (1966). While the book dealt with the children and certain family attitudes, Miss Shaw's reminiscences of day-to-day trivia were less gossipy than any of the "backstairs" books already published or planned, and her anecdotes of life as a nannie were restrained.

In December Mrs. Kennedy bought a riding horse and attended a Christmas party at the Hodson Community Center in the Bronx. The day after Christmas she and her children left for the skiing at Sun Valley, Idaho.

By any and all appraisals, "Jackie" had made little news for the daily press; nevertheless, life was far fuller for her within the fan magazines. For example, an extended note of sentimentality was achieved by Christopher Kane in the September *Modern Screen* piece: "Why Bobby Needs Jackie."

> The chain which binds Jacqueline and Robert Kennedy together is forged of mutual agony; it is so strong that a word like love seems inadequate to describe it. But for all the talk of how much she leans on her brother-in-law, there has been little recognition of how much HE needs HER, of how reciprocal the relationship is.

"The Day John Met the Queen!"—compiled by anonymous *Movieland and TV Time* personnel—concentrated on the young boy's greater interest in a guardsman than the Queen. "Anonymous" made another inauspicious appearance in *Movie Mirror* with "Jackie Kennedy's Story Plus Personal Photos: He Wanted Me as a Wife." This sample of moral default masqueraded as a "Jackie" interview and told so much in the subtitles it was unnecessary to read the full article: "Reminisce with Jackie as She Talks of the Past. Then Share Her Dreams of the Future and What She Prays for."

By now a calendar fact of fan magazine publishing was evident. If Mrs. Kennedy did something in May that could conceivably interest the fans, it would be interpreted in the September and October issues distributed for sale during the months of June and July. An examination of October issues reveals that "Jackie" did no more in June than she had done in May to excite the imagination of these peculiar magazines. So Myron Fass, publisher of *Inside Movie* and an entrepreneur whom we shall meet again, had to spice his October issue with a "Jackie" cover and the boldest type.

Although Sophia Loren asked a uberous question, "Can They Jail a Pregnant Mother?"—most of the cover advertised a

SPECIAL
JACKIE
BONUS
HER SECRET
LIFE IN LONDON
PLUS
HER PUBLIC AND
HER PRIVATE
DATES IN N.Y.

The revelations were reminiscent of Ed De Blasio's article in the August, 1963, *Motion Picture*—"Jackie Kennedy's Bohemian Year in Paris!"—which also had delivered nothing. Similarly, an enormous carminative conjecture was attempted by *Inside Movie* concerning visits by "Jackie" to the opera and her attendance at a performance of *The Right Honorable Gentlemen* with Roy Jenkins, identified as "the writer." That the play was written by Michael Bradley-Dyne did not concern "Anonymous," who was off on a more significant flight of fancy as he revealed how "Londoners were abuzz at the thought of a possible romance."

October's *Movie Life* never revealed what danger its subjects faced in "Jackie and Sybil: The Untold Story of the Terror They Faced." But more was offered by Hillary May in "The

Day Jack Cried in Jackie's Arms," published by *Photoplay* in the October issue:

> John Fitzgerald Kennedy did not know that he was weeping. He could not have known, for tears were unfamiliar to him; the salt sting in his eyes was new. He had not wept since his childhood—and not often then, for Kennedys did not cry; Kennedys learned in the cradle to be brave . . . All he had been through in the hospital and before, all the suffering yet to come, lying flat on his back for months while the world raced by and left him behind, would not make him well. . . . His wife, Jacqueline, arrived for her daily visit, opened the door silently and took in all that she saw. She took from her bag a white handkerchief, and with infinite gentleness, wiped her husband's cheeks. At the touch, he looked up at her. "Was I crying, Jackie?" he asked.

For November and December, two magazines dusted off the Hyannis Port-Sinatra-Farrow-Colbert-Russell-Lawford-Jackie playlet. *Modern Screen* used Laura West's "What Mia Learned from Jackie about Sinatra," wherein Mia Farrow, as she sailed the stream-of-consciousness, conjectured about the *possibility* of meeting Mrs. Kennedy aboard the *Southern Breeze*. *Movieland and TV Time's* "Why Jackie Denied Meeting Sinatra" purred smugly: "It is an . . . unfortunate mistake, but one that is understandable, for there was a great resemblance, as you can plainly see in the accompanying picture."

Photoplay for November reverted to the sure-fire "medical angle" in "Jackie, Amnesia Victim—A Doctor's Report on Her Loss of Memory," by Milburn Smith, who analyzed some of Mrs. Kennedy's testimony before the Warren Commission. Smith, rather than the "doctor," emphasized that after President Kennedy was shot, movie film showed and eyewitnesses saw "Jackie" climb over the rear seat of the car, but she had not remembered *why*. Certainly, this was evidence of "amnesia."

The next month, the same magazine ventured out on a limb again: "Jackie's Prayers Are Answered—Two Years Too Late":

> For Jackie Kennedy November and December are the cruelest months, reviving memories of her husband killed and her dead son. At the end of the first week in August, she will kneel and pray to God, even as two years ago, in the maternity suite at Otis Air Force Hospital, she prayed for a miracle: even as two years ago, clutching Jack's hand as she left the hospital, she prayed for strength; even as two years ago, when the little boy and his little sister were reburied next to their father, she knelt at graveside and prayed not only that God would eternally bless the souls of her loved ones beneath the earth, but also that He, in His infinite wisdom, might spare other fathers and mothers the heartbreak that Jack and she had suffered during those agonizing August days in 1963.

Such stuff was not what November's *Movie Life* offered its readers in "Jackie and Liz Fight to Keep the Same Man," who turned out to be—of all people—their hairdresser, Alexandre. Nor could *Modern Screen* for December be accused of morbidity when it invited its readers along for a fun evening. However—"We Go to Jackie's Wild Discothèque Party" was only a warming-over of a *Time* story (October 1, 1965) of a conversation between Mrs. Kennedy and Killer Joe Piro, a dance instructor: "All my nieces and nephews do these dances so well. I'd like to do them well too."

Movie Life—first to inform its readers of Alexandre's importance to "Jackie" and "Liz"—returned the next month with another teaser: "Revealed: Caroline and John-John's Secret Dream" by Edward Coventry. Would you believe the "dream" was about Maud Shaw's house on the "rugged sandy shoreline in the seaside town of Sheerness, at the mouth of the Thames, in Southeast England," where it was claimed the children had once gone for a weekend?

CHAPTER TEN

"If the American Public Didn't
Want It, We Wouldn't
Sell a Damn Magazine."

MYRON FASS, Publisher, *Movie TV Secrets*

PROBABLY the most unsatisfactory way to define fan magazines is to catalog them as old or new. Equally unsatisfactory is to attempt a value rating based on their writers, for by now it is evident that the names we have met in preceding chapters write for all the fan magazines. Format, typeface, clarity of photographs, and advertising carried are equally unrewarding and melancholy areas of investigation. Could then some rating of these magazines be made on the basis of an unblushing insolence more or less criminous to its human subjects and their activities; or what regard they may have for propriety, relevance, timing; or the degree of responsibility a fan magazine feels toward its simpleminded purchasers? None of these can be used because all the magazines are guilty of heteroclite editorial policy and all adhere to a code whose principal tenet is to do violence to every standard of editorial ethics and human compassion.

Such a code is inconsistent and jerry-built; in one area only is there a united standard of conduct, and this is markedly evident when the fan magazines take it on their editorial shoulders to prescribe forms of behavior usually associated with matriarchal or hypocritical societies. For example, *Popular Movie* (January, 1966) ran "Married Men Only—The Dating Rules Jackie Must Obey!" by Florence V. Brown. It is audacious on several major counts; both are important to the title of the article and bring to mind two pertinent questions. Why should any publication like *Popular Movie* assume it has the authority to decide what rules of social behavior are acceptable? Does such an article appeal to teeny-boppers—at whom the magazine is slanted—or childish minds in older bodies? Both questions are meaningful to youth, and their implications weight the following paragraph of indictment in Miss Brown's homily.

> There is one thing that has baffled many of her friends, however. She seems to have made one hard and fast rule that governs her social life—married men only. Although she could have her choice of eligible bachelors to escort her to the Metropolitan Opera, to the opening of an art exhibit or on a skiing trip, *she chooses as her companions only those men who are cultured, socially prominent—and married* [italics added]. What, her friends ask each other, is the reason for this self-imposed restriction? Or is it entirely self-imposed?

Now that Mrs. Kennedy has been charged, some of her famous *married* companions are named: Leonard Bernstein, with whom she attended a preview of *The Sandpiper,* Robert Kennedy who accompanied her to a private screening of *Goldfinger,* and an appearance with her mother-in-law and Senator and Mrs. Edward Kennedy at the seasonal opening of the Metropolitan

Opera. In the curious minds responsible for *Popular Movie,* the company of married brothers-in-law is forbidden to a widow. In the zany world of fan-magism even the presence of a respected mother-in-law does not permit a widow to go to the theater with a brother-in-law and his wife. God help us—these are the rules laid down by Florence Brown, whose presumptiveness is revealed in her penultimate paragraph:

> However, the greatest obstacle to Jackie's involvement with another man, the reason she clings to the security of dating only those men who are out of reach because they are already married, is her own fear. Her fear of giving her love again and making it possible to be hurt again. Another heartbreak like the one she experienced after Jack's death might be too much for even a woman as courageous as Jackie to bear.

As if to prove that *Popular Movie* was right about "Jackie" only dating married men, *Modern Screen* bragged in January of how "We Join[ed] Jackie and Bobby For an Evening of Football" at Shea Stadium. And that was it.

Still, because it was 1966, new "Jackie" slants were expected by readers. From *Modern Screen*—of whom fans often expected more—the January offering was founded on the old editorial practice of associating "Jackie" with other persons-of-the-moment currently famous in fan magazines. Thus "What Jackie Did for Sonny and Cher" is never divulged by Jane Ardmore, for she was much too busy with her account of how the popular singers were flown to New York for "one memorable evening" at a party where Mrs. Kennedy was present. Sonny and Cher were welcomed by their hostess, who "threw open the door . . . just like Loretta Young!" Lyrical with wonder, Miss Ardmore describes "servants running around everywhere and beautiful people with diamonds dropping and sparkling, and almost the first person they saw was Jacqueline Kennedy wearing a magnificent floor-length gown, and the hand she held out to them had an emerald ring and on the wrist a fabulous diamond bracelet, and she was saying how much she liked their singing . . ."

Now Sonny and Cher were caught up in a round of introductions, and Cher is quoted by Miss Ardmore with relish as she recollects how their hostess, Mrs. Charles Engelhard, " 'who is just a doll, was introducing me to her daughter Annette, who is a real gas, and everyone was talking at once, about clothes, and about false eyelashes.' "

If social critics are dismayed, then hasten to point out that such articles appear only in "those" magazines, how do they explain the influence of "those" magazines on the respectable middle-class periodicals, such as the *Ladies' Home Journal,* which on January 18 of that same year took almost a full column in the Los Angeles *Times* to advertise that its February issue would feature "a fresh start for Jackie. . . . 'She has her old piz-zazz back,' says a long-time friend," and "life with Caroline and John-John"—which reintroduced as spokeswoman "Maud Shaw, the English nanny who helped raise the Kennedy children." Keeping the Kennedys company in this issue were their magazine relatives, the Burtons, stars of the *Journal*'s "world's most unhappy marriage?" For the good ladies who bought the *Journal* the editors promised an exciting lagniappe: a revealing report on *Who's Afraid of Virginia Woolf?*"—identified by the magazine as a "shocking film."

February fare among the fan magazines was even richer than that offered by the *Journal.* Specifically, *Photoplay* featured a "Jackie" hysteric by George Carpozi—"The Big Hurt that Keeps Them Apart"—stimulus for which was that eighteen months had passed since "Jackie" had last seen Lady Bird, but the "big hurt" that separated the First Ladies was never revealed.

Our old and trusted friend, "Anonymous," appeared again in the February *Movie Mirror* to tell us in confidence "How Jackie's Mother Stopped Her from Marrying." This rather old bromide told of a time before she met John Kennedy, when "Jackie" was briefly engaged to G. W. Husted, Jr.

"Jackie Asks Your Help—Please Accept Her New Husband" cried *Inside Movie,* which must have accompanied thousands of ladies as they were led to the hair-dryers. With hot winds blowing about their ears, housewives looked for equivalent temperatures among the coverlines suggesting torrid articles. Alas, although the tagline swore that "NOBODY ELSE COULD GET THIS STORY," none of the men mentioned in the article was news to the ladies.

But the ladies loved the article, and when their nails were dry, they reached for *Inside Movie*'s March number and "White House Nanny Tells Kennedy Family Secrets." Maud Shaw revealed nothing new. But nothing new was demanded, editors and writers understood this well. As she was fussed over at the beauty parlor by *her* hairdresser and *her* manicurist while they gabbed about "Jackie" and how to read between the lines, the matron felt that she had been levitated into the jet-set world where she could spend some magic hours before returning to home and a sink filled with unwashed dishes. With her hair sprayed and hands gloved to keep her nails from chipping, Mrs. America could wish to quiet hell her "mother [had] stopped her from marrying" a clod. If this had happened, she might have known a different life: skiing at Aspen, riding to the hounds in Virginia, being offered a blooded mare by an Indian prince. . . .

By the middle of January, 1966, it was evident that no replies would ever acknowledge my inquiries of the previous year, and in an effort to understand the women who purchased fan magazines, I began to ask questions directly of them. Teen-age girls usually bought their magazines at newsstands, which made it difficult, even dangerous, to speak with them. However, most supermarkets in metropolitan Los Angeles display large racks of magazines; and with the assistance of former students of mine, or friends, some of them members of the Writers Guild of America, West, we undertook to speak directly to anyone who bought a fan magazine in a supermarket.

Fourteen investigators assisted me in this survey, between January, 1966 and July of 1967, and in our experience only thirty-five men were ever seen buying a fan magazine. Only three refused to answer our standard question—"How come you're buying a fan magazine?" The replies of the other thirty-two can be stated as, "My neighbor's wife reads this crap and she asked me to get it for her. Frankly, he'd rather have her read this than run around, drink, or smoke pot."

During 1966, and through June 1967, more than 1,880 women who purchased fan magazines were engaged in conversation at market magazine stands.

The following tables may help establish how many and approximately how old were those who bought fan magazines and why:

Number of persons spoken to in supermarkets between January, 1966, and June, 1967:

Men	35
Women	1,882
Total	1,917

Ages of men (approximate):

20–35	18
36–50	11
over 50	6
Total:	35

Ages of women (approximate):

under 20 years of age	164
21–25	379
26–35	500
36–45	438
46–50	265
over 50	136
Total:	1,882

Why 35 men bought fan magazines:

For neighbors	24
For own wife or daughter	4
To see what women read	2
Cover looked interesting	2
Unsatisfactory replies	3
Total:	35

Why 1,882 women bought fan magazines:

For neighbors	977
For sister, other relative, or friend	104
For self	801
Total	1,882

Reasons for personal purchase of fan magazines:

To get interesting lowdown on people	854
Going to beauty parlor or other entertainment in next several days and have to have something to talk about	647
For scrapbook on a particular star	137
For Jacqueline Kennedy scrapbook	41
Articles are funny	34
Just something to read that won't give you a headache in these awful times	25
Unsatisfactory, or refused to answer	144
Total:	1,882

Almost every girl under the age of twenty (all ages approximate) replied, with some belligerence, that reading these magazines was fun and it gave them the lowdown on lots of people who weren't really so smart after all because everything they did was found out. Slightly older as well as much older women also were defensive, and more than half of them claimed to be buying the magazines for a friend, a neighbor, a stupid sister-in-law, or someone who wasn't feeling well and wanted something light to read that would give them a good laugh. Because all our investigators would nod in sympathetic understanding, the standard explanation was often amplified to include a denigration of the magazines as junk or trash; but then there would be a change of attitude and the purchasers would observe that in their opinion the magazines told a lot that other magazines or newspapers didn't. The mysterious "they" also said such magazines "really had the goods on the stars who were crazy to believe they could do the things they did and think they could get away with it."

When the discussion would finally turn to Mrs. Jacqueline Kennedy, almost all women expressed indignation at the magazines for their intrusion on the former First Lady. Then, without exception, they would turn devil's advocate and suggest strongly one or more of the following defenses of the magazines: (1) "Jackie" liked the publicity and probably had a publicity agent who engaged writers to do stories that were offered free to the magazines; (2) if "Jackie" had nothing to hide why should she or her friends be concerned with what the fan magazines wrote about her; (3) if "Jackie" didn't want to be written about in the fan magazines she shouldn't do the sort of things that interested fan magazines; (4) "Jackie" shouldn't be so concerned about getting married in a hurry; (5) a woman like "Jackie" should be more discriminating in her choice of friends and the places she visited; (6) no fan magazines wrote about Bess Truman or Mamie Eisenhower because they were ladies, and if "Jackie" wanted to stay out of the news she need do no more than emulate Bess and Mamie; (7) the fan magazines were the best reminders to "Jackie" that she was a human being and no better than anyone else when it came to a magazine calling the shots against well—things; (8) why should "Jackie" feel she was above criticism; (9) the fan magazines made "Jackie" a better mother because they watched her carefully and everyone knew that rich women weren't the best mothers; (10) many people kept "Jackie" scrapbooks and the best sources for stories and loads of pictures were the fan magazines.

By the end of March we had interviewed enough women at supermarkets from Hollywood to Santa Monica, or recruited them by cooperating beauticians (who were paid five dollars for every woman they could persuade to attend an in-depth interview) to schedule group discussions. To attend a discussion such women had only to admit reading fan magazines and be willing to discuss their contents.

Meetings were held on the following dates:

Date of meeting—1967 (10)	Women at meeting: (80)
April 5	8
April 26	7
July 15	8
August 11	9
September 23	6
October 9	9
October 20	10
November 16	7
November 29	7
December 11	9

Date of meeting—1968 (7)	Women at meeting: (53)
January 24	6
February 17	10
March 8	8
April 26	9
October 9	6
November 18	7
December 18	7

Not until the fourth meeting (August, 1967) were the interrogators (including myself) sufficiently skilled to make the most of such discussions, which averaged about three hours. Most of the cooperating researchers were women, and they offered the use of their homes and provided light refreshment. For most meetings, seven or eight women willing to volunteer information were present, and they were asked to complete short questionnaires which need not be signed. The women were encouraged to write rather than print their replies; if they felt any question to be improper they could leave it blank. About one woman in every twenty refused to complete the questionnaire; perhaps an equal number decided that they preferred not to participate in the discussions and left.

The following information was gathered:

Age: about 70 percent were between the ages of twenty-five and thirty-five.

Education: less than 8 percent admitted to no more than a grammar school education; almost 80 percent claimed to have graduated from high school. The rest—12 percent—claimed some college education. None claimed to have received degrees. (It should be noted that calligraphy, sentence structure, spelling, and organization of thought belied most of their statements.)

Married or unmarried: all claimed to be married; some admitted to more than one marriage.

Children: less than 5 percent had no children.

Last employment: before they had borne their first child.

Job held: without exception all claimed sales experience or employment as typist, file clerk, receptionist; their salaries averaged between fifty-five and eighty dollars a week.

Husband's education: all claimed that their husbands had graduated from high school. Not quite 10 percent claimed that their husbands had some college education. Only two claimed professional status for their husbands.

Husband's income: this ranged between eight and eleven thousand. Four claimed annual incomes of over fifteen thousand dollars.

Church affiliation: less than 10 percent listed any church affiliation. All admitted they were Christian.

Political affiliation: 33 percent were Democrats; 48 percent were Republicans; 19 percent claimed to be independents.

Motion Picture attendance: 8 percent went to the movies at least once every two weeks; 17 percent attended movies at least once a month; 55 percent saw no more than one movie every four months; 14 percent saw only one movie a year; 6 percent never went to the movies. All watched movies on television.

A full display of current fan magazines was placed on tables within easy reach. On completion of all the questionnaires, each was asked if she wished to be introduced to the others. There were women who preferred anonymity, but for the most part most offered their names; some of them became quite friendly and exchanged telephone numbers.

Questions had an established order and notes of responses were taken by the research volunteers and myself.

Do you like or dislike movie actresses more than television actresses?

By and large, television actresses were preferred, with Mary Tyler Moore, Lucille Ball, and Dorothy Malone the ranking favorites. Mia Farrow was least favored. The women divided equally on their feelings for movie actresses, with about half preferring Debbie Reynolds and Elizabeth Taylor. An overwhelming majority disliked Ava Gardner, Doris Day, and Sandra Dee. Almost all liked Hayley Mills and Deborah Kerr. In unison, they dismissed Jayne Mansfield and Raquel Welch.

Most of the women agreed that "liking" an actress did not mean they would enjoy having her as a friend or neighbor. Actresses were too pampered and conceited to be "real people." The only actresses who could be credited with any intelligence were Audrey Hepburn and Dina Merrill. Almost all agreed that Miss Hepburn was lovely, but among those who did not like her, most took exception to her diction. "She speaks like she's too good for the whole world," one woman said. "She must think she's Adlai Stevenson or Eleanor Roosevelt."

Would you prefer to be Elizabeth Taylor or Jacqueline Kennedy? Prior to the assassination of President Kennedy, most agreed they would have preferred to have been born Jacqueline Kennedy. Older ones agreed that when Elizabeth Taylor had made her early movies—between *National Velvet* (1945) and

Father of the Bride (1949)—she had been one of their favorites. About 10 percent of the women would have preferred to be Elizabeth Taylor if they would not have to accept her weight problem. None of the women appeared to show much disturbance over the accidental death of Mike Todd—Miss Taylor's husband.

Who contributes more to your understanding of the present —Elizabeth Taylor or Jacqueline Kennedy?

This question proved difficult. When I explained that we considered both women to be products of our time, the discussion became more animated. An overwhelming majority agreed that sex was a prominent factor in American life and that Elizabeth Taylor—like Ingrid Bergman—was an emancipated woman. However, the best features of American life were incorporated in Jacqueline Kennedy.

Who contributes more to your imagination—Elizabeth Taylor or Jacqueline Kennedy?

Again the subjects were divided about equally. Elizabeth Taylor certainly did the more adventuresome things and shrugged off any attempt at censure. The marriages of Miss Taylor; her battles with gossip columnists—particularly Hedda Hopper; her romance and marriage to Richard Burton; that she could become so ill and still win an Academy Award as Best Actress; and that she was really beautiful and lived in real life like Cleopatra—these endeared Miss Taylor to many women.

On the other hand, Jacqueline Kennedy was an aristocrat and moved in circles where Miss Taylor would only have been accepted as an entertainer. Jacqueline Kennedy was the equal of Elizabeth II of Great Britain, which could never be said of Elizabeth Taylor.

Do you dislike either of these women? Or both? Why?

Most took exception to "dislike." They preferred to think of themselves as constructively "critical." Elizabeth Taylor took what she wanted out of life—even the husbands of other women —and this should not be permitted. Elizabeth Taylor broke whatever rules of conduct she found repressive because she "could get away with it." Without exception, all resented her receiving a million-dollar salary for a picture. Most agreed that if Elizabeth Taylor ever divorced Richard Burton and attempted to remarry, her children should be taken from her by the courts.

Jacqueline Kennedy "pretended" democracy but she was a snob. And they didn't like her "little-girl" voice, she was a "culture vulture," a woman who did too much traveling. Many resented her wealth and wondered how much she actually gave to charities, if this sum was greater than her contributions to the opera and other cultural activities without meaning to "average people." One woman suggested that Mrs. Kennedy welcomed the discussion generated by the Warren Commission Report because it kept her in the public eye and "got her lots of publicity." About six women resented Mrs. Kennedy putting her children in private schools, but most agreed that private schools were better than public schools. More than a dozen defended the enrollment of *their* own children in private schools.

Do you agree or disagree that the women we are discussing— Jacqueline Kennedy and Elizabeth Taylor—get the press coverage they deserve?

To a woman, all agreed that the star and former First Lady were being given fair coverage. However, if either "did not want to be written about they shouldn't do things that get them written about."

Do you read gossip columns? If so, whom do you enjoy most?

Until her death in February of 1966, Hedda Hopper had been an overwhelming favorite; Sheilah Graham was second, and Louella Parsons a poor third. Some enjoyed Sidney Skolsky. Fewer enjoyed Walter Winchell. Very few found Dorothy Manners an adequate replacement for Louella Parsons. About three women were acquainted with Mike Connolly of the *Hollywood Reporter* and Army Archerd of *Daily Variety*. One maintained that Mike Connolly really went to the "in" parties and knew more about Hollywood than all the other columnists combined.

If you were Jacqueline Kennedy or Elizabeth Taylor, would

you enjoy or resent the coverage in the gossip columns and fan magazines?

A majority said they would resent the coverage—if they had something to hide. Which inspired the next question: *What did either of these women have to hide?* A majority averred that their conduct left much to be desired, although Jacqueline Kennedy was better behaved than Elizabeth Taylor—at least she appeared to be. . . .

Among the fan magazines, which do you think are the most reliable? The least reliable? Motion Picture was rated more reliable than *Photoplay* by a scant majority. *Modern Screen* was voted less reliable. Standards for these judgments could not be offered. Rather, the composition of the covers seemed to help form the opinion of those present. Among the least reliable magazines were those that had too long titles and looked like *Confidential.* Magazines devoted to singers, rock-'n'-roll performers, or juvenile actors and actresses were wholly unreliable. In the main, these judgments were subjective and founded on instinct.

Do you think fan magazines have a right to publish intimate and private details of the lives of their subjects? Why?

This portion of the discussion always inspired laughter. Magazines were in business to convey this coverage. If they didn't some other magazine would. People had a right to know as much as they could about the people they were interested in. People who were afraid of stones shouldn't live in glass houses. As to *why* magazines had a right to report the intimate details of the life of their chosen subjects, some women suggested that a free press guaranteed this right. Furthermore, the fan magazines made people in show business "toe the line." And this was for their own good. But—it was suggested—Mrs. Kennedy was *not* in show business. . . . Reply was immediate: "Then she shouldn't do things that show business people did." *What were these things?* Evidently—"the things that put her in the magazines!"

Why do you buy and read fan magazines?

"Because their subjects are interesting people," seemed the

favored reply. All concurred that through the fan magazines they learned about jet-set activities and what it was like to be able to go anywhere and afford anything.

Others said such magazines made them feel good; although they were only "little people who didn't count," their lives were far better than those of the rich and famous. Proof of this was that rich and famous women were always ill, usually lost their husbands and lovers, were always having trouble on their jobs and with other people on their jobs, and were always feuding with other rich and famous people over their fair share of scripts, publicity, parties, and good roles. Somehow, it seemed to the ladies that wealth and fame traveled hand-in-hand with unhappiness; "you can't have one without having the other."

More than half the women who participated in the discussion agreed that knowledge about the stars enabled them to "keep up their end of conversations. . . . No one wants to sit around and have nothing to say. . . . It's fun to talk about the stars and even 'Jackie' because it makes you look like you're up on things."

Who are your favorite writers of fan magazine articles? My volunteers quickly learned to restrain their astonishment that not one of the women who had participated in the seventeen group meetings could name *any* fan-magazine writer. Most attempted to open a magazine and look, but this was not permitted. An occasional woman would suggest that Hedda Hopper and Louella Parsons had written articles, but they could not give the gist of such articles. When the name of Walter Winchell was offered, the article he had written could not be identified. This portion of the discussion usually annoyed the subjects, so another question was asked:

Who could offer for discussion some activity about Mrs. Kennedy that has not been covered in the fan magazines?

This drew an absolute blank. Promptings such as—with whom had Mrs. Kennedy and her children gone skiing at Gstaad; how much money had President Johnson asked Congress to approve for the operation of Mrs. Kennedy's New York office; what foreign country had she visited with her children during Easter (1966); where had Mrs. Kennedy and her children been stranded by an airline strike; what was the name of the book Mrs. Kennedy had attempted to bar from publication; what famous newspaper columnist had succeeded in getting a lengthy interview with Mrs. Kennedy which was published in three installments by a New York newspaper; when did the Navy intend to launch a vessel named the *John F. Kennedy* (this had already been done in May)—all of these drew blank stares, then expressions of anger. These women were busy and didn't have time to read everything about Mrs. Kennedy and her family. Besides, they really didn't care about Mrs. Kennedy and her family who were too much in the news anyway—and what made them think people were that interested anyway?

It was immediately evident that readers of fan magazines were wholly uninformed about "Jackie's" activities unless they excited the interest of fan magazine writers. Their concentration, like that of the fan magazines, was only on her widowhood, what it was like to be young, beautiful, and without a husband, and when she would remarry. One woman, wrathful at this exposure of her ignorance, said that "Jackie doesn't want to marry again, but she wants all the fun of marriage." Almost immediately she regretted her outburst, asked forgiveness of everyone, and left.

A coffee break became a diplomatic necessity at every session. During it the ruffled ladies were mollified with small flatteries and assurances that none of the researchers had been able to answer more than one or two questions, and had concentrated for long periods of time on this study.

What is conclusive is sad: each woman admitted reading little more than fan magazines, seldom watched a television newscast or listened to the news on the radio. This condition inspired the next question:

What shows did they enjoy most on television? In order of preference, for 1967, the ladies were pleased most by "Jackie Gleason," "My Three Sons," "Gomer Pyle—USMC," "Get Smart," "The Lucy Show," "The FBI," "Beverly Hillbillies," "Green Acres," "Bonanza," and all the movie nights. Favorite shows for 1968 were "The Lucy Show," "Red Skelton," "My Three Sons," "The Dick Van Dyke Show" (reruns), "The Dean Martin Show," "Beverly Hillbillies," "Green Acres," "Daktari," movie nights, and seasonal sports events. The talk shows of Joe Pyne, Merv Griffin, Johnny Carson, and Joey Bishop were also enjoyed. Some few watched "CBS News" because they thought Jerry Dunphy and Bill Keene were cute.

What, if anything, did they enjoy on radio? Without exception, all those who listened to radio enjoyed the radio talk-shows most, especially those where the radio personality—Joe Pyne, Bob Grant, Jack Wells, Michael Jackson, and Steve Allison—"told people where to get off." Of this group, Pyne, Grant, and Wells were overwhelming favorites because they were "good Americans and not afraid to take on do-gooders, atheists and Communists." Jackson and Allison were less favored because they were "liberals" and insisted on "discussing facts."

Would they go to a movie that starred Jacqueline Kennedy? Yes, but only to see if she could act. If she couldn't act "they would be the first to tell her." At least twice women asked if I had knowledge of Mrs. Kennedy accepting a movie contract and they demanded to know if I were employed by a company who determined audience acceptance of "Jackie" as a star? My denials were never quite believed.

Would they encourage teen-agers to read fan magazines? To a lady they demurred. Such magazines were filled with too much sex and other depictions of adult delinquency to be read by anyone of innocence. Only adults who had experienced enough of life to know fully the distinction between right and wrong should be permitted to read fan magazines. For teen-agers, fan magazines were as bad as comic books; and "they could never help anyone get an education and go on to college."

The discussion was almost at an end. What else would anyone care to contribute? Almost a third of those present observed that they had learned to read *into* fan magazines stories—which to defend themselves against legal suit "had to do most of their story-telling between the lines." With practice a reader could construe "what had really happened."

About a third agreed that most stories were timeless and old fan magazines were as interesting as those of recent date. They could be read again and again.

After the meeting of November 16, 1967, one woman lingered to tell me that the stories of stars in the fan magazines had done much for her emotional health and libido. Years of reading about the illicit romances of the stars had made her realize that none of them had suffered at the box office or in the opinion of the general public; thus she had been able to relax and enjoy sexual activity, which heretofore she had considered shameful.

At the July, 1967, meeting, and for the balance of the year, I was tempted to call to the attention of the women in the discussion groups an article that had appeared in the Los Angeles *Times* on May 15. My assistants and I had discovered how angry our participants had become when it was suggested that they were careless readers and uninformed, so we never referred to the article directly. But John J. Goldman's piece is so pertinent it merits full reproduction here:

MRS. KENNEDY A STAR, HELPS KEEP
MANY U.S. MAGAZINES IN PROFITS

NEW YORK—On the 10th floor of a red brick building on New York's lower 5th Ave., a Jackie factory flourishes.

An assembly line of writers, editors, and researchers for a firm that publishes fan magazines toil here daily, turning out stories about Mrs. Jacqueline Kennedy. Old newspaper clippings are studied, latest biographies are read, pictures of Mrs. Kennedy are carefully chosen.

The factory's work, and the work of other factories, appear in magazines this month across the nation with these headlines:

"JACKIE SAYS: CAROLINE WON'T DATE TOO SOON."

"THE SECRET MEN IN JACKIE'S LIFE—THE ONE SHE'LL WED."

"CAN JACKIE PUT PETER AND PAT TOGETHER AGAIN?"

It's a profitable business. Two and one half years after the assassination, public thirst for stories about Mrs. Kennedy remains unquenched.

It's a Scramble

The biggest magazines scramble to write about her. Just this month, for the third time since Dallas, *Life* featured the former First Lady—this time astride a white horse—on its cover. *Look* has used Mrs. Kennedy three times. In June, her name will be on the cover of *McCall's*.

And on U.S. newsstands, at least 35 fan and movie magazines put Mrs. Kennedy on the cover every month.

"Jackie Kennedy indisputably falls into the category of the star," said an official of Macfadden-Bartell Corp., publishers of *Photoplay* and other movie and TV magazines with more than 3 million circulation. "We run Mrs. Kennedy frequently, and Mrs. Kennedy sells."

Headlines Count

For many smaller fan magazines, an extra catchy Jackie headline, an extra striking photograph, makes the difference each month between profit and loss.

"I try to have her on the cover every month," said Myron Fass, a 40-year-old former commercial artist who publishes *Movie TV Secrets* and other fan magazines from his lower 5th Ave. office.

"If you take Jackie off your cover and you put someone else on," said Fass, "sales go down. If you put David McCallum on the cover, there might be a 20% drop in sales." (McCallum, co-star of TV's popular "Man from UNCLE," is one of today's biggest teen-age attractions.)

Profits Are Target

The potential profits and public thirst have spawned the Jackie factories.

The boom is based on sound economics. One survey shows that 86% of the women who buy family magazines are married and have children. Mrs. Kennedy has great identification.

Competition is cutthroat; magazines stop and start monthly.

"All you need is a line of credit and you are in business," said a consultant in the field.

Like any business, there are certain formulas. To spur sales, Mrs. Kennedy is always labeled Jackie.

"We always use Jackie," explained Fass, doodling on a sketch pad in his wood-paneled office hung with his own paintings of children and a leggy modern dancer. "Jacqueline is not American. If anyone saw her on the street, they wouldn't say 'there's Jacqueline,' they'd say 'there's Jackie.' "

All stories about Mrs. Kennedy must be positive, as a part of the formula. Publishers find that derogatory articles about her just don't sell.

"She has pushed Liz Taylor, the phenomenon before her, off magazine covers," said Fass. "Liz was a 'bad girl.' Jackie is always positive. We never have a negative Jackie line on the cover. She is the First Lady, I mean the former First Lady."

Stories generally say that Jackie will find happiness; she has suffered enough!

Since the Jackie magazines depend 90% on over-the-counter sales, the piece de resistance, the true stock and trade of any Jackie factory, is its supply of catchy cover lines. These are designed to stand out on newsstands in the jungle of other Jackie publications and make readers buy that book, generally for 35 cents.

"It takes a great psychologist to be a cover line writer," said Fass. "The simplicity has to touch a great mass."

Fass knows his psychology. For the briefest moment he thought, then leaned back in his chair and with no difficulty poured out a stream of lines:

"The new young men in Jackie's life" . . .
"We reveal Jackie's secret guy" . . .

"You can help plan Jackie's wedding" . . .

"Of all Jackie's dates, the man the children love best."

New cover lines are a closely guarded secret. Tours of Jackie factories—if they are allowed at all—are conducted almost on the run.

Stories themselves are constructed from many sources. Larger magazines pay reporters to follow Mrs. Kennedy when she makes a public appearance. *Photoplay* assigned two correspondents to be near her when she visited Spain recently.

Everyone Interviewed

In the search for new anecdotes, new scraps of information, even old dressmakers and nursemaids have been interviewed.

Smaller magazines with less money follow newspapers and carefully collect each other's stories. Often they feed on each other.

"For example, if I write Jackie Kennedy loves Ringo Starr of the Beatles," said one Manhattan author familiar with techniques, "six or seven months later, someone else will write 'why Jackie jilted Ringo.' "

A necessary gambit is the suspense ending. Since Mrs. Kennedy's private life is very private, this is vital.

One Report

After discussing Mrs. Kennedy's social life, the standard technique (from the already out July issue of *TV World,* published in Manhattan by Michael and Stanley Morse):

"We can't say for sure yet.

"One thing is certain, though.

"Jackie will undoubtedly make an important decision in the very near future.

"One way or the other."

How did it all begin? Publishers generally agree it began with the assassination. "She's the heroic person who gets dragged down. It's the old Greek tragedy," said one editor.

When will it end? "I suppose if Jackie married an older man, she would dwindle," said Fass. "It happened to Debbie Reynolds. There was a period when Debbie Reynolds was on the cover of every movie book.

"We don't do anything the American public doesn't want. If the American public didn't want it, we wouldn't sell a damn magazine."

March in fan magazine land attempted to prove, at least through *Photoplay*, the truth in Ralph Waldo Emerson's trenchant observation that "a foolish consistency is the hobgoblin of little minds." In the by-line to "The First Man Jackie's Cried Over Since Dallas," Harriman James is identified as the author. But after all the tears are shed and Mrs. Kennedy is reported to have wept "at a secluded table in one of Manhattan's most elegant restaurants," the reader is uncertain whether the cause of her tears was Bennet Cerf or an author published by Random House who intended to do a "minute-by-minute account" of the assassination. If this event took place, it was unreported by the daily press and other media, which may lend substance to the statements of ladies at our meetings who insisted that "people had a right to know as much as they could about people they were interested in."

At this time it is proper to ask: *who* writes for fan magazines? What are the characteristics of a fan magazine writer, who—to sell stories to Myron Fass and his peers—must compose pieces as rife with bathos as they are unfeeling of privacy or bereft of sense? Would any writer want his real name on such a contribution, especially if he had been assigned to write about "Jackie"?

A Hollywood publicist, who for obvious reasons asked that his name not be used, had this to say: "In Hollywood, a fan magazine writer who has a legitimate assignment from a fan magazine and interviews the stars must submit the story to the studio and players for their okay. But most of the sensational stories are dreamed up in New York offices for the fan books."

Ezra Goodman, in *The Fifty-Year Decline and Fall of Holly-*

wood (1961), has his own comments to make on this "dream" practice:

> "Today," says a voluble but retiring fan magazine writer whom we might as well call Mr. Anonymous, "the fan magazines have completely adopted the *True Confession-Confidential* magazine style. It goes way beyond *True Confession* and that sort of thing. What they have now is fiction writers back in New York who have not been to Hollywood and know nothing about Hollywood. Most of the time, anyway, they're written from newspapers. Sometimes they have someone in Hollywood send them 'notes.' The fan magazines say 'we go on the assumption and contention that we cannot write the truth about most of the people in Hollywood because it is so sordid and horrible. So we make them look better.' But they make them look like assholes. They just make it all up. It's 100 per cent fictionalized."

"The fan magazines pay ridiculously low prices for material, except for an occasional big name," says a current fan writer who must also remain hidden at the bottom of his barrel. "Of course, if a big name like Fannie Hurst consents to do a piece, then it probably goes through her agent who extracts as much loot as possible. But the average-run hack writer, like myself, is lucky if he gets a hundred lousy bucks for a story he had to dream up in the first place. I have a kid in college, two in high school, and one that slipped in just three years ago. I thought I could get out of this rat race in 1952 and finish a novel I started when I was in college. But freshman year I had to quit and I've been supporting my family ever since. I used to have a pretty good reputation around town—and still work in an advertising agency—but when the studios stopped calling me after they let their big stars go—I finally realized that the taint of the fan books had colored me 'brown.' My agent couldn't get me a decent magazine assignment to do in the slicks, for whom I had occasionally worked, so I turned to advertising copywriting.

"I still sold—and do now—to the fan mags, under about three dozen pseudonyms. Few of the fan book writers today use their real names. Not only because they are in a rut and can't get out, but because they'd get a few punches in the nose by some of the guys they've smudged over the years. The husbands of the stars are pretty sensitive too about some of the crap written about their wives. Just say I came to Hollywood in 1932 to become a screenwriter and ended up a nothing-writer. Sure I'm bitter. But I suppose I've lived off the crumbs of the fan books so long, I can't come up with a decent compound sentence anymore."

There has been some disagreement between the editors and publishers of fan books over the use of Mrs. Kennedy on the cover and in sensationalized articles inside. Editors have been known to resign over the publisher's insistence that Mrs. Kennedy constantly appear in their publications. However, in all honesty, it must be stated that the fan magazines use popularity polls to determine *who* should get preferential star-treatment. If letters from readers and various polls indicate that Mrs. Kennedy is the lady who sells magazines, then the magazines have no alternative but to feature her as often as possible, and as often as she continues to delight the fans.

After the writer we interviewed admitted that he wrote "under about three dozen pseudonyms," the *Film Daily Yearbook* for 1966 was consulted, specifically the section titled "The Working Press." The following names, with which we have become familiar, are not listed: George Carpozi, Kate Christiansen, Edward Coventry, Charlotte Dinter, Florence Epstein, James Gregory, Jim Hoffman, Harriman Jamis, Christopher Kane, Stacy Kytell, Jay Richards, Leslie Valentine—and others.

Really then, what difference would it have made if the ladies in our discussion groups had remembered the names. If a shadow is given a name, does it become visible, or viable?

CHAPTER ELEVEN

"Behind the Year's Hottest Headlines— the Real Stories"

Screenland Annual 1966

Despite the unpopularity of reality with an increasing number of citizens who find cozy and/or erotic comfort in fantasy—fact and its documentation are never wholly ignored by pushers of emotional narcotics. Some reference, therefore, to reality suggests that a précis of Jacqueline Kennedy's activities for 1966 will enable the straight folk, hardnosed in their preference of fact to opinion, to have a better understanding of fan magazines and how life's raw materials are utilized by "Jackie factories" to manufacture whopping fantasies. Was it Aristotle who suggested that as the island of knowledge grew ever larger, the shorelines of ignorance expanded?

No mythology, even when it concentrates on zoomorphic elements and places the human condition in a lesser position of importance, can totally ignore reality. To be intelligible and popular and capable of easy propagation, myths must be simple and readily understood by autodidacts, for they rely heavily on those empirical experiences that best stimulate wonder and excite the libidinous imagination. After a community has surrendered itself to fantasies, legends, and myths, if its apostles intend to popularize their mysteries and gain new converts, the missionaries charged with the propagation of faith must choose evangelists with proven capabilities for lunacy as well as hyperbole, inasmuch as only the most fervent of these can convince a strange people that their realities are inferior to the golden calves offered by the munshis from below the horizon. It is their task to convince the movers and shakers among the heathen that the new combination of myth and fact is more appealing than the old.

Certainly, in the light of reasonable affinities, no modern myth can ever be lastingly popular in a mechanized community unless it will show a profit. No modern myth will ever become a popular placebo unless it can—in some situation of grave personal or community emergency—provide comfort and emotional surety against a real situation of danger or cataclysm. Jacqueline Kennedy is real; "Jackie" is a myth. The myth is far more popular than the reality. To keep the myth ever broadening and popular, the fan magazines make efficacious use of only those realities that lend themselves to profitable exploitation of their particular areas of fantasy.

Briefly then, after a ski vacation at Sun Valley in early January, Mrs. Kennedy made plans for more skiing abroad. She and her children were accompanied on their flight to Switzerland by John Kenneth Galbraith, his wife, and other friends. Unfortunately, on their first day at Gstaad, Mrs. Kennedy and her children were mobbed by a small army of tourists and a vanguard of at least twenty-five carloads of reporters and photographers. Reasonable, then stronger pleas for privacy were made before Mrs. Kennedy bargained with photographers, a successful tactic she had employed at Sun Valley. It was agreed that she would permit photographers a period of twenty minutes to take pictures, then they would leave. And so, with shutters clicking and flashbulbs popping, Mrs. Kennedy pulled John-John on his sled and played with Caroline in the snow. However, when the session was over, the photographers disavowed their agreement, refused to leave the slope, and Mrs. Kennedy returned to the lodge in tears.

Shortly thereafter she departed for Rome, where she was the guest of Antonio Garrigues y Diaz Canabate, Spain's ambassador to the Vatican. The visit to Rome was especially enjoyed by Mrs. Kennedy, who for the first time in years, was able to walk along a crowded street and not be hounded by people after they recognized her.

While Mrs. Kennedy was in Rome, President Johnson asked the Congress to approve its usual grant of $50,000 for the operation of her office in New York. Although some opposition was voiced by a minority of elected representatives, who reasoned that their approval of this grant for a third year might make it a permanent expenditure of government, the sum was appropriated. But in April Mrs. Kennedy informed Representative Edward P. Boland of a considerable drop in mail addressed to her; therefore, $30,000 would cover her expenses for the calendar year. Some months later she suggested curtailment of the entire allowance, and funds were cut off as of July 1, 1967.

On February 2, Mrs. Kennedy had an audience with the Pope and some conversations with Cardinal Amleto Giovanni Cicognani, Secretary of State of the Holy See. These meetings and conversations displeased fundamentalist Christians, especially those who saw in religious liberalism signals of considerable danger to their own myths of quantum bigotry. Several days later, Mrs. Kennedy returned to Gstaad, where she thanked the Swiss community for its hospitality (the following month she sent a $1,500 check for improvements to the town's social institutions). After her children and she returned to New York, the only news for March considered noteworthy by the more normal press was her attendance at a concert, her appearance as a spectator at the St. Patrick's Day Parade, and some Easter shopping toward the end of the month.

On April 4 she left with both children for an Easter vacation in Argentina, where she was given an official welcome and luncheon by President Arturo Umberto Illia. For the remainder of her visit, Mrs. Kennedy was a guest at the ranch of Senor M. A. Garcano at Cordoba, where visitors were kept at a minimum as the former First Lady rode, visited a chapel, and thwarted young John's attempt to swim in the nude. Real unpleasantness developed after a South American magazine ordered a cameraman to add a telephoto lens to his equipment, which he was to use after he had breached security on Senor Garcano's estate. The photographer stalked Mrs. Kennedy and Caroline as they went to a secluded pond to swim, and he photographed them as they changed into their swimsuits behind shrubbery. Every photograph appeared in South American publications, but the most embarrassing snapshots were not reproduced in the United States. When concerned people asked why Mrs. Kennedy was treated so unceremoniously by the foreign press and their photographers, the reply became self-evident: the press representatives of her country, where her husband had been elected to its highest office, treated her as shabbily.

Not quite two weeks later she returned again to New York, placed both children in school, and packed again for a visit to Seville, where she would be a guest of the Duchess of Alba during the Spanish holidays of April. On the night of her arrival a charity ball was held in the palace of the Duke of Medinaceli. Among the international guests were the reigning Monagasques, Prince Rainier and Princess Grace, whose meeting with the former First Lady might have been meaningful to the fan magazines if they had not concentrated on *châteaux en Espagne* conjecturals of a romance between Ambassador Garrigues and "Jackie." While the fan magazines made natural and unnatural efforts to gather every scrap of information that could be used to gauge how this international love-match would fare, Mrs. Kennedy attended a bullfight, where she was hemmed in by excited crowds and members of the press. Similar attention was focused on her when she visited Seville's six-day Feria. Mrs. Kennedy's attendance at a bullfight subjected her to censure by the New York City Humane Society just a day before she was the honored guest at a dinner party given by our ambassador to Spain, Angier Biddle Duke. Before Mrs. Kennedy left Madrid for London and home she denied flatly reports of any marriage plans—and most certainly those involving Senor Garrigues. For the fan magazines this was indeed sorry news.

Some small glimmer of hymeneal intelligence of value to the owners of "Jackie factories" was an announcement that Mrs. Kennedy's half-sister, Janet J. Auchincloss, was engaged to Mr. L. P. Rutherford.

For a good part of May, Mrs. Kennedy devoted herself to riding, and among the shows she entered was one sponsored by the St. Bernard's School at Gladstone, New Jersey. She, her mother, and Caroline received ribbons for their participation but John failed to place in the events for children. Plans for the summer included a month's stay in Honolulu. An airline strike delayed their departure for the mainland in July, but settlement enabled Mrs. Kennedy to return in ample time for the marriage of her half-sister. Immediately thereafter she accompanied both her children to Hyannis Port.

August was a quiet month, as was September, with nothing more newsworthy than the choice of a fall wardrobe from Valentino and her presence with both children at the wedding of her press secretary, Pamela Turnure.

Speculation as to where and with whom Mrs. Kennedy would spend the Christmas holidays was settled in early December when Robert Kennedy announced that she would accompany his family to Sun Valley. On December 9 some unpleasantness occurred before the apartment house where Mrs. Kennedy lived: a woman unknown to the family began to behave irrationally and had to be removed to a hospital for psychiatric observation. An added damper to the holiday spirit was another sale at auction by Charles Hamilton of two more inconsequential letters written by Mrs. Kennedy. Later he lamented the low prices they brought and related this fall in price to a diminution of interest in the former First Lady.

Legal efforts undertaken in December by Mrs. Kennedy to bar the early 1967 serialization and publication of William

Manchester's book, *The Death of a President,* compelled the plaintiff to cancel her Sun Valley trip. The issue was doubly unpleasant because Mrs. Kennedy had chosen Manchester over qualified biographers, and it was public knowledge that she and her family had given him full personal cooperation. The most significant portions of Mrs. Kennedy's complaint charged that the book would cause "irreparable injury [and result in] sensationalism and commercialism." Particularly offensive, in the opinion of the former First Lady, was Manchester's interpretation of the sad return to Washington from Dallas and the descriptions of open hostility between followers of her husband and those of Lyndon Baines Johnson.

Knowledgeable publishers and attorneys agreed it would be difficult to bar the publication of so important a book and pointed up what precedents had been established when Mrs. Kennedy had failed to keep Maud Shaw's book from sale. Indeed, this was a bitter time, and with both children Mrs. Kennedy left for Antigua, where they were the house guests of Paul Mellon. After pleas for privacy were ignored, police guards were posted at the beach to assure Mrs. Kennedy against incursions of unwelcome photographers.

On December 27, Pablo Casals was ninety and among his congratulatory telegrams was one from Mrs. Kennedy. The next day the Gallup poll announced that for the fifth consecutive year the American public had named her as the "most admired woman in the world."

Our understanding of fan magazines tells us that an article in the February, 1966, *Screenland*—"How Jackie Is Changing Luci Johnson's Life" by Judi R. Kesselman—was written no later than in August or September of 1965, so this would be old news. An examination of this dreary account proves our inference true, for it is a thin piece about how Luci, in her admiration of "Jackie," had become interested in Catholicism, was converted to that faith, cut her hair in the "Jackie" style, and began "to wear her clothes with a dash akin to Jackie's."

April's fantasies for 1966 were still rooted in some facts of 1965, and no more than two examples need be chosen to illustrate how imaginations, even when they flagged, could always find some inspiration in motherhood. Marie Crawford's lachrymatory "Jackie's Fear: Why Can't My Daughter Be Like Other Little Girls?" in *Motion Picture,* offered nothing new in her rehash of Kennedy grit and the family's "fierce determination to win," a rugged family characteristic that brought neither satisfaction nor joy to the little girl when she won "a medal for deportment or French at school." Indeed, she achieves these honors automatically, "as though her spirit has been broken." Naturally enough, this psychological condition worries Caroline's "vivacious, out-going mother."

Another old fact presented again in *Photoplay*'s collection of April conjurations included "Innocent Jackie Dragged into Divorce Case" by Chrys Haranis, who gave her attention to the old news of the Lawford separation before she added some rambles on an old dunking of Peter in a swimming pool, and how the actor had telephoned Marilyn Monroe shortly before her suicide.

Not until the September issues, normally distributed at the end of June or the first week of July, do we find anything current, although it is wrenched out of time's normal continuum. For the September *Movie Stars,* which offered its readers a peek at "Jackie's Secret Heartache at Luci's Wedding," introduced this keyhole piece with the observation that "August 6th is the big date. . . . Luci Baines Johnson will become the bride of Patrick J. Nugent." It is reasonable to suggest that purchasers and readers of these manufactures pay no attention to time, for it is indeed without consequence in fantasyland. But to get to the piece: certainly "Jackie" would receive an invitation to the wedding; but she might decline because if she "were among the wedding guests, her picture would be snapped as often as the bride's." To give the bride her very special day of sentiment and memory, Jackie would be elsewhere, suffering another variety of heartache as she speculates on "the day when she will watch Caroline walk down the aisle . . . and walk into a new life."

Two articles about "Jackie's" Hawaiian vacation indicate how the event was covered in many of the fan books for October. *Photo Screen* offered a Mavis London revelation, "The Romance Jackie and Peter Won't Talk About." "For months," Miss London wrote, "he had been away from the Kennedy scene—a stranger to family meetings and parties. Then suddenly, it was announced that Peter Lawford would be welcomed back into the clan." In this case "the clan" was not the "rat pack" once led by Humphrey Bogart, but the Kennedy family. "He was going to take two of his four children on a Hawaiian holiday with their Kennedy cousins, Caroline and John Jr., and their aunt, Jackie Kennedy. Why the reunion? Was it really a simple vacation, or was it a jaunt planned because the Kennedys were disturbed about Peter's off-scene romance with a young Hollywood starlet?" Then, as if to prove she was a reporter capable of seeing all sides of a vapor, Miss London added: "So far, nothing further has been noted in the romance of Peter and [the starlet] although there have been some recent hints that the pair are no longer seeing each other as steadily."

"Jackie's Terrible Ordeal in Hawaii" by James Gregory for *Silver Screen* was subtitled, "IT WAS A WONDERFUL VACATION—UNTIL CAROLINE, AND THEN JOHN, MET WITH NEAR-TRAGIC ACCIDENTS. THE MAGIC SPELL WAS BROKEN AND JACKIE HAD TO FACE MORE OF THOSE HEART-RENDING MOMENTS SHE KNOWS SO WELL." Is the full coverage of Caroline's mishap while swimming, and John's falling into the embers, as dramatic as the subtitle? Reading will prove that the extended caption conjured up more "ordeal" than the article.

Important current news for November's fan magazines (distributed in late August–early September) was the wedding of Janet Auchincloss at the end of July. *Photoplay*'s treatment by Charlotte Dinter—or Lisa Reynolds—carried a remarkable tagline to introduce the article: "She tries not to think of it, but she cannot help it. Over and over Jackie Kennedy must ask:

OH GOD, HOW MUCH LONGER MUST I HURT THE PEOPLE I LOVE?"

As Charlotte Dinter and/or Lisa Reynolds interpreted the nuptial events: "The wedding—which was meant to be one of the most memorable Newport, Rhode Island, had ever seen— became a fiasco instead—a disorderly, howling mob scene. . . . Throughout the ceremony, Janet wept repeatedly. When she and her young bridegroom emerged from the church at last, they looked as if they had been at a funeral rather than a wedding. . . . The cruel and thoughtless people who had made a shambles of their day had not even come to see them, but to catch a glimpse of the bride's half-sister—Jacqueline Kennedy."

This interpretation of events was not borne out by the facts, but of what concern would this be to the fans, who were given in the rest of the article a serving up of old events for serious speculation: had "[Jackie] used political connections to coerce her church" into annulling Lee Radziwill's first marriage; and had she hurt her neighbors everywhere by moving next door and inspiring sightseeing buses and tourists to hold carnival on their lawns and streets?

In fantasyland there are many mansions, all of them, it seems, occupied by mutants, for who could recognize the subjects of November's *Photoplay* as people of this earth? Another question is also in order. If a being of another planet could beam up a copy of this issue, would he conclude that he was looking at a fan magazine devoted to the coverage of an industry of major earth entertainment? Judge the magazine's table of contents for November:

Two December stories dealt with young John Kennedy. *Movie TV Secrets* offered "John Jr. Asks Jackie—Am I Like My Daddy?" The title told all and the reader could pass immediately to Nanette Bolton's "Jackie Saves John Jr.'s Life . . ." in *TV Photo Story*, which somehow associated the assassination of John Kennedy with the accident suffered by his son in Hawaii some two and a half years later.

CHAPTER TWELVE

"From Most of Us to Some of You
...A Disenchanted New Year..."

Esquire, December, 1966

COSMOPOLITAN for December, 1966, advised readers to fortify themselves against holiday trauma by meaningfully empirical, albeit selfish, Christmas presents: visits with psychiatrists. Other evidences of existential cynicism could be found in almost every popular magazine fit for viewing by guests during the season of joy. As they suffered what was for them the worst of times, some closet cynics could find humor in *Esquire's* irreverent cover, which offered Hugh Hefner, Billy Graham, and Timothy Leary as the three "wise" men. The conceit would have been more meaningful if the cover had shown how the wise men received instruction from the mentor—Lyndon Baines Johnson—who had received an overwhelming mandate from the electorate in 1964. Truly, as *Gal Friday,* a short-lived magazine for the single girl mindful of sex, and what role it played in the office, pointed out—the season of peace on earth, goodwill, and the rest of that ticky-tacky sentimentality was just what the "con men, pickpockets, shady operators and swindle[rs had been waiting for]. They had been planning all year, just like the department stores." Which condition, if accepted, drew much of the sting from *Esquire*'s wishes for the season: "From most of us to some of you, then, a very, very alienated Christmas, a disenchanted New Year; some degree, if you insist, of peace on earth; and whatever you may find to your advantage in good will toward men."

When events of December, 1966, and the months to follow, which saw the serialization and trade publication of William Manchester's book, are viewed through the spectacles of hindsight, *Esquire*'s holiday wishes for the season and coming year were uncannily omnipresent. Certainly they were for the former First Lady, when on December 16 her attorneys were granted a "show cause" order against William Manchester, Harper and Row—his publishers, and *Look*, which planned to begin its 60,-000-word serialization of Manchester's *Death of a President* on January 10, some four months before the book would be distributed.

Again, reference must be made to *Esquire* (June, 1967) which offered an irreverent composograph for its cover of Jacqueline Kennedy and Eddie Fisher on a sled, with a comment attributed to Mrs. Kennedy that made the composition appropriate to an extended article by John Corry on the Manchester-Kennedy controversy. "The Manchester Papers" is devoid of sympathy for Mrs. Kennedy and the family of the slain President; nevertheless, Corry's observations do much to explain why during the winter and spring of 1967 Mrs. Kennedy was subjected to her customary savaging by the fan magazines. What made the press attack unusual was that it was joined by an increased number of respectable examples of public media, which in the past could have been counted on to ventilate the mind rather than to punch destructive holes through the reasoning process. In his discussion of ideas at work, John Dewey observed in *The Quest for Certainty* (1929) that "To magnify thought and ideas for their own sake apart from what they do . . . is to reject the idealism which involves responsibility."

That this was, unfortunately, the prevailing condition weights the irony of Corry's observations:

> Speculation is frivolous, of course, but it is entertaining too. What if, say, *American Heritage,* or *The American Scholar,* or *The Sewanee Review* had bought the serialization? These are not magazines that find their way into dentists' offices, where they lay [*sic*] for months, idly thumbed by just anyone. They do not languish in pool halls, where they are shuffled through between games, or in barbershops, mixed in with comic books under the girlie calendars, or in drugstores next to *Photoplay,* where teen-agers can slurp Cokes and riffle the pages.
>
> What if the serialization was to be read only by the academic community, not by women in housedresses who write letters to the editors saying that Jackie is entitled to her privacy and then hang slack-jawed on each last word printed about her. What if Jackie Kennedy's letter to her husband, for example, was not to be read by grocery clerks, bartenders, cops, hustlers, sailors, widows, fat ladies, caddies, teen-age girls, retired men and American Legionnaires? Would it have made a difference? Sure.
>
> Burke Marshall [an assistant attorney-general for civil rights in the Kennedy administration] once said, "To have her personal life spread out just like in a movie magazine is distressing to her." Next to a passage in a *Look* galley proof about the last night that Mrs. Kennedy and her husband spent before the assassination, Dick Goodwin [who had served as assistant special counsel to President Kennedy in 1961] noted that, "Mrs. J. F. K. feels very strongly about this. Their sleeping arrangements, embracing, etc., will all be taken by *Modern Screen,* etc., sensationalized, cheapened. Asks if you will please take this out." . . . The word please was underlined.

Ted Sorenson, who had been privy to the former President and helped write many of his more remembered speeches, called the book, in part, "tasteless and distorted [with] inaccurate and unfair references to other individuals." This judgment set the general tone for the brief filed in behalf of Jacqueline Kennedy, wherein she complained that Manchester's book and its popular serialization would reveal to the morbidly curious "all the private grief, personal thoughts and painful reactions which my children and I endured in those terrible days [. This] does not seem to me to be essential to any current historical record. . . . As horrible a trial as it will be, it now seems clear that my only redress is to ask the courts to enforce my rights and postpone publication until the minimum limits of my family's privacy can be protected."

Because in the months prior to publication her side of the matter failed to elicit the hoped-for responses, Mrs. Kennedy instructed her attorneys to file suit to enjoin publication unless five remedies were heeded by the author and his publishers. Saliently among the remedies was her insistence that copies of letters she and Caroline had written not be published in Manchester's text; nor was Manchester to use any of the material she had given him during the course of taped interviews in April, 1964; he was also to return the tapes.

Some six days later, on December 21, the litigants adjudicated their differences, and Mrs. Kennedy was the legal victor, because Look's publisher excised offensive passages of about 1,600 words. That she had dared brave the publicity attendant on the filing of a suit impressed only a minority of the press, which had begun to feel that the juicy profits accrued to the fan magazines since they had discovered "Jackie" should be more equitably distributed among a greater number of buccaneers. Another unhappy result of her determination to sue was the mounting assaults to breach her privacy, so that her stay in Antigua became less of a vacation than a public contest to land reporters and photographers on the beach.

One day Mrs. Kennedy had to remain in the surf for a quarter-hour while Secret Service agents rid the area of photographers and other representatives of the curious. In retrospect, the Manchester affair only charged the public's curiosity, only whetted the public's appetite for unexpurgated and pirated editions of the *Look* articles as they were published abroad. As Cleveland Amory observed in *Status and Diplomat* (February, 1967), "Mrs. Kennedy . . . succeeded in publicizing the very things she did not want publicized, far beyond any publicity they would ever have had if she had not sued; furthermore, taken out of context as they have been, they stick out like sore thumbs."

Amory's judgments may have held true for the press that published *immediately* after the event. It did not hold true for the fan magazines which in January, February, and March of 1967 pursued their full-time careers of otiose stupidity and profitable malice. Thus, *Photo Screen* for January offered "Jackie" on the cover as she thought of herself in the company of her assassinated husband, all under the title of "Jackie's Miracle Dream—'WE'LL MEET AGAIN!' " Certainty of a hereafter enabled Helga Bowers to give her interpretation of events from President Kennedy's inauguration through his death and the mourning of his friends and family as it is still observed. Other activities also receive attention, but these were no longer necessary to the education of the lemmings who moiled their way to newsstands to buy the latest interpretation of "Jackie's" real-life ordeal. Even Miss Bower's conviction that the former First Lady's religious faith led her to believe "she [would] be reunited with her loved one [which made] it possible for her to go on and face every new day," no longer had the emotional zap to help readers experience the pullulations required of them to reap the fullest benefits from their fantasies of a fundamentalist heaven.

In another Mary-Worth approach to life, *Motion Picture* introduced its "Jackie" feature with the question, "What Would Jack Want Me to Do?" which treated distressing books and publications such as the Warren Commission Report and the publication in October, 1966, of *The Pleasure of His Company,* a memoir by Paul B. Fay which especially disturbed Mrs. Kennedy and other members of his family. However, Arthur Krock praised Fay's book because it "correct[ed] the impression . . .

that is disposed to make of Kennedy a plastic saint. . . . It contains something all the other Kennedy books lack—his quality of mirth, both in giving and receiving." To conclude his review of books, for *Motion Picture,* Darnell Patterson mentions *in passim* William Manchester's work in progress. Summing up, Patterson chided Mrs. Kennedy for her activities as a censor and with the heavy-handed severity of a Dutch uncle advised her to "remember that sooner or later Caroline and John will embark on their own voyage of discovery about the father they loved so well and lost so early."

Other strictures for the month were applied by *Movie Stars and TV Close-Ups* in an anonymous offering, "JACKIE AND THE KENNEDYS TODAY—Who She's Closest to . . . Who She Won't See . . . The Kennedy She Must Protect Her Children from . . ." and *Photoplay*'s mini-melodrama by Sharon Beasley, "The Night Lady Bird Forced Jackie to Stay Home." In the first of these, Robert Kennedy was identified as the "closest" man and the people "Jackie won't see" were "Mr. and Mrs. Joseph Kennedy." But *who* was "the Kennedy she must protect her children from?" Revelation involved refined psychological casuistry that must be admired, inasmuch as this Kennedy proved to be their martyred father, the ties to whom had to be "sever[ed], in order to protect her children and insure their futures."

Far simpler and therefore more to the liking of the average fan was *Photoplay*'s article about "Jackie's" intention to attend the opening night of the Metropolitan Opera season on September 16 for the premier performance of Samuel Barber's *Antony and Cleopatra.* Then—oh, fate!—she learned that Lady Bird Johnson, "looking every inch the First Lady in an exquisite white Grecian style gown and accompanied by Philippine President Marcos and his attractive wife," also was to be present, and "for weeks the 'in' crowd had been looking ahead to this night of nights, anticipating a reunion of two of the most celebrated women in the world—one a president's wife, the other a martyred president's wife." But "Jackie" had been invited to join Samuel Barber in the celebrity box! Acceptance of this invitation of regard would reduce to secondary importance the appearance of Mrs. Johnson and her distinguished guests. "People began jumping to conclusions all over the place." What would "Jackie" *do?* If she put in an appearance, it would be construed as a slight of Mrs. Johnson, a certain evidence of discord. Therefore, as a former First Lady, " 'Jackie' was *forced* to" absent herself from the opera because she remembered with "regret the furor that was caused . . . when she and Princess Grace of Monaco attended the same debutante ball in Seville [where] the Princess and her husband . . . were the guests of honor [until] Jackie arrived." No indeed, Sharon Beasley opined, "Jackie" would never embarrass Mrs. Johnson, so good taste, rather than an official command from Lady Bird, had "forced Jackie to stay home." Of such straw is spun the chaff of fan magazine stories.

After she returned from Antigua, the second week of January, Jacqueline Kennedy and her attorneys met to resolve her legal dispute with Manchester and his publishers, and on January 17, the text of the settlement between the principals became a matter of public knowledge. Meanwhile, the Kennedys waited uneasily for the national reaction to Manchester's serialization in *Look,* and they were visibly relieved that after the well-publicized dispute the four-part serialization stirred little controversy. Manchester's hard portraits of President Johnson, Governor John Connally of Texas, and the city of Dallas were dismissed by William S. White and Senator John Tower as "guilt by geography" and "knee-jerk" liberalism. *Stern,* the West German weekly magazine which had bought foreign rights from *Look,* published the sentimental letter sent by Mrs. Kennedy to her husband, and for those readers whose curiosity prompted them to purchase a copy of the German publication and have the letter translated, it was a disappointment.

There were two more installments to be published in February, but readers of fan magazines certainly preferred their February offerings to anything *Look* might publish. The assassination was old news; most readers of fan magazines were willing to accept the conspiracy theory; what they demanded, therefore, was less analysis of old events and the assignment of Efram Zimbalist, Jr., to the case, for he would certainly solve its ramifications and bring the culprits to justice *after* he had bested them in an exciting shoot-out.

More important, undoubtedly more demanding of attention was—what did Mrs. Kennedy intend to do about providing a father for Caroline and John-John? Healthy, secure children required two parents, and this prompted *TV and Movie Screen*'s Helen Martin to lift some hastily manufactured rocks of darkness and let in what she believed to be light. "Revealed! Jackie Can No Longer Live without a Husband," certainly appealed to many mothers, especially the lines that quote the former First Lady as telling how "since she has no husband [to help with their children], she does the next best thing: she depends upon pediatrician Dr. Spock's books for advice." Miss Martin now undertook an impassioned prose paean to sell marriage to the widow: "Jackie surely feels the need of a husband [and] there is not a single valid argument against Jackie remarrying. It's her move now."

Motion Picture's Terry O'Bryan agreed. In the February issue—wherein he competed with writers responsible for "Eddie Sues Liz So He Can Marry Connie Stevens," "How Billy Graham Led Hayley Mills Back to God," and "Sinatra in Wild Fury over Mia's Late Hours!"—O'Bryan revealed the identity of the true villains who kept "Jackie" from experiencing again the happiness of marriage as a couple of mean little kids, her children. So—"Now It Can Be Told! How Jackie's Children Keep Her from Marrying"—transported readers to "the elegant morning room of the stately town house in the most exclusive section of London," where they became invisible eavesdroppers to the discussion among Caroline, John, and a "nice lady," who informed the children that " 'Someday your mother will meet a very handsome man. A good man. He will love her, and he will love you and John. He will want to take care of you all.' " Did the children dislike the "nice lady" because they recognized the regionalism as southern and they, too, were infected with a distrust for Dixie? Such speculation must take a secondary position to the events immediately following, as O'Bryan reports them: Caroline and John ran to the "top of the formal stairway" where, as they were embraced by their mother, Caroline wailed that she " 'didn't want another daddy. I *won't* have another daddy.' " And John joined his sister in protest. " 'We don't need a new daddy.' "

What was to be done with such stubborn and selfish children? A mysterious "Mr. X" supplied the answer. First, they would have to be instructed that their father was a man, not a god. Second, "Mr. X" continued, " 'we must remember [that] Jackie's sister married a prince. Perhaps Jackie will find such a man— a man charming enough to win her love and her hand, and princely enough to conquer [*sic!*] the respect and trust of two wonderful little children.' "

As noted in preceding chapters, fan magazines appear some six or more weeks before their cover dates. In the opinions of their publishers and editors, the events set off by Manchester's book were sufficiently important to demand the removal of some articles from the March issues—which appeared in the middle of January—and substitute newly written material. But all that George Carpozi revealed in March's *Photoplay* in "What Jackie Took out of the Book" was some ability to rewrite the points of dispute between the principals in the gaseous style of fan magazine prose. What difficulties George Carpozi only touched on, however, were developed fully by Michael Pearse in his efforts for *Modern Screen,* which combined a cover photo of "Jackie" with coverlines of anguish—"Tearfully Jackie Cries: You're Telling Too Much! You're Hurting Me and My Children!"

Where Carpozi's article was only slightly bitchy, Pearse relished the problems the Kennedys had had with Manchester and hastened to tell the world that "Jackie Kennedy was a loser. The big loser. Even winning, she loses." To prove how much she had lost, Pearse reported innovatively that "to Manchester, who'd transferred his devotion for the President to the President's widow, this rejection by Jackie was a blow." This weedy suggestion planted in the brainpan of his readers, the rest of the article is devoted to the author's simmering and savoring of all the points at issue between the Kennedys and Manchester, before he whipped in a high church conclusion through his citation of *Proverbs* 31: 10–12, 20, 25, 29. Somehow this brings to mind the burning of Joan of Arc, when mighty prayers were recited as she was offered up to the flames.

Where March balm to heal the burns was applied by the *Ladies' Home Journal*'s publication of Stephen Birmingham's "How the Remarkable Auchincloss Family Shaped the Jacqueline Kennedy Style," psychic wounds were salted by the March 11 publication of "Jackie Kennedy: A View from the Crowd" in the *Saturday Evening Post*. Proof of "Jackie's" distress with this article (which we have discussed) is evident in the second installment of the interview she granted to Bob Considine and Frank Conniff, a national editor for the Hearst chain of newspapers, to whom she observed:

> ". . . the stories . . . the strangest stories that haven't a word of truth in them. . . . I guess [the writers] have to make a living, but what's left of a person's privacy or a child's right to privacy?
>
> "That piece in the *Saturday Evening Post*, for instance. . . .
>
> "Why a map, a detailed diagram showing just where my children are at various times of the day?" Jacqueline asked.
> "Why is it so important to a story to give our address, or the name of the children's schools, times of classes. Why?"

The interview, a journalistic plum, appeared on March 12, 13, and 14 in the New York *World Journal Tribune* and in other newspapers associated with the Hearst Corporation. When the logical question was asked—why the Hearst Corporation?—knowledgeable persons replied that Frank Conniff, an old friend of Joe and John Kennedy, had advised Mrs. Kennedy well during the Manchester imbroglio and she had, therefore, honored his request for an interview. In a later statement, Conniff was pleased to tell how Mrs. Kennedy had trusted him, had faith in his choice of reporter, and had not asked to read copy before it was sent to press. Reporter and editor admired the former President's widow, sympathized with her plight, and the article presented a portrait which, in a civilized climate, would have aroused the national conscience to demand an end to a scrutiny that had long since become harassment.

There was some chagrin in the offices of fan magazines when Vance Bourjaily's *The Man Who Knew Kennedy* (1967) proved to be a novel of how the assassination affected two fictional men, one of whom is presented as a man who had known the President as a boy and later been hospitalized in the same naval ward. Happily, there was a bright side to the journalistic picture, as the fan magazines saw it. Namely, there were increasing evidences of a pluralistic disregard for compassion as more and more of the better magazines commissioned "Jackie articles"— which lent themselves readily to overhaul for restatement in the journals loved by the fans. Without question, Stephen Birmingham would be seen by people who would talk freely to him; none of them would ever speak to a writer or editor of a fan magazine. What they had to say for "respectable" publication could be lifted, redressed, and served up again. In addition, the Considine articles had mentioned negatively only one magazine —the *Saturday Evening Post*. The proprietors and employees of the "Jackie factories" could breathe easily.

Photoplay for April dared pull out all stops and use a cover composition of what passed for a framed oil portrait of John F. Kennedy and a photo of "Jackie" in the foreground to sell an article on "The JFK Diary" by Harriman James. The editors deemed it worthy of four coverlines: "① Why he thought Jackie would ruin his career. ② Why he had to smuggle liquor into his dad's home. ③ His impatience with Bobby. ④ His mother-in-law trouble."

The source of all these revelations was not a "diary" but Paul Fay's *The Pleasure of his Company*, a book that already had offended the Kennedys. Now, the article certainly offended Fay who must have been astonished to see what a fan magazine writer could get away with.

Far more interesting than James's article is an advertisement in the same issue that measures 3½ by 5½ inches. Taken by the Kenmore Company of Millford, New Hampshire, it was aimed at stamp collectors.

JACQUELINE KENNEDY HONORED
On New Commemorative Envelope!

YOU shared her sorrow during that tragic weekend in 1963! Her queen-like dignity and sense of duty gave heart to millions. And ever since, you've wanted to own something to recall her greatness. Something to treasure . . . to show your grandchildren when you tell them the story of John F. Kennedy. Now, at last, Jacqueline Kennedy is honored on a Special Commemorative Envelope! Issued on Pre-Dedication of the new $2,270,000 JFK Memorial, this beautiful Envelope is officially postmarked at Arlington, site of the National Cemetery, on the 3rd Anniversary of the President's assassination. As long as the limited supply lasts, we'll send this valuable Commemorative Envelope to introduce you to Stamp Collecting—World's Most Rewarding Hobby. Also, selections of JFK and other fine stamps from our Approval Service for Free Examination. You may return selections without buying and can cancel service anytime, but the Jacqueline Kennedy Commemorative Envelope is yours to keep.

Less important were the April presentations of *Motion Picture* ("How Jackie Has Hurt Lynda Bird & Luci") and *Modern Screen*'s "Can Lynda and George's Wedding Bring Jackie Back to the White House?", an article that must stand out for its wishing on a star, namely Hamilton. Because fabulist Aileen Mehle, a "Society Columnist" (*sic!*) known as Suzy in more than sixty newspapers, was also doing her thing for *Modern Screen* in a section titled "Society and the Stars," fans approved of her making much of the romance between the President's daughter and the young movie star.

For people who really cared about "Jackie" and were left unfulfilled by the April fan magazines, fat nourishment was offered by the March 26 and April 2 issues of the *National Enquirer,* a weekly that had bought the *American* rights to Drew Pearson's article for West Germany's *Die Zeit.* The April installment was featured full page in this tabloid: "JACKIE LEFT JFK TWICE," and both installments were so successful that the *Enquirer,* which billed itself as "The World's Liveliest Paper," devoted much of its May 14 issue to an embrangled pudder of "How Jackie Went From . . . MOURNER TO SWINGER."

If Suzy was going to give space to "Jackie" in her *Modern Screen* pieces, that magazine's Dorothy Manners (hailed as "Hollywood's greatest columnist") also serviced fans who really cared in one department of her eight-page monthly stint of gossip entitled "The Letter Box." There, it must be noted with some satisfaction, she gave short shrift to the question put by a fan from Salt Lake City, who wrote: "Will *Jackie Kennedy* and *Bobby Kennedy* play themselves when the *Manchester* book is made into a movie?"

In the same issue was a discussion of "Jackie's Real Marriage Plans" by M. Williams, wherein the writer concluded that although "British seer Maurice Woodruff predicted her betrothal to a 'non politico' . . . her own family . . . report that they don't think Jackie will marry again." *Modern Screen* presented Ruth Waterbury in her mantle of historian as she invited fans to "Relive Them!—Weddings of the Century." These, as chosen by Miss Waterbury, were the nuptials of some liliaceous Beautiful People: Grace Kelly and Prince Rainier, Jacqueline and John, Frank Sinatra and Ava Gardner, Elizabeth Taylor and Eddie Fisher, Elizabeth Taylor and Richard Burton, and Sammy Davis, Jr., and May Britt. In its posture for the month of May, which was indignation, *Motion Pictures* exhorted its readers to "SIGN THE PETITION. WE BACK JACKIE. WE EXPOSE THOSE WHO ARE TRYING TO BLACKEN HER NAME." Most of Jae Lyle's article was devoted to a reprint of hate letters from "The Voice of the People" in the New York *Daily News,* which concentrated their venom on one of the paper's columnists, Ted Lewis, for his sympathetic piece

Do you believe Jackie is no different from any of us, that she has the right to act according to the dictates of her heart? It doesn't matter whether or not you are a fan of Jackie, whether or not you think she has made mistakes. If you feel Jackie is having her name blackened for no reason other than that she is human and has human emotions—here is your only opportunity to let her know you support her. Be sure to sign this petition and rush it in to us. We will pass all signed petitions on to Jackie's office in N.Y.

WE BACK JACKIE
c/o MOTION PICTURE
205 East 42 Street
New York, New York 10017

I think Jackie is being attacked unfairly and has suffered enough.
I believe it's time she knew how many of us sympathize with her.

Name_____

City_____

State_____

on "Jackie's" problems with William Manchester and his rhetorical query whether the Kennedy-Camelot legend would survive. In addition, the article quoted the findings of the Harris poll. By three to one, good citizens believed Mrs. Kennedy's image had suffered because of her controversy with William Manchester. But *Motion Picture* backed "Jackie"! And their polling page proved it.

Why any Hollywood star should be concerned with the games of scandal played by the fan magazines, which promised much on the cover and then delivered less stimulus than a pinprick, brings up the collateral question of security. Are the stars so insecure, so devoid of ego strength that in their determination to give offense to no one, they suffer inordinately over the smallest suggestion of unauthorized publicity?

As a mass entertainment, scandal is a social by-product of all communities. However, as a direct result of instant communication, the influence of scandal as an entertainment is unprecedented. Not only are the words that suggest ideas supported by group acceptance of a contemporary standard, whatever it may be, but ideas are strengthened or dismissed in direct proportion to their acceptance by society. Whether the acceptance is bovine and dispirited, or fervent and enthusiastic, is often related directly to the modern community's reliance on scandal as a relief from boredom and mechanized regimentation. Scandalous social relationships, the statistical possibilities of such relationships, the community importance of those who practice such exciting relationships, the charismatic qualities of the principals and whether their activities are viewed as evidences of despair, pleasure, or merely outright defiance—all of these must be taken into account when they are judged by society.

Then—*who* are the judges? In the case of fans for whom the lives of movie and television personalities are of greatest importance, it is too evident, sadly so, that absurd stories quickly calcify into even more absurd beliefs that have great influence in gaining new converts to absurdity (why then, *shouldn't* "*Jackie Kennedy* and *Bobby Kennedy* play themselves when the *Manchester* book is made into a movie?"). Absurdity, when the community wills it so, can become stronger than religion in the lives of the ignorant. As V. Gordon Childe, a prominent archaeologist, once observed: "Few of us have any better grounds for believing in germs than for believing in witches. Our society inculcates the former belief and ridicules the latter, but other societies reverse the judgments." Which becomes even more meaningful when we look to Leo Gurko's views in *Heroes, Highbrows and the Popular Mind* (1953): "Magazine editors, unlike radio and film producers, do not feel that they are producing a deficient product for a public whose taste is low, whose mental resources are slight and whose craving for simplification is endless." Absurdity, then, as long as it is not blatantly anti-scriptural, is never judged too harshly for its travesties of logic. Rather it is treated with kindness and often accepted as an essential component of the national pharmacopoeia devoted to the care and well-being of every sort of human stupefaction. Thus, as human evolution has come full circle from the most primitive hominoid of *pithecanthropus erectus* to *homo sapiens*, the role of man as a developing creature has seemingly concluded. However, devolutionatory types have appeared—the Nielsen and sub-Nielsen men—and there is little doubt that they will shape the world of the future. In such a time, a turtle or dog may be the most intelligent creature in a spaceship whose home base is earth.

One of *Weekly Variety*'s offerings for 1966 included an article "How Stars Handle Scandal," in which Bette Davis remarked "Members of the press are people with a job to do who are trying to earn a living." Less understanding and of an opposing view is James Drury, a principal of "The Virginian," who, with some evident pleasure, observed: "A lot of the press is angry with me. That suits me fine. I hate stupid people. And the press who prey on personal lives must be too dumb to make an honest living."

At the moment, more actors and actresses of prominence are in sympathy with the conclusions of Jim Drury than with the tolerance of Bette Davis. In an interview with Roderick Mann for the *London Express Service* (later reprinted in the Los Angeles *Herald-Examiner,* May 28, 1967), Ann-Margret said: "I've won it twice [the Hollywood Woman's Press Club Sour Apple Award, which is given to the year's most uncooperative actress]. How about that! Now they're murdering me, of course. They write complete lies about me. . . . You just wouldn't believe the bitchiness of our business."

And after Barbara Parkins of television's "Peyton Place" (and later *Valley of the Dolls*) was informed she had been awarded a Sour Apple, she told the *Intelligencer* how pleased she was to be a member of a good and distinguished company that included Marlon Brando and Elizabeth Taylor. Challenged because she refused to give interviews to fan magazines, Miss Perkins fairly spat: "You devote an hour to an interview and they take one line and build a story around it—terribly distorted."

There is, however, another view, best presented by Dorothy Manners, who in defense of her peers said that a player "has no private life once they are in show business, and that no star has been ruined by the press. Elizabeth Taylor would be at Forest Lawn, instead of running around Europe getting a million dollars a picture." Then, to prove—despite her allegiance to angels —how expert she was in the use of basilard and kidney dagger, Miss Manners continued: "Taylor has a very bad press—even the Vatican press has called her an immoral woman."

During this time of pots and kettles calling each other black, a significant example of confusion was published in the *Film Daily* for January 3, 1967, whose masthead informs readers that it is "the international newspaper of motion pictures, founded May 8, 1918." *Film Daily* devotes itself to news of consequence to distributors and exhibitors of movies. When it publishes widely divergent views of the importance and value of fan magazines, especially if they are run side-by-side, this converts the polarity of positions into stances of frigid hostility.

In the discussed issue one banner ran across the full page: "FAN MAGS FILL 50% OF SEATS? Surprising survey reports them better than 23 magazines." In lead paragraphs of the article, William Tusher reported the findings made by the

Communications Research Center in Chicago. In a study of twenty-five magazines that included *Reader's Digest, Life, Look, Time, Newsweek, Saturday Evening Post,* and "17 other mass circulation publications. . . . *Modern Screen* and *Photoplay* accounted statistically for the sale of slightly more than one out of every two tickets to motion picture theaters. . . . Remaining publications whose effect on movie attendance was sifted were *New Yorker, Playboy, True, Argosy, McCall's, Hot Rod, Redbook, Seventeen, Woman's Day, Better Homes and Gardens, Good Housekeeping, Ladies' Home Journal, True Story, TV Guide, U.S. News and World Report, Cosmopolitan,* and *Family Circle.*"

Understandably, Tusher continued: "Richard Heller, editorial director of *Modern Screen,* was quick to recognize the landmark significance of these findings.

> "I was flabbergasted and delighted," he told the FILM DAILY. "I have always maintained that fan magazines sell a great many more tickets to movies than any other publications. I am absolutely certain that people who make movies and those who sell and distribute them have little inkling of how important fan books are to the success of their films.
>
> "This report was not designed to elicit these figures, but they clearly show that a movie maker may derive some prestige from promoting features in books like *McCall's, Redbook, Seventeen, Good Housekeeping, Ladies' Home Journal, Life, Look,* but they sure sell a hell of a lot more tickets through fan magazines."

The headline of second importance in this issue of the *Film Daily* is "Fan Mags Have Hurt Industry: Ferguson." Howard Lipton's article elaborated on a statement of Robert S. Ferguson, Columbia Picture's vice-president in charge of advertising and publicity, to explain why, in recent years, some of the major picture companies had sharply curtailed or canceled all advertising in fan magazines. Although Ferguson neither denied nor discounted the findings of the Communications Research Center, he said that Columbia would continue its ban on advertising in fan magazines.

> "They've hurt the industry as a whole," Ferguson stated, asserting that some of the "hideous photos, etc., in effect cater to the cheapest elements in the country and hurt the industry."
>
> Some of the material they print is "low, disreputable and on the order of *Confidential* magazine," Ferguson stated.
>
> "Once they were an excellent help but not now. Furthermore . . . at the present time they hurt our image. I believe they encourage censorship, condemnation of the industry by outside groups and restrictive legislation."

Media polls, surveys, rating, previews, and reports—all are designed to measure public reactions to film and television products. Decades before General Foods undertook its first survey to determine public reaction to its new cereal products or Lever Brothers distributed free samples of soaps and powders to stimulate consumer allegiance, Hollywood invented "sneak previews." Television also uses Preview House in Hollywood to test viewer reactions to pilot films and advertising commercials. Every seat in Preview House is equipped with a battery of buttons which enable a viewer to register instantly his positive and negative responses to cast, plot, and developing action. For the record, this audience is as often wrong as right; and one of its most glaring failures was its unflattering reaction to "Batman." Overwhelmingly, the audience disliked the pilot films, but "Batman" became the major hit of the 1965 television season, and has had a considerable influence on thought, style, and the popularization of middle class "camp."

It is possible that the human engineering undertaken at Preview House, and the polls conducted by fan magazines, merely reflect the shoddy equipment of its subjects, who may be, as we have suggested, Nielsen and sub-Nielsen types. Concerned because the conclusions of our coffee klatches with the ladies who read fan magazines fully contradicted the findings of the Communications Research Center, I turned again for advice to Dr. Lewis Yablonsky, Chairman of the Department of Sociology at San Fernando State College. Were the ladies at our first two meetings somewhat less than truthful about their movie attendance? Only 10 percent had claimed they paid to see one or less movies a year.

In the past, Dr. Yablonsky had advised me on research procedures. Now, as a graduate student who still reported to him on an academic project of considerable importance to me, I turned to him again—as teacher and friend—for assistance in the preparation of a four-page form embracing twenty-two questions which I intended to send to prominent people in motion pictures. Through these questionnaires I hoped to gather the reactions of movie and television principals to fan magazines. Between May 4 and 9, 1967, sixty questionnaires were sent out over Dr. Yablonsky's signature. By May 25, twenty-nine replies had been received by him.

The following paragraph appeared on the last page of the questionnaire.

> NOTE: If you are willing to be quoted by name, please sign the following:
>
> The undersigned gives full permission for the utilization and quotation of all comments made herein for the purpose of a class paper, a book, monograph, article or any other publication.
>
> _____
> (signature)
>
> _____
> (date)

Many who filled out the questionnaires gave permission to be quoted; understandably, others did not. One publicist at a major studio demanded many reassurances that his name would not be used if we quoted in part from his revelatory letter to Dr. Yablonsky.

> For your student's information, also, one fan magazine editor, who edited eight fan books, finally quit his job over his publisher's insistence that a Jackie Kennedy story be coverlined on each issue. After being jobless for a period (other than writing fan mag stories), he recently took over the editorship of two other fan magazines, finally resigned to the fact that Mrs. Kennedy stories will have to be included in these two fan books! . . . I haven't really the vaguest idea of who buys fan magazines. . . . Personally, I've never bought one in my life, wouldn't waste my money on them.

Of another tone is a letter sent to Dr. Yablonsky by the publicity director for the West Coast studios of one of the major film corporations:

May 8, 1967

Mr. Lewis Yablonsky
Professor of Sociology
San Fernando Valley State College
Northridge, California

Dear Mr. Yablonsky:

Inasmuch as all media of dissemination is part of my activity, I am not in a position to give you an impartial point of view regarding the fan magazines, particularly in regard to their influences in my motion picture taste.

However, we in the motion picture industry look upon the fan magazine as a publication in which the reader is a died [sic!] in the wool movie-goer and consequently an important area of publicity for our films as well as our players.

It has always been axiomatic that the fan magazine reader is an avid fan and hero worshipper who can be counted upon, percentage wise, to be a regular movie-goer. Obviously, we cannot turn our backs on a media that influences entertainment tastes.

For summarization, the variety of answers to questions were first weighted by percentages.

*Question
Number:*

1. *As a youth, or miss, did you read fan magazines?* (YES: 43% NO: 34.7% NO ANSWER: 22.3%)

2. *If so, which magazines were your favorites?* (*Photoplay:* 13% *Modern Screen:* 13% OTHER: 1% NO ANSWER: 73%)

3. A. *Did the fan magazines influence your choice of movies?* (QUALIFIED YES: 30.7% NO: 47.6% NO ANSWER: 21.7%)
   B. *Do they influence your television viewing?* (YES: 0% NO: 65.3% NO ANSWER: 34.7%)

4. *Did fan magazines influence your choice of career?* (YES: 4.4% NO: 73.9% NO ANSWER: 21.7%)

5. *Do you now read fan magazines?* (QUALIFIED YES: 21.5% NO: 43.8% NO ANSWER: 34.7%)

6. *Do you "personally" subscribe to fan magazines?* (QUALIFIED YES: 4.4% NO: 73.9% NO ANSWER: 21.7%)

7. *Do you "personally" buy fan magazines?* (QUALIFIED YES: 4.4% NO: 73.9% NO ANSWER: 21.7%)

8. *Do you think fan magazines aid and assist a performer's career?* (QUALIFIED YES: 30.7% NO: 39.1% SOMETIMES: 13.1% NO ANSWER: 17.1%)

9.   *Do you think fan magazines are an asset to the industry they cover, and reflect fairly and accurately the work, career, problems and progress of the industry?* (QUALIFIED YES: 4.3%   NO: 65.2% NO ANSWER: 30.5%)

10. *Do you think fan magazines are well written?* (NO: 65.3%   NO ANSWER: 34.7%)

11. *Do you think fan magazines are intelligent in their purpose?* (QUALIFIED YES: 4.3%   NO: 60.8% SOMETIMES: 4.3%   NO ANSWER: 30.6%)

12. *Do you think fan magazines offer intellectual fare to their readers?* (QUALIFIED YES: 4.3%   NO: 69.7%   NO ANSWER: 26%)

13. *Do you think fan magazines are an asset to the publishing industry?* (QUALIFIED YES: 13% NO: 43.5%   NO ANSWER: 43.5%)

14. A. *Do you think readers of good education and taste read fan magazines?* (QUALIFIED YES: 4.4% NO: 60.8%   NO ANSWER: 34.8%)

    B. *What do you think is the educational level of the average reader?* (GRAMMAR SCHOOL: 90% HIGH SCHOOL: 10%   COLLEGE: 0%)

15. *Do you like fan magazines?* (QUALIFIED YES: 4.4%   NO: 65.1%   NO ANSWER: 30.5%

16. *Do you, personally, fear fan magazines and their influence?* (YES: 4.4%   NO: 65.1%   NO ANSWER: 30.5%)

17. *Have fan magazines helped your career?* (YES: 0% NO: 65.3%   NO ANSWER: 34.7%)

18. *Do fan magazines enable their readers to gain intelligent knowledge about your industry/profession and its leaders or stars?* (QUALIFIED YES: 4.3%   NO: 69.7%   NO ANSWER: 26%)

19. *Have you, or anyone you know, been helped careerwise by fan magazines?* (QUALIFIED YES: 26% NO: 47.6%   NO ANSWER: 26.4%)

20. *Have you, or anyone you know, suffered career injury or embarrassment because of a fan magazine?* (YES: 26% NO: 60.8% NO ANSWER: 13.2%)

21. *Do you resent the prominent inclusion in the fan magazines of people who are "not" actors and actresses?* (YES: 21.7% NO: 43.5% NO ANSWER: 34.8%)

22. *In your opinion, what has been the effect of the fan magazines' concentration on Mrs. Jacqueline Kennedy?* (GOOD: 4.3% BAD: 30.7% NO EFFECT: 30.7% NO ANSWER: 34.3%)

Replies to the eighth question, which asked if fan magazines enhanced a performer's career, revealed that the "YES" responses (30.7%) were qualified in every case. Some typical answers include the following. One young Oscar winner: "Probably only at the beginning, when publicity is necessary." Arthur Knight, Professor of Theater Arts at the University of Southern California: "That's not what they are designed for." Director Delbert Mann: "Possibly can help in publicizing a performer and keeping his name before a segment of the audience." A well-known producer-director: "Only minor exposure —movie-magazine readers don't follow up at the box office." A motion picture reviewer: "Possibly difficult to trace. Can't recall a single instance of article or magazine contributing solely, or to a significant extent, to a career." A Hollywood publicist: "I think they did more in the old days than they do now. They're more destructive than helpful now. They put sensational titles and story headings on stories about players, then deny the title in a single sentence somewhere near the last paragraph, but damage is done since many readers glance at the cover page titles or at first page of the stories and don't get to the end. In early days fan magazines were constructive, writing biographical stories about stars. Now, more and more they tend to select their own angle based on a single incident, distort it out of any semblance to truth for the sake of sensationalism."

Burt Prelutsky, film reviewer: "For performers all publicity is good. The people who read such magazines write fan letters." A well-placed lady in film institutional activities: "Most movie magazine writers emphasize shock effect to attract readers and this includes details of actors' private lives. This may aid a performer's career by making him seem more warmly human to his fan public, but other movie magazine articles hurt his career." Producer Norman Felton: "If a performer has inherent qualities of personality (as well as talent) which will interest an audience in him (or her) the magazines will help popularize the performer (with those of a certain cultural group who read them)."

The ninth question, which asked if fan magazines were an asset to the industry and reflected an accurate picture of Hollywood, drew these replies. A well-known actor: "They are filled with gross and tasteless distortions of the truth about performers' private lives." Motion picture reviewer: "Their publicity value for neophytes may be majorally useful for the industry, but as reflecting anything more than a publicist's fantasies, forget it." A publicist: "They do not reflect anything about the work, careers, problems or progress of the industry. They reflect more on the personal life of the player, frequently to the player's disadvantage. Particularly if the player refuses to do fan magazine interviews, the magazines do a series of destructive stories about the player deliberately and with malice aforethought." A newspaperman: "Neither an asset nor liability, since the people who read them are not notably influenced by them. They certainly do NOT reflect the current Hollywood." A leading recording artist: "They are destructive—misleading—and full of contrived falsehoods."

The eleventh question, which asked if fan magazines were intelligent in their purpose, inspired these replies. Vocalist: "They feed upon youngsters' and others' mostly healthy (but sometimes morbid) curiosity about stars' personal lives." Oscar winner: "No, because they are generally based on supposition, not fact." Bert Prelutsky: "Yes, because their purpose is to make a profit." Male star: "Yes, they aim to sell copies to their readers. They do, by catering to the taste (lack of taste) of their readers." Film reviewer: "Their purpose is to entertain in the most simple way and intelligence is no part of this." Writer: "They are often *ingeniously* written to avoid libel or to say nothing. But I can't regard this as well written." Actor George C. Scott: "They appear to be almost totally motivated by sensationalistic designs." Norman Felton: "As intelligent as they need to be to attract those who are usually interested in movie magazines." Publicist: "Believe it or not, after many years in the film business, I admire, personally and professionally, many stars. Because these stars are unsensational in their private lives, they almost never rate a story in the fans. Because of the sensationalism of fan magazines, many players, even young ones who need publicity, refuse to do fan magazine interviews."

The sixteenth question ("Do you personally fear fan magazines?") elicited many responses. Young movie star: "Yes. The time and mediums to correct these lies are often lacking." Writer-producer: "Possibly a deleterious effect on taste." Reviewer: "No. I doubt that at their most nearly libelous they can adversely affect an important career." Publicist: "No. I don't think they have enough influence to warrant fear of them. Film audiences are more intelligent than fan book editors. When a picture is good, when the performances are fine, people flock to see the picture." Producer: "I don't *fear* them but—I'm always pleased when I see them cover my films and actors (business-wise)." Male movie idol: "No. Only to the extent of distortion of the truth." George C. Scott: "No. Of course not!" Writer: "I'm not interested in reading lies, half-truths and ballyhoo written by hacks."

"Have fan magazines helped your career?"—the seventeenth question, garnered many comments. Star: "The material I have read about myself is either completely untrue or grossly exaggerated. How can this help?" Norman Felton: "I'm a director-producer and they have had, I suspect, only a small indirect influence on my career." Publicist: "I'd rather see a good newspaper story or national magazine story on a picture or player than any in a fan mag. However, all publicity is grist to the mill of alerting the public on films and their players and, in all fairness, I presume controversial stories sometimes inspire more interest than staid stories." Writer: "I am a writer. Movie magazines ignore the screenplay."

The eighteenth question, which asked whether fan magazines enabled their readers to gain intelligent information about the movie industry, its leaders or stars, motivated a publicist to write at length: "Certainly, they don't disseminate 'intelligent knowledge' about the motion picture industry. That is not their business. Their business is to promote the sale of their publications by any means possible, which, to them nowadays, means writing as provocative, as sensation-packed stories about players as they can." A female star: "Hollywood can be exciting, but no place and no group of people could possibly be as superhuman, famous, inhuman or infamous as these magazines would have their readers believe." Male star: "Movie magazines give a highly distorted picture of the 'industry' and those in it."

The nineteenth question, whether movie magazines had helped the career of the person involved, or that of someone they knew, drew a qualified "yes" (26%). Norman Felton: "Yes, I venture to guess that Richard Chamberlain, Robert Vaughn, David McCallum, Gary Lockwood, among those whom I've had on television series, have been helped." George C. Scott: "I have not, but I cannot speak for others." Newspaper reviewer: "Yes, some youngsters (Ryan O'Neal, before the magazines turned on him, for example) say the early puff stuff has been helpful." Bert Prelutsky: "Yes. It helped a friend of mine pay the bills while he tried to write better things."

"Have you, or anyone you know, suffered career injury or embarrassment because of a movie magazine?" was the twentieth question. Young female star: "It's most embarrassing to have deliberate lies made up about your personal life. I have felt frustration and anger when combating them." Male movie star: "Embarrassment, but not injury on the part of several actresses I have known." Norman Felton: "No, although I'd bet it has happened to some that have been hurt." Oscar winner: "I find them embarrassing because the 'interviews' are usually made up and do not reflect the ideas or opinions of the subject." Organizational lady: "Interviews, on which so many movie magazine stories are based, have often been misleading and slanted by the impression made on the interviewer who is frequently a stranger to the person he has interviewed."

The twenty-first question, "Do you resent the prominent inclusion in the movie magazines of people who are *not* actors and actresses?" drew this reply from a publicist: "Certainly. I see no reason for their inclusion in fan books. People who buy fan magazines buy them because they are interested in film stars. Incidentally, the top fan mags write stories only on the top ten in their readers' poll. That is, those who write in to them, asking for stories on favorite stars. Many intelligent film-goers won't write letters to magazines requesting stories on their favorite stars, so those stars aren't written about." Movie star: "I resent the fact that any person should have to have lies printed about them. Jacqueline Kennedy, for one, should not have been made a saint only to have every segment of her life torn apart and degraded to line the pockets of these avaricious publishers."

"In your opinion, what has been the effect of the movie magazines' concentration on Mrs. Jacqueline Kennedy?" was the twenty-second question. (Good: 4.3%; bad: 30.7%; no effect: 30.7%).

ARTHUR KNIGHT: "Bad. It drags her down to the level of Ann-Margret and Annette Funicello."

NORMAN FELTON: "I don't know of any effect on Mrs. Kennedy."

GEORGE C. SCOTT: "I find it inconceivable that a woman of such caliber and high character would find herself damaged *in any way* by scandal-mongering."

BERT PRELUTSKY: "Good. I don't like Mrs. Kennedy. At best, she bores me. Maybe if the magazines keep it up in ten or twenty years there will be another who feels about her as I do."

MOVIE STAR: "Good—for the magazines' circulation. Obviously no effect on Mrs. Kennedy."

REVIEWER: "Surely the dullest readers must now see through the technique of a catchy cover-line supported by no facts whatsoever—or contradicted by them. Still, they still sell, don't they?"

PUBLICIST: "I don't really know. Obviously, they, the magazines, feel it bolsters their circulation. I, and most people I talk with outside the business, think the fan books' concentration on Mrs. Kennedy diminishes her dignity. I cannot see how it helps her nor the late President's senator-brothers."

OSCAR WINNER: "Let's face it, it's damned undignified."

The twenty-third question, which elicited the most opinions, asked only for any comment the recipient might wish to add:

Producer: "Movie magazines are an anachronism in the world of the 1960s. They serve no purpose other than to attempt to titillate the reader with presumably sensational items and stories."

Publicist: "Fan magazines do not 'interpret the movie industry,' they only reflect and sensationalize the life of film stars—the personal life of stars. But they are not alone in this trend. Regrettably, national magazines, in pursuit of more circulation, are now following the trend to sensationalize. They no longer write definitive biographical stories of stars. They, too, prefer sensational angles on players who make sensational news. There has always been immorality—no more among screen players than businessmen or clerks—but, except for flagrant indiscretions, these have been ignored or discreetly handled press-wise in the past. Discretion seems to have become a lost art in every walk of life, as well as journalism."

Organization officer: "Most writers in this medium are content to put together most any narrative which will sell. The interpretation of stars and other personalities is seldom based on studies in depth and their only value is pap for readers and advertising for people and pictures—that is, if the names are spelled correctly."

Producer-director (who explained why he preferred to remain anonymous): "These books, as we call them, are merely out to hustle a dollar at anyone's expense—integrity and truth have nothing to do with their policy—sensationalism—smear—dirt—garbage—inane point of view. Don't care to waste time in battle in such a lowly arena—these lies will continue as long as idiots have nothing better to do."

Reviewer: "The persistence of the fan mags—almost in spite of their own inadequacies—says a good deal, I think, for the persistence of interest in films and players. Yet in a time of rising educational levels and general sophistication, the fan mags must somehow upgrade or write for an ever-younger audience. In a curious way, their increasingly 'confidential' approach is probably a response to a changing audience. The wrong response naturally."

Female movie star: "If fan magazines did not exist it would be no loss to our society. I can and do understand people's desire to become personally involved in a public figure's life, but to have this desire fed with destructive lies does no one good. There are many magazines which feed this desire well or at least with some taste—the various 'teen' magazines such as *Teen, In, Ingenue, Seventeen,* etc., of course, national feature magazines."

Thomas M. Pryor, editor of *Daily Variety,* wrote:

Dear Sir:

I have not filled out the questionnaire because in my case "yes" and "no" could be misleading. In a professional capacity as reporter, critic and editor I have occasionally looked at fan magazines with a critical eye for some 35 years, which covers a span from relative youth.

Until about 15 years ago the fan magazine served a purpose in helping to promote a low intelligence level interest in motion pictures by giving circulation to the glamour pap that press agentry created to invent and sustain the fanciful image of Hollywood.

During the 1920s and 1930s, and until approximately 1950, the fan mags were pretty much under the control of the motion picture industry via the publicity departments of the different studios. All that changed, however, when the studios abandoned contract players and star stables.

As part of the neo-realism era of the motion picture, and because studios lost control with cutbacks in ad budgets, the fan mags turned to the sensational personal revelation, Often, however, the headline for the cheap, quick sell was bolder than the story content.

I don't know of a fan mag having ever ruined a performer's career. At best, except for a rare article, the fan mag is not really concerned with the problems, artistic or otherwise, of the film business.

The fan mags flourished as a tool of motion picture industry publicity. The era of their greatest success is gone; they have failed to date to grow in terms of maturing public interest in films. Too often they hint at scandal, and, as in the case of Jacqueline Kennedy, reveal shocking irresponsibility and bad taste for no other purpose than to attempt to turn a fast buck.

I have no objection to being identified with any of these comments so long as my remarks are not used out of context.

Cordially,
/s/ THOMAS M. PRYOR
Editor

Charlton Heston, national president of the Screen Actors Guild, also responded by letter, which is quoted in part.

Dear Professor Yablonsky:

I am happy to render my opinion of movie-fan magazines for the benefit of your student's thesis on them. I think I can do so much more succinctly without resorting to the questionnaire you supplied. In reply to your query, he may quote me at his discretion.

I never read any of the fan magazines as a youth, and had no interest in their content, although I was an avid movie-goer. When I first began working in films, some effort was made to see that articles about me were published regularly in these magazines, or "fan books" as they are called in the profession. My own distaste for the editorial content of these publications coincided with a growing realization throughout the industry that their influence was declining rapidly. I thereupon abandoned all effort at having my affairs or my person reported in them. I believe articles about me still occasionally appear, but I seldom read them. The stories written are generally invented quite freely and aimed at the sub-teen public. It could perhaps be said that exposure in the fan books might be of some publicity value in the early part of a young performer's career, but it's a recognized peculiarity in the industry that, with the exception of Elizabeth Taylor, none of the performers regularly featured in the fan books are in fact box-office attractions for the ticket-buying public.

The standard of writing in these publications, as well as their regard for journalistic honesty, is even lower. Their recent necrophilic preoccupation with the widow of the late President Kennedy is an appalling example of their execrable taste. I cannot conceive of these magazines having any influence among literate people. They certainly possess none whatever within the industry, with this possible negative exception: it might be argued that the proliferation of these publications has been a factor in preventing the successful publication of a serious American magazine on film. . . .

Most sincerely,
/s/ CHARLTON HESTON

CHAPTER THIRTEEN

*"This is 1967 and virginity is as
old-fashioned as a chastity belt."*

Helen Weller, West Coast Editor of *Modern Screen*

IMMEDIATELY after events of any consequence, history—for participant or spectator—becomes subjective experiences, for in their eyes nothing beyond the periphery of personal interest can be more consequential. The same holds true for institutions; they may retain their outward appearances but the inner workings, as they are manipulated and realigned, will alter and shape the institution to meet new forms demanded by the social scheme of things. Thus we have seen how people and events shape the *new* interests and contents of fan magazines, as they swell their balance sheets with evidences of financial health. Such success cannot be ignored; and we have seen how socially acceptable and popular middlebrow weekly magazines undertook qualitative and quantitative analyses of fan magazines to learn why they had become so popular and if their finger-licking-good stories were worthy of imitation.

The better magazines have used fan magazines' plan, style, and design to get their proportionate share of publishing profits. One might say that host magazines turned to their parasitic fellows for sustenance and growth, which in logical biology or economics seems an unnatural practice. But as publishers and editors of respectable and middlebrow magazines ordered the inclusion of "Jackie" articles, they were delighted to find that these issues increased their sales. Whenever "Jackie" pieces were prominently advertised and featured, sales rose significantly.

In publishing, as in life, the wheel continued to turn, and the fan magazines reverted to their nature of true parasites. Magazines that could be left on coffee tables without loss of social position assigned important writers to do pieces on "Jackie" and spent considerable sums on research and advertising. Subsequent activity for the fan magazines was obviously predictable: they ingested articles from *Life, Look, Esquire, Ladies' Home Journal, Cosmopolitan, McCall's, Redbook,* and even foreign publications, if they could be read or translated without difficulty.

An article by Robin Douglas-Home in the February 1, 1967, issue of *Queen,* a breezy English fortnightly (published since 1861) that combined features of the *New Yorker, Town and Country, Harper's Bazaar* and *Vogue,* became parent to more than several articles in American fan magazines. In May, *Modern Screen* thought so well of the credentials of Douglas-Home, a journalist identified as nephew of former Prime Minister Alexander Frederick Douglas-Home, and a "close friend of the Kennedys," that it revealed in "Jackie's Real Marriage Plans," one important conclusion of the British writer: the former First Lady would never remarry!

Photoplay also turned to *Queen* for a June rewrite by Helene Gardiner, "THE MAN WHO IS TRYING TO MAKE JACKIE & BOBBY ENEMIES." Immediately identified in the lead paragraph as the very same Robin Douglas-Home, *Photo-*

play deplored the *Queen* article *Modern Screen* had thought was so great. According to *Photoplay's* interpretation, Douglas-Home scored "Jackie" for being " 'obsessed' about her place in history." In his role of a Polonius wholly devoid of homiletic ability, Douglas-Home recalled the unsolicited, market-basket advice he had offered the former First Lady. " 'I've tried to explain that she is going into a self-made trap . . . if Bobby does get into the White House there will be no further use for Jackie. In any case, Ethel would see to that. She would have to. There can't be two First Ladies in Washington. And in any case, there isn't much love lost towards Jackie.' "

To prove beyond all doubt that "Jackie's" enemies were domestic as well as foreign, *Modern Screen,* in June, made a quick shift of position. It identified Douglas-Home as a foreign agent of spite; but a feature piece also revealed how even "family" could not be trusted fully. "JACKIE *ATTACKED* BY HER OWN RELATIVE!" shrilled Rachel Gardner (could she also be Helene Gardiner?) as she assembled all the people—"the false friends"—who were determined for one reason or another to get "Jackie." According to Miss Gardner, "Robin Douglas-Home [had] revealed that Jackie's 'emotional balance' went after her husband died. . . . The Manchester book mess cost Jackie all kinds of popularity on the public opinion polls. Writer Cleveland Amory's mad at her because she said that bullfights were beautiful. . . . Writer Inez Robb [a columnist syndicated by United Features] is irritated because Jackie asks for privacy. . . . Interviewers say there's no way you can write about her and make her like it. . . . Even nightclub comedians are needling the widow of the late President."

All told, Miss Gardner suggested, this sorry state of affairs got even worse when Gore Vidal, cheerfully identified as a relative of "Jackie's" by a stepfather several marriages removed, attacked her. "The Holy Family," subtitled "The Gospel According to Arthur, Paul, Pierre, William and several minor apostles," in the April *Esquire* was an iconoclastic but rational appraisal of books about the late President that offered him up for worship as a plaster saint. Less reasonably, the article censured John Kennedy's widow and brother for their interference with William Manchester. Of all the books published about the late President, Vidal enjoyed only Fay's sympathetic presentation of John Kennedy. Vidal also swiped at the deification of the former First Lady, whom he identified as a woman cast by wise and ignorant alike into a ternary form that comprised Isis, Aphrodite, and the Madonna. Nor did he fail to give the back of his hand to the three Kennedy brothers, John, Robert, and Edward. Throughout Miss Gardner's tremulous editorial discussion of the Vidal article—which was written by someone who could be called a *relative!*—there is an undercurrent of private glee that this attack had been made in a "better" magazine by a well-known writer of whom it could be said, as had been said of Falstaff by the Hostess (2 *Henry IV,* II, i, 14-17), "In good faith, 'a cares not what mischief he doth, if his weapon be out: he will foin like any devil; he will spare neither man, woman, nor child."

It is fair to assume that *Movie Mirror's* ungenitured writers had read nothing at all the previous month, because they decided to be loyal to Mrs. Kennedy in June—the traditional month of weddings—by thinking only of her welfare and how marriage could help her. Although the magazine wished her well, "Jackie's" mother (in "Her Own Mother Reveals: WHY NO MAN CAN MARRY JACKIE AND BE HAPPY") lamented—or so the anonymous writer wrote—that no man could marry her daughter without finding his stature diminished, his position subordinated to "her glory." However, all was not lost; there *were* eligible types: "A royal person? Perhaps. A famed actor? Quite likely. A statesman? Probably."

But of all the June pieces the medal for outrageous behavior must be awarded to *Motion Picture,* which was showing increased editorial evidences of a hard line in its treatment of Jacqueline and the other Kennedys. The anonymous piece, "Jackie in Acapulco!", dealt with the unhappy accident of the past March, when her small boat capsized. What distinguishes the article is the proud inclusion of a photograph of the magazine's "supercameraman," Stan Einzig, who jumped from a plane and opened his parachute just above the action "to record another episode in the Kennedy War on Publicity."

July issues of fan magazines are uniformly dull and concerned with old news from which every drop of sensation has been distilled. The only items worthy of notice are several letters in response to the poll taken in May, 1967 by *Motion Picture* to gauge the extent of its readers' sympathy for the former First Lady. More than a thousand replies were received and these were sharply divided. Mary Smith of Chicago, for example, concluded that "Jackie is being attacked fairly because she deserves all she is getting. She asked for it."

Again, the publication cycle of fan magazines precluded coverage of current events, especially as Mrs. Kennedy had gone abroad to attend the funeral of Lady Sylvia Harlech, victim of an automobile accident, whose husband had been the British ambassador to the United States from 1961 to 1965. Some two weeks later Mrs. Kennedy journeyed to Ireland for a six-weeks stay in the country she described as "this land my husband loved so much." With her were Caroline and John, and close friends Mr. and Mrs. T. Murray McDonnell and their seven children. After a warm welcome by Irish officials at Shannon Airport and Dublin, the entire party traveled by chartered bus to Woodstown House, Waterford County, which had been rented by Mr. McDonnell. The large Regency mansion of some forty rooms fronted a secluded beach. Privacy was assured by a brace of FBI agents, thirty armed detectives, and two hundred policemen who guarded the roads.

Swimming, riding, and visits to local landmarks were enjoyed, and Mrs. Kennedy was an honored guest at a dinner given by Prime Minister John Lynch before she departed alone for a six-day visit to Italy. Shortly thereafter, Mrs. Kennedy, her children, and the McDonnells flew home, arriving in time for the celebration of the former First Lady's thirty-eighth birthday at Hyannis Port—and some criticism from Gabrielle Chanel. The French designer scolded Mrs. Kennedy for her preference for youthful designs and noted how—in her opinion—slavish imitation of "Jackie's" dress made American women less chic than their European sisters.

While Chanel and her peers debated this monumental problem, Myron Fass announced his plans to run a cover and a feature story in *Inside Movie* on Caroline Kennedy, who at nine had to be reckoned with as a sub-subteen pace-setter of style. Fass observed that his teen-age readers had registered disappointment over Mrs. Kennedy, who had lost their favor since the Manchester affair. However, Caroline still had "the magic," and if Caroline had to replace her mother in the sale of the magazines produced by Myron Fass's "Jackie factory," so be it. The publisher was a man who always harkened to the felicitous judgments of his eudaemonic readers.

To fortify the inherent good taste of *Inside Movie* readers, Fass revealed how his agents had discovered remarkable evidences of Caroline's style sense. The staff of Lilly Pulitzer's boutique in Hyannis Port had told them that Caroline had been choosing her own dresses for six years and had a "fantastic" color sense. More significantly, *Women's Wear Daily* had featured a photograph of Caroline, her brother, and mother as they took part in the dedication of the aircraft carrier *John F. Kennedy* on May 27, and the editors had agreed that Caroline's dress with its tight waist was "the beginning of the end of the A line." And the lead item in Jack Bradford's "Rambling Reporter" column for the *Hollywood Reporter* (August 24, 1967) informed its readers of "One of the most surprising rumors to hit this desk in some time: Little Caroline Kennedy's ready to begin her screen career! !"

That none of this was a nonsense reserved for a minority of Americans was indicated by *Cosmopolitan*'s May issue that, as it instructed women in the conceptual differences among the various forms of love: agape, philia, and eros, also kept its eye on the hemline as it was worn by "Jackie" Kennedy; "7 Pages of Jackie Kennedy and Her Fabulous Clothes" cheated only a little, for six pages were devoted to Mrs. Kennedy, but the seventh took note of the influence of Caroline and John on children's style.

That hot summer of 1967, *Photoplay* catered to necrophiles in its account of "What LBJ Did to Jackie the Night Jack's Body Was Moved," and to readers who loved tragedy or near-tragedy in "Jackie Nearly Drowns!" Maidens who sought instruction in the art of snaring a mate could read "Jackie, Joan, Rose, Ethel: What They Did to Catch a Kennedy." *Motion Picture* identified "Jackie" and Barbara Stanwyck as "Women without Love," who "always date men they can never marry!" And Caroline received some attention in the September issue, when readers were given an inside account of "Close Friends [who] Discuss Jackie's Terrible Mistake with Caroline."

While *TV Radio Mirror* used its September number to gloat over how "Jackie's Sister Flops as Actress," *Modern Screen* still considered "Jackie" rather than Caroline to be the newsworthy one. In the role of marriage broker interested in romance rather than a fee, the magazine presented Rudolph Nureyev as "the strange man in [Jackie's] life," a suitor with verve and style and archetypically deserving of the widow's hand.

More determined than ever to seek out Jacqueline Kennedy, whom the publishers of *Women's Wear Daily* believed had become inherent to its omnipresent reason for being, the paper made the former First Lady an important component of its five-day-a-week publishing schedule. Logically enough, then, in October, after "Jackie" had accepted the invitation of Prince Norodom Sihanouk to visit Cambodia, and she had left for Montreal to attend Expo '67, the *Daily* reported most important international news: the recently widowed David Ormsby Gore, Lord Harlech, would marry again—and to Jacqueline Kennedy. United Press International also carried this dispatch. Although it was denied by Lord Harlech and Mrs. Kennedy's secretary, a later announcement that the eligible, elegant, and royal widower would join Mrs. Kennedy and her friends in Cambodia only reinforced the rumors. The reticence of the principals could be attributed to the obvious: Lady Harlech had been buried only three months before; or, perhaps they were selfishly determined to make their own announcements.

But the October *Photoplay* could not see Lord Harlech—a

straight-arrow type—as a suitor. Rather, under a fulsome title, "Her mother and sister say it's impossible—but we find three men Jackie *can* marry," Fred O'Brien presented a trio of candidates approved by the magazine's matrimonial selection board. The first was identified as "The Architect"; the second, as "The Hotel Executive," who in appearance was "a cross between a younger Franklin D. Roosevelt, Jr., and Sonny Tufts"; the third candidate (first introduced by Walter Winchell) was presented as "The Man With The 'Inside Track.'"

November demurrers of *Photoplay*'s choices were published by *Motion Picture* and *Movie Mirror,* which backed Lord Harlech as its candidate for the hand of "Jackie." *Modern Screen* decided to avoid conjecture and concentrated on real history: the "break-up" of Lynda Bird and George Hamilton, "two practical, conservative people [who] are playing a love game so dangerous, so risky, that Elizabeth Taylor and Richard Burton would never have chanced it."

But for true historians, the November *Photoplay* must be given first place. Billed as the "SPECIAL COLLECTOR'S IS-SUE," its featured offering was a fully illustrated piece, "The Day the Great Ones Died." Included, naturally, was another derivative reminiscence of the assassination of John Kennedy and reflections on the demise of other great ones of his time. The "great ones" were Gary Cooper, Marilyn Monroe, Humphrey Bogart, James Dean, Nelson Eddy and Jeanette Macdonald, Mario Lanza, Clark Gable, Jean Harlow, Franklin and Eleanor Roosevelt, Pope John XXIII, Errol Flynn, Tyrone Power, and Alan Ladd.

The December issues could not do much with "Jackie" in Cambodia, although a range of newspapers between the New York *Daily News* and *The New York Times* gave considerable attention to dispatches claiming Mrs. Kennedy's visit had official government sanction and diplomatic purpose. Knowledgeable people were aware that Prince Sihanouk had broken diplomatic relations with the United States in March, 1965, after he charged American troops in Vietnam with consistent violations of his country's frontiers. As a matter of record, the enthusiasm of the Prince's welcome contrasted radically with his harsh, even intemperate criticism of American foreign policy in Southeast Asia. The warm meetings between Jacqueline Kennedy and the Prince, the honors and entertainments provided by him, might harbinger a thaw in the relationship between the host country and the United States. And throughout, Jacqueline Kennedy was accompanied by Lord Harlech.

In December, when *Modern Screen* ran an article—"Lynda's Wedding Prayer: Dear God, Help Me Be Brave"—a letter to Dorothy Manners asked the Hollywood gossip to "please write something about how George Hamilton is taking Lynda Bird Johnson's marriage to another man." More than likely, thousands of fan magazine readers were just as concerned about Lynda's leaving George for Marine Captain Charles Spittal Robb. Letters such as these were welcomed by columnists and editors, for they proved beyond dispute that there were enough people who cared about such matters to assure a healthy future for the magazine.

Such letters also refuted an article by Walt Anderson in the *Los Angeles Magazine* (March, 1967). "Twilight of the Columnists" quoted Sheilah Graham as saying the gossip column was doomed. The entertainment editor of the Los Angeles *Times,* Charles Champlin, told Anderson that he doubted if the paper would replace Hedda Hopper, whose column had died with her because "unlike Louella Parsons she had never groomed a successor. And our thinking was that her kind of Hollywood column had outlived the Hollywood in which it arose by about twenty or twenty-five years anyway."

That there were other grave diggers became evident on December 17, 1967. The Los Angeles *Times,* in keeping with that paper's avowed intention to report the sociology of show business rather than show-biz, ran a lead article in the Calendar Section by Aljean Harmetz, who had written for *Photoplay*. In it, she quoted Helen Weller, the West Coast editor of *Modern Screen,* whose circulation was more than a million copies a month, as saying that "finding a movie star to put on our cover every month is a hard sweat." To prove how readily other principals could be found, and with much less sweat, Mrs. Harmetz noted that this month, "gallantly staring down from the covers of *Motion Picture, Modern Screen* and *Photoplay* . . . are the faces of Jackie Kennedy, Lord Harlech, Lynda and Lady Bird Johnson and Marine Capt. Charles Robb."

Pat Campbell, president of a coven with the deceptive name of the Hollywood Women's Press Club, and the West Coast editor of *Motion Picture,* with a circulation of 750,000 copies, lamented that "this year we've had Jackie Kennedy on our cover four times and the Lennon Sisters four times; and even one of the covers of Jackie bombed." Miss Weller also confided to Mrs. Harmetz that "our circulation is really 50 million. Each copy [of *Modern Screen*] is read by 50 or 100 people. That ubiquitous woman under the hair-dryer. It doesn't matter if she pays for it. . . . Our stories are real-life soap operas."

Granted even half the truth of Miss Weller's statement, if soap opera is the format of the fan magazine story, then who but the stars themselves could suppy the most sudsy scripts of love and abandonment, joy and despair, marriage and adultery and divorce, cavalier disregard for all conventions, and the wildest oscillations of schizophrenic behavior ranging between catatonic withdrawal and paranoid exhibitionisms, including public assaults, divestiture of clothing, and imitation of the unique behavior of Sir Charles Sedley?

Does Nancy Anderson, *Photoplay*'s Hollywood editor, speak for her peers when she avers that readers of fan magazines find "most actors and actresses suffocatingly dull"? Why? "Primarily, because they are dull." Helen Weller saw current actors and actresses as members of "the colorless brigade. Drab, scared little people with a lopsided idea of their own careers." The fault lay not only with actors and actresses, Miss Weller elaborated her descriptions, but with unimaginative press agents who foolishly advise clients that privacy is preferable to their exploitation by fan magazines and gossip columnists. Now Helen Weller is truly spokeswoman for the lamia who pit at the Hollywood Women's Press Club when she advised actors and actresses to ignore personal image and give the public what it wishes.

"Image, hell!" Miss Weller is quoted. "Swing a little. This is 1967 and virginity is as old-fashioned as a chastity belt. Liz Taylor is a lusty, busty, gutsy girl who buys yachts and airplanes for pleasure—and she's the biggest star in the world."

If stars, with the exception of Elizabeth Taylor, are insufficiently lusty, busty, and gutsy, does this mean that Jacqueline Kennedy, Lord Harlech, Lynda and Lady Bird Johnson and Marine Captain Charles Robb are blessed with the characteristics that make Liz big news and box office? Is there any truth in the concluding statement, again attributed to Miss Weller, that "everyone's complaining about those Jackie Kennedy covers except Jackie"? Or is her intellectual blindness so complete, her hide so thick, her conscience so transparent that she truly believes "the Kennedys have enough power to stop covers. But they have someone they want to elect in 1972 and—unlike actors today—they're smart enough to know the values of a star."

Then on December 31, "Calendar" published James Garner's article in which he savaged the magazines and their correspondents.

"Practically every fan story is salacious, muckraking drivel aimed to suggest scandal in the life of a favorite actor," Garner wrote, "or to suggest that some part of his psyche is twisted and morbid, or that his past is soon to catch up with him . . . and God have mercy on his soul."

> I was told by a reliable source that Debbie Reynolds, a few years back, gave freely in fan magazine interviews in an effort to combat false stories when she was having personal problems. However, the fantasy stories continued despite her cooperation and protests. Mia Farrow made herself available to fan writers until her patience gave out after a steady diet of similar hard-to-swallow phony stories about her private life.

Understandably, the reaction of the ladies to Garner's scorn was neither mild nor temperate nor reasoned. En masse, weighted by hardness of heart, the mordacious dames scorned

James Garner as a petulant and disappointed actor of little consequence, piqued because their magazines refused to give him cover-space.

Defense of Garner came from a most unexpected source. Russell Baker of *The New York Times,* as was his custom, offered his annual selection of the "ten grossest excesses of 1967." In his list, which included the 1967 football season, Charles de Gaulle (who had stiff competition from Gamal Abdel Nasser, General Hershey, George Wallace, H. Rap Brown, and Joe Pyne), *The Story of O* ("the dullest dirty book ever written, it set pornography back fifty years"), *Casino Royale* (which "exemplified the utter boring vacuity of the put-on carried to excess"), he also included "Jacqueline Kennedy on magazine covers."

It has long been held by a broad consensus of responsible critics that Southern California is neither civilized nor representative of reason, and these propositions were propounded with vigor by H. L. Mencken who once indicted the region for swapping a real and civilizing culture for institutions of appeal to midwestern boobs and the wives of retired automobile salesmen who delighted in the activities of fake swamis clad in bed-ticks. That Mencken was not suffering from dyspepsia was proved by interviews related to the retirement on January 22, 1968, of Mrs. Aggie Underwood, the assistant general manager of the Los Angeles *Herald-Examiner.* George Putnam, principal newscaster for KTLA, asked Mrs. Underwood to reflect on her forty-two years of journalistic experience and tell him what were the two biggest, most important stories she had ever covered. Without hesitation, Mrs. Underwood gave them as (1) the breaking of the Eddie Fisher–Elizabeth Taylor romance and (2) the paper's acquisition and publication of Lana Turner's love letters to Johnny Stompanato, the gangster murdered in Miss Turner's home.

CHAPTER FOURTEEN

"Jackie, Don't Marry That Englishman!"
A warning from Psychic-Astrologer
George Dareos.

Movieland and TV Time, February, 1968

OTHER devoted fans, in numbers legion, are staunchly devoted to Welk and the Four Sisters. They read the magazines, and the impastic knowledge gained from these tunnel-vision journals filled with disordered maunderings, enabled them to agonize deliciously with the brave warblers and their families. Oh yes, there was anguish and suffering aplenty. Indeed, between the months of January and October of 1968, details of the premarital pact forced on the husbands of the Lennon Sisters were revealed to the world.

Peggy (who confided to *TV Radio Mirror,* "I was born to be a mother!") undertook a period of penitential suffering for brave Kathy, who could never have a baby. Indeed, unfulfilled motherhood was but one of the sufferings Kathy had to bear;

while she coped with *another* secret marital problem she wouldn't talk about, she was also engaged in a great personal struggle to keep her husband and save her marriage. Janet, too, was having troubles. Married less than two years, she cried, "I'll never leave my husband again!"

Closest to Kathy, thus most privy to her problems, there were *reasons* why Peggy, Diane, and Janet could not help her through many domestic crises. Nor could any of the sisters—including Kathy, with enough troubles to plot every television soap opera on the three major networks for at least a full season—help pregnant Peggy, dissolved in tears because her baby son might catch cold. Then there was Diane's brave fight to save her "special" adopted child from heartbreak. Was the dolor of Janet, Peggy, Diane, and Kathy the reason why their eighteen-year-old brother said, "I'll never marry a girl like my sisters"?

For those who cannot enjoy a full program of gloom, it is possible to report some bright spots. For example, Diane had solved her mother-in-law problem. Although Janet by her very own self had brought tears to the eyes of Jo Ann Castle (a singer billed on the Welk Show as "the queen of the honky-tonk piano"), all the sisters had banded together to persuade Jo Ann to get married! But to be serious for a moment: was Lawrence Welk mistreating the Lennon Sisters—or were they just ungrateful minxes who had become worldly? Was it injury or carapaciousness that kept the four sisters from posing for photographs with good Maestro Welk, while Peggy and Kathy *approved* their husbands' resignations from the orchestra of bubbly musicians?

Because there was conflict among the Maestro, the Four Sisters, and two of their husbands, could Welk be blamed for asking—praying—that five other thrushes with his musical aggregation (the only true rival to Muzak) might replace the Lennons in the affections of the program's viewers? Could the fans be blamed if they asked for more and more information about who had kept the Lennons out of the movies, especially at a time when there was such an aseptic need for CLEAN PICTURES? Or for more information about the baddies who terrorized them? And whether they would have to *return* to Welk for protection?

Weighty problems all. So it was spiritual solace to read the story the Lennon family asked *Movie Mirror* to write—a piece about their vow "never [to] be separated on Christmas."

Although a superficial perusal of fan magazine covers in 1968 could have convinced the casual investigator that the Lennon Sisters were their exclusive civilized concern, a substantive analysis reveals the fuller truth: the girls were of secondary chemical interest to the pulps, their writers, and readers. Without question, the Lennon Sisters were important—more so than Lynda Bird Johnson, about whom stories were written to reveal her "intimate love story, marriage and honeymoon"; of "the love promise Lynda refused her husband" before she joined with her sister Luci to send "their husbands off to war." But after all was said and done, the major circulation emphasis was still geared to Mrs. Jacqueline Kennedy.

Some feeble attempt to link the lives and fortunes of "Jackie" and Lynda was made by January's *Motion Picture,* which assigned Joyce Franklin to compare "Jackie and Lynda's weddings [and] how each bride learned to love on the rebound." But the major editorial thrust was to get "Jackie" married to someone who had taken the fancies of Americans concerned about such things. The former First Lady had been widowed long enough; people loved romance, but they loved it even more when it led to a marriage service splendid enough for everyone to enjoy. Prolonged, extended, final widowhood was too grim for the American public to accept, especially as medical and social statistics, as set forth in all the coffee-table magazines, proved that women outlived men in the United States and became neurotic if they were denied male company. Very few women wanted to return to the single state after they had known the joys of marriage, although everyone knew that men, the beasts, were only interested in ONE THING. This explained why young and old beasts concentrated their scoring attempts on divorcees and widows: traditionally, they were the easiest targets.

"Jackie" *just had to get married!* She owed it to her children, her family and friends, her nation, but principally to her fans, whose loyalty had never wavered. Unanimously, the fan magazines arrived at their decision: if the lady was reluctant to assume again the obligations of marriage, the fan magazines would have to nudge her through the church doors. As a matter of policy, their outright marriage brokering had to be garnished with hesitations, misgivings, second thoughts, seemingly reasonable alternatives, determined but altruistic concern for the lady alone and, finally, approval and blessing of "Jackie's" new husband. He had to be someone the entire nation and, incidentally, the world could accept with pride. And if he were found, he had to be married to "Jackie" before he fell prey to some international adventuress, because everybody just knew how too many men over forty were often entrapped by designing blondes, with foreign accents and Playboy cleavage, who used seductive scents for evil.

There were three more considerations. First, more often than not, "Jackie" had appeared in public with *married* men, and this was a practice the magazines and their good readers could not condone. Second, although men were pursuers, they were notoriously shy of marriage, so the man the magazines favored had to be persuaded to pop the question because of the third consideration—it was said that men proposed marriage, but only with reluctance.

One man "Jackie" seemed to favor and one the magazines, even the most insular and isolationist, found nothing really wrong with was Sir David Ormsby-Gore, Lord Harlech, a suitor described by January's *Movie Mirror* as "a suave, brilliant diplomat, and a titled English aristocrat." It was titled at length, "Did Jackie Finally Say 'Yes'? The Man Who Is Going with Her Tells All! How Bobby Really Feels about It!" and Elena Gregory took pride in smelling out romance, especially since the public had been fooled so often by "Jackie," already "badly burned by the criticism the public heaped on her for going out with 'unsuitable' escorts." In high good spirits, Miss Gregory offered her readers real news: the Auchinclosses and the Kennedys—Bobby included—favored Lord Harlech. This was progress and readers could begin to buy rice because "Jackie" had already said "yes" to the lord and now had only to fix the day when she would again become "a complete woman—a *wife* as well as mother once more."

Photoplay for that month offered a fatuity filled with hedges and deadfalls by one of its most practiced of "Jackie" technicians, George Carpozi. In "Jackie—Photoplay Answers the 2 questions Everybody's Asking about Her: 1. Have the Kennedys Had It with Jackie? 2. Is She Really Going to Marry Lord Harlech?"—Carpozi cites an undated, unsubstantiated interview with William Manchester, who is supposed to have said: "It is more than obvious that one member of the Kennedy family is trying hard to embarrass Jackie."

Without question, this was far less important than the engagement fever which had gripped *Photoplay* and other febrile dizzards, to the end that Carpozi must bear the responsibility for the lowest taste in January, when he called attention to the significance of "Jackie" as a mourner at Lady Harlech's funeral. "Although accompanied by Bobby and her two sisters-in-law, Mrs. Stephen E. Smith and Mrs. Sargent Shriver, Jackie's presence at the funeral served to instigate talk about a possible future romance between David and Jackie." Yet in the end, *Photoplay*'s spokesman approved Lord Harlech as a second husband for "Jackie" because he was not only a lord and a man of good lineage, a political figure of impeccable reputation and national service, but was also chairman of a new television organization incorporated to provide programs for Wales. One of the partners in this enterprise was Richard Burton, "a man no one can accuse of being stodgy. . . . And wherever Richard goes, so goes his wife, Elizabeth Taylor. It would truly be a new, fun, fun world for Jackie—for the Burtons are fun, fun people who love a party as much as a brawl." At last, hopefully, the subliminal effort of some five or six years to associate Mrs. Kennedy with Elizabeth Taylor might succeed.

Using its cover for maximum worth, *Modern Screen* offered a Susan Wender article to indicate that *perhaps* approval was less than unanimous. "Why Jackie Isn't Safe with the English Lord

She Dates. Exclusive! Despite Denials Jackie Will Marry Royalty." Readers who turned to page 32 with feverish anxiety were quickly reassured: all was well in the Romance Department. For, as Susan Wender saw the matter, David was *so right*. Why, then, was "Jackie" no longer safe in his company? Well—there wasn't a single reason for her to say "No!"

As fitted a self-anointed matchmaker, far better equipped to mate people than a computer, Susan did not see "the English lord she dates as a threat to Jackie's emotional peace of mind." Rather, as Susan evaluated the possibilities for matrimonial hang-ups, there was "in fact only one thing that can come between Jackie and David—and that is Jackie's own reluctance to give her heart, so long possessed by death, to life and love again."

February issues were anticipated by the fans, which explains why so many of them were surprised when *Modern Screen* preferred to make its article for the month by Bobbie Bates a slashing attack on Lee Radziwill as an actress. Indeed, Miss Bates insinuated that diplomatic pressure had been applied to Pope John XXIII by "Jackie" and her influential friends until he had agreed to an annulment of Lee's first marriage to Michael Canfield. However, if Lee continued to gad about with Truman Capote, and another divorce resulted from her theatrical and peripatetic activities far from home and hearth, well—Bobbie Bates doubted if Jackie had as much influence with John's successor.

The success or failure of Lee Radziwill as an actress preoccupied none of the other magazines because they all were concerned with more important matters. With the exception of some unregenerate Anglophobes, all the fans agreed that "Jackie" should marry David, so when might the nuptials be celebrated? Lord Harlech's year of mourning would be over by calendar May, 1968.

Photoplay thought so much of Lord Harlech as a suitor that it chose to grace him with a substantial honor: a colored cover photo. For good measure, and as circulation insurance, he was joined by "Jackie," Caroline, and John-John, three established stars.

Still, there was something wrong! The coverlines did not match the photograph, for Kay Wendell sounded a strong, run-on, apocalyptic warning in "Jackie & the Man She Travels With—Why Lord Harlech Is So Wrong for Her and the Children." Summed up, Miss Wendell warned all to prepare themselves for domestic and patriotic clouds already bigger than the Atlantic Ocean.

> To begin with, since he would never be in danger of becoming Mr. Kennedy, and he has his own career to follow —if he married Jackie, they would have to live in England. This would mean that John-John and Caroline would live in Great Britain. The thought of a martyred president's children living outside the United States might be too much for some. . . . Kennedy spent several boyhood years in England, but he was raised an American, and the feeling is very strongly felt that an American president's children should be raised American. There would be something rather sad about John-John attending Eton (Lord Harlech's school) instead of following the American traditions of his father.

Other cultural tocsins were sounded by Miss Kendell. She expressed disapproval of David's participation in any business venture with Richard Burton and, incidentally, that wife of his. Then there was also the problem of Lord Harlech's individualistic children. How could "Jackie" be stepmother to Julian, twenty-six, a male model and dabbler in antiques? Or Jane, twenty-four, married to a men's mod fashion-designer? And twenty-year-old Victoria was "the swingingest debutante of the year on both sides of the Atlantic"! Even Alice, only fifteen, was already aping Victoria's life style! Not to mention Francis, a boy of thirteen, enrolled at Eton and given to wearing Bob Dylan caps and blue denims! How could "Jackie" be expected to deal with Jane and her husband Michael, who had been arrested for sleeping in a field with a bouquet of flower people? True, they were only sleeping, but why in a field, why with hippies, why on the ground? Miss Kendall's readers shuddered. Better to forgive England her debts, to salvage her empire and shore up her currency, than to give them "Jackie."

The most interesting of the lord's children, all of whom had been covered by Miss Kendall in two paragraphs, became the subject of a full feature in the February *Movie Mirror,* which assigned John Rimmington to file a London exclusive under the scare-title of "THE HIPPIE WHO MAY BECOME JACKIE'S STEPDAUGHTER TELLS ALL! ! !"

Mrs. Michael (Jane) Rainey lived hippily in a "luxury flat in the fashionable part of Westminster" with her husband (who designed men's fashions for his mod boutique in Chelsea) and their infant son, Saffron. Jane was fully willing to discuss her LSD and pot experiences, but what she had to say about rumors of second marriages for her father and Mrs. Kennedy was of minimal value to gossips: although they had seen each other socially, this was "no reason for everyone to suppose there is a romance brewing."

Rimmington was far more interested in offering some anthropological insights into the folkways of socially acceptable hippies than in the romance of two people past thirty who, except as museum pieces, didn't really count with the Now Generation. So the pad was described: dim lights, colored cushions strewn across the lounge floor, and redolent clouds rising from burning josh sticks. In this exotic setting, which really grabs you, Jane and Michael sat in the lotus position. Jane wore a long robe over red silk knickers tucked into her boot-tops. And Michael—get this! the son-in-law of a real lord!—wore a shirt with a Byronic collar and hip-huggers of flower-petaled fabric. And he also wore beads, sported long hair, and he was growing a beard! Could anyone imagine him playing touch football?

The final and most lethal chop at respectability was Rimmington's conclusion that Jane and Michael and baby Saffron enjoy their groovy bag; Saffron, his mum and dad were fully at ease—not ashamed for even a second.

After some long attention to fan magazines, it is logical to arrive at a dismal conclusion: everyone associated with their creation and digestion is being more dangerously narcotized than if they were on a diet of hashish and peyote buttons. Although it will take more than one generation to know fully what mental and physical deteriorations LSD babies will suffer as adults and what mutations they will transmit to their children, the narcoleptic results to brain and social orientation, as well as the emotional titubations, are almost immediately evident in the cases of creatures who live by and for fan magazines. A startling and shocking example was published in the February issue of *Movieland and TV Time* which used its cover in warning: "JACKIE, DON'T MARRY THAT ENGLISHMAN! (A Warning from Psychic-Astrologer George Dareos)."

To teeny-boppers, chicks, and birds in their training and cantilever brassieres, eyes ringed with black and shaded with blue, and bird-nest hairdos, to young matrons and even women in their forties, the name and personality of George Dareos meant nothing. But in Hollywood with its bumper crop of astrologers and palmists, life readers, fortune-tellers, and clairvoyants, crystal-gazers, mediums, hypnotists, necromancers, numerologists, and prophets, George Dareos is a senior guru, very important. Way back in 1925 he looked in his crystal ball, then told Rudolph Valentino the worst: Natacha Rambova had left him for good and final.

Valentino had been taken to George Dareos's apartment by Vilma Banky, with whom he was starring in *The Eagle.* Why had she recommended Dareos? Well, he had been consulted by Norma Talmadge and her husband, Joseph Schenck. And wasn't Joseph Schenck the guiding genius of United Artists, to whom Rudolph was under contract?

By 1928 the dependence of movie stars on practitioners of the occult had become so dangerous that Will H. Hays decided to consult with James Quirk about reasonable steps they might take to shake the stars sane. Quirk suggested a *Photoplay* exposé of quakery and a naming of the principal fakers who battened on the film industry. Although the suggestion appealed to Hays, he balked at Quirk's intention to name the fakers' dupes, no matter their importance as stars. Such specificity had never been the intent of the industry's czar. But Quirk realized how important the subject was for circulation. So he informed Hays of his intention to do the article, with or without official blessing.

Photoplay's feature for December, 1928, was Harry Lang's "Exposing the Occult Hokus-Pocus in Hollywood. The Truth about the Strange 'Psychic Guides' Who Influence the Destinies of the Stars—It's a Great Racket." The article was everything Quirk hoped for, and it named Joan Crawford, Eric von Stroheim, Pola Negri, Virginia Valli, Constance and Norma Talmadge, Billie Dove, Florence Vidor, Gilbert Roland, Mable Normand, Claire Windsor, Olive Borden, Jetta Goudal, Eleanor Boardman, Richard Dix, Charles Chaplin, Richard Arlen, Tom Mix, Eileen Pringle, Anita Stewart, Ralph Ince, Mae Murray, Ramon Navarro, Corinne Griffith, and Lupe Velez as stars who depended on psychics for guidance. And many of these stellar people were clients of George Dareos, formerly butler to a Hollywood star addicted to frequent consultation with a Pasadena medium. After Dareos compared his earnings as a manservant with the medium's takings, he decided to set himself up as a seer. The 1928 telephone book listed him as a psychoanalyst; but warming to his interviewer, Dareos confided that through his mother's line he was related to English peers and ranking governor-generals in the colonies.

The editor's choice was sound, for immediately making use of every hepatoscopy available to seers, Dareos warned that it would be a great mistake for "Jackie" to marry in 1968. Let there be no doubt of it, the lady of his prophecy had "a strong physical nature, and she feels she cannot go on living alone as a widow without close male companionship."

> She is brilliant, highly sexed. . . . [and] I see a great and brilliant future for her where she will make a lot of money if she is able to remain a single woman and bypass marriage to the Englishman. . . . If she had been a man, she would be the President of the United States. . . . I do feel that she had a warning ahead of what happened in Dallas. As she is very psychic. There are two more marriages ahead of her, in any case. . . . Should she have another child, she

may have twins. . . . As she goes along she will write books that will make a great deal of money for her.

I warn her strongly against alcohol. It could become her downfall. She could late in life become an alcoholic. She need not have this happen to her; for to be forwarned is to be forearmed.

It was time now to discuss the children, so Dareos saw John-John's mother training him for a career of public office. Although the boy's future would be brilliant, Caroline's was highest destiny, for she would be romanced by "Prince Charles of England, a Scorpio, [who would] attract her Sagittarius Sun. . . . However, Caroline would never consent to become a second Duchess of Windsor. If she should marry anyone but an American, the American people would resent this. This also applies to her mother."

Editors waited for the bomb to drop. Certainly, this time, there would be some reaction—vocal, punitive, or both—to such outrageously stupid graffiti. There was nothing. Which meant, thankfully, only one thing: the offended principal, her family, and friends were resigned to the great sea-serpent absurdities of heated imaginations. The material, really, all the passable members of the Hollywood Women's Press Club agreed, had to be treated as science fiction. Quite evidently, "Jackie" understood this. She was an intelligent being and a lady—and ladies did not sue. This conviction brought relief to all the factories, their assembly lines and fabricators, vendors and colleagues in associated industries.

Baring unforeseen events, fan magazine issues for March indicated how "Jackie" would be handled through year's end. Undoubtedly, she would become the bride of Lord Harlech and also help Bobby Kennedy become the next President of the United States. Would then "Jackie's" marriage to the lord—for no one believed she would listen to Dareos—interfere with Bobby's campaign for his party's nomination and a majority vote in the electoral college? No question about it, this was the real stuff of high life and drama.

It is now time to get along with the manufacture of "Jackie" history for March. While *Photoplay* led off with an old-fashioned article to acquaint its readers with "Bobby Kennedy—The Man Nobody Suspects," *Modern Screen,* in a burst of creative versatility presented three important players in Stacy Kytell's cover story, "Will Bobby Stop Jackie from Marrying Lord Harlech?" Few people doubted their love because "Jackie . . . in his presence glows with a relaxed warmth unseen in her for years. . . . But whether—and when—they can acknowledge that love . . . may depend on Bobby Kennedy's giving them his go-ahead [for] her engagement to a man so recently widowed . . . could affect . . . Bobby Kennedy's own political future, and that of his brother Ted."

If Bobby's motives were Machiavellian, such projections were necessary to politics and politicians. However, if their wives, as Bobby's Ethel, were good women with ideals of *Kinder, Küche, und Kirche,* the time their husbands spent with *other* women might give the sweet helpmeets reason for anxieties. So Daisy Charles's article in the April *Movie Mirror* was as naturally logical as falling into the gutter. "JACKIE KENNEDY: WHAT ETHEL KENNEDY HAD TO TELL HER CHILDREN ABOUT THEIR FATHER AND 'AUNT JACKIE'" was obviously inspired by Robin Douglas-Home's earlier article for *Queen* magazine. Daisy believed that "Jackie" and Bobby had pledged themselves to immortalize the memory of John Kennedy—and this work of canonization demanded all their energies and time. But the older children were asking questions of their mother, and Ethel was unable to explain why she couldn't accompany Daddy on his political trips. "Wasn't she lonely now with Daddy away so much? And . . . how did Mommy really feel about Aunt Jacqueline getting all that glory instead of her?"

How—Daisy asked—could Ethel be expected to reply gracefully, how could she make sweet reasoned response when "the light burning late in their parents' bedroom signified a lonely weeping mother waiting, sleepless, for the return of their father"? Was political office and "glory" worth a good woman's broken heart? Although Ethel was willing to do *anything* because she understood the need for personal sacrifice to make "glory" possible, and her religion had taught her that it was more blessed to give than to receive, there was still the hard question that "one of the teen-agers asked. . . . What if people should start wondering why their mother was staying home while their aunt was with his father? What about that?" Would people who asked such questions vote for their father?

Photoplay's readers might not, for in the April number, they were asked to cast votes to decide if "Jackie is wasting her life." To make possible an informed electorate is the duty of the nation's press; fully aware of the magazine's civic responsibility and that an informed citizenry is a free citizenry, Leslie Valentine reported, with cheerful grief, a significant ambitendency: "Jackie Kennedy is no longer the queenly symbol of courage and honor." For example, an article appeared in the Miami *Herald* under the headline, "Why Must We Idolize Jackie When She Doesn't DO Anything?" A count of the letters-to-the-editor inspired by the article ran five to one against the former First Lady. Such arithmetic led *Photoplay* to inquire if its readers were one in ambivalence with those who took the Miami *Herald?* A ballot was offered, autochthones who took such matters seriously were invited to vote and add their astigmatic insights.

Readers could turn with relief to *Movie Mirror* and enjoy the May divertimento with the biggest cast of featured players to date, all beholden to the stagecraft of Milt Robbins. The principals—"Liz-Burton-Jackie-Lord Harlech-Bobby"—were featured in color on the cover ("WE HAVE THE EXCLUSIVE PICTURES") over and under the catchy title, "The Affair that Broke Jackie's Heart! What Really Happened . . ."

A clever semanticist, Milt Robbins did not use "affair" in the accepted sense of an amorous relationship or clandestine episode between people not married to each other. Rather, he employed the word in the non-U sense of a classy dinner or entertainment where waiters did not pass toothpicks from a plate on which a dollar had been placed because tips had been

```
┌─ ─ ─ ─ ─ ─ ─ ─ ─ ┐
│                   │
│     I THINK       │
│  JACKIE KENNEDY   │
│    (check one)    │
│                   │
│  ☐ is wasting her life │
│                   │
│  ☐ is not wasting her life │
│  COMMENT (if you wish)── │
│                   │
│  ───────────────  │
│                   │
│  ───────  ───── │
│                   │
│  ───────────────  │
│                   │
│  ───────────────  │
│                   │
│   Please check:   │
│                   │
│  ☐ Male    ☐ Married │
│                   │
│  ☐ Female  ☐ Single │
│       Age──        │
│  CLIP & MAIL TO:  │
│  Jackie Kennedy Poll, │
│  Post Office Box # 1705, │
│  New York City, N.Y. 10017 │
│                   │
└─ ─ ─ ─ ─ ─ ─ ─ ─ ┘
```

included in the catering costs. So the "affair" turned out to be the movie premiere of *Doctor Faustus,* which starred Elizabeth Taylor and Richard Burton. Was there a woman anywhere who wouldn't want to be *intime* with so many stars! Why, even Jill St. John and Jack Jones would be there! And David too—because he was Richard Burton's partner in that television deal. Bobby would also be a guest. That was why "Jackie" couldn't go—because "Jackie and Bobby have begun to drop out of each other's lives. . . . [Recently,] every time a photographer wanted to get a picture of just her and Bobby—alone—Bobby motioned more people over to get into the picture. It seemed clear that

he didn't want to be linked too closely to his sister-in-law."
Wholly sympathetic, Milt Robbins explained how "very much
against his will, [Bobby] is in a terrible position. He can't take
a chance of having voters turn against him. And he can't allow
himself to stand in Jackie's way. . . . And Jackie will soon be
free to marry her David."

This was far cheerier reading for the fans than Maxine Cheshire's column in the Washington *Post* (May 12), where she
reported that "Jackie's" stepfather, Hugh D. Auchincloss, told
close friends there were no plans for a marriage between Jacqueline and Lord Harlech. "Alas," he is quoted by Miss Cheshire,
"it would be wonderful for everyone if it were true, but it
simply is not going to happen. . . . [It is] wishful thinking."
Wishful thinking might also be the best description of a story
in that May's *TV Radio Talk,* which warned its readers against
putting all their money on Lord Harlech because Rudolf Nureyev was still in the running. All of this was summed up on the
cover as "LEE RADZIWILL'S DILEMMA: Her jealous feud
with Jackie—Their love for the same man!" This cover also
asked of its readers: "Are the Lennon Sisters turning hippie?"

We must assume the retooling, at this time, of most of the
machinery in Myron Fass's "Jackie factory." During this period
of changeover, *Movie TV Secrets* had to reach for anything
available, so the editors ran a composite photo of Jacqueline
Kennedy and Caroline under a coverline, "JACKIE: Should I
Let CAROLINE Go to Dallas?" Hailed as the "STORY OF
THE MONTH," it was no more than a hodge-podge of scio-
listic mutterings of what "Jackie"—if she was an ignorant
woman—*might* tell Caroline if she ever decided to visit Big D.
Far more interesting were NEW Peyton Place scandals unearthed by *Movie TV Secrets* and several full pages of advertisements taken by Frederick's of Hollywood who—under the
catchy caption "Hollywood's Beauty Profile Tricks!"—offered
underwired bras with push-up pads to cover the bare essentials,
matching minipants tied at the sides, the BLACK MAGIC
nightie of exquisite black lace with nude sheer underlining, leg
pads to give unimpressive limbs a sculptured look, and SHORT

'N SHAPELY—a padded panty designed for slat-seated broads who desired callipygian contours.

What was good enough for fan magazines was even better for the June *McCall's*. There they were on the cover—"Mrs. Kennedy and Lord Harlech in Cambodia"—and for those who took the trouble to read, "Jacqueline Kennedy's Secret Mission for the U. S. in Asia." Two writers, Bernard and Marvin Kalb, confided "how a pleasure trip, ostensibly to see the ruins, was in reality a delicate and deftly executed diplomatic assignment." Mrs. Kennedy had visited Cambodia the previous November to build—the writers insisted—a small bridge for the convenience of diplomatic travelers between Pnompenh and Washington. Maybe so. But *Modern Screen* in April made much of its coverline, "JACKIE KENNEDY ATTACKED BY PLAYBOY PRINCE." And Campbell Zakomin, who should know, revealed that in January, 1968, only two months after "Jackie's" visit, Prince Norodom Sihanouk, chief of state of the Buddist kingdom of Cambodia, had made a mockery of Mrs. Kennedy's diplomatic efforts. The following month, May, *Photo Screen* in its account of the "affair that broke Jackie's heart" mentioned *in passim* Bobby's anger at his sister-in-law's trip to Cambodia because she had traveled with two men, one of them still in mourning, and at the airport welcoming ceremonies Prince "Snooky" had "presented Jackie to all the Communist bloc diplomats."

Modern Screen featured Susan Wender's piece, "Jackie Calls off Wedding to Help Bobby Run for President." Inasmuch as "Jackie's" marriage to David would interfere with Bobby's political strategy, he had ordered "Jackie" and David "to cool it" during his presidential campaign, had forbidden any discussion of a wedding date until some five or six months hence, and instructed them neither to announce their engagement nor to breathe a word about the honeymoon cottage they'd chosen in Bermuda.

The June *Photoplay* carried an article, "The Night Jackie said 'Yes' to Lord Harlech," by George Carpozi, which described hand-holding on a balcony during a romantic evening

JACKIE'S WEDDING DRESS!
See The Designs on Page 64

BURTON NEARLY SHOT TO DEATH
How His Drinking Saved Him

PHOTOPLAY

JUNE
50¢

JACKIE'S WEDDING DRESS

See designs in full color on page 64

◄ PLUS ►

The Night Jackie Said "Yes" To Lord Harlech

LENNONS FIGHT WELK

* **Are they mistreated by him—or ungrateful?**
* **Why two of their husbands quit the band**
* **Why they won't pose with Welk for pictures**

HOW LYNDA & LUCI SENT THEIR HUSBANDS OFF TO WAR

continued from 65

When Jackie Kennedy weds

Lord Harlech, I think

she should wear (check one):

DESIGN ☐   DESIGN ☐   DESIGN ☐
#1   #2   #3

Clip and mail to: Jackie Kennedy's Wedding Dress, Post Office Box 5037, Grand Central Station, New York, N.Y. 10017.

at the plantation of Mr. and Mrs. John Hay Whitney in Thomasville, Georgia. The cover featured the Lennon Sisters and headlines of their strife with Lawrence Welk—but it also displayed a sticker (which blocked off three of the four sisters) to let readers know who and what was really most important.

Wedding dresses were shown on pages 63 through 65, and readers were invited to choose "Which of the three designs of the following pages should Jackie wear for her forthcoming marriage to Lord Harlech?"

The dress lengths varied from ballroom to mini; all resembled frocks that had been remaindered as just plain low-class by Frederick's of Hollywood or Lili St. Cyr, whilom stripper and now a designer of "French Delights" underwear. A ballot was provided to record the reader's vote.

Almost all Americans are aware of the assassination of Robert Kennedy shortly after midnight on June 5, 1968. But it was not until August that the big-three fan magazines acknowledged the assassination in a manner designed to please the fans and disgust anyone capable of pity or taste. *Motion Picture* published a "jinx photo" of Andy Warhol and friends gathered around three identical photographs of Robert Kennedy. This was apparently important because on June 3, Warhol had been shot by a woman because he had refused to film her script. Within thirty-six hours Kennedy was also shot (but by a stranger), and *Motion Picture* saw something astrological in the coincidence.

Photoplay used its cover to tell of "THE WARNING BOBBY IGNORED BEFORE THE BULLET HIT." Cal York, a fictitious name for nondescript staff writers, told of a warning expressed by John Lindsay in *Newsweek* that Robert Kennedy would be shot. York reported this as if he were covering an appointment in Samarra, "Bobby the senator expected to be assassinated, and did not have to be told by anyone that he might be!"

Modern Screen offered "Bobby's Death—What Will Happen to Jackie and Her Children NOW? The Story No One Has Told"—a résumé by Marion Jones of the assassination of Robert Kennedy.

Only *TV Movie Screen* in the August issue was seemingly unaware of Senator Kennedy's death. Instead, it offered scoops on how divorce haunted Kathy Lennon unless she could make her husband forget the other woman; how Doris Day suffered secret torture because of persistent feelings that she could have saved her husband's life; how Ava Gardner was led to confess that Frank needed her and Mia could not stop her plans to remarry the singer; and a big chunk of really boss *news* about Bobby Kennedy: "Hollywood's Married Beauties and What They Do for Him."

That the article was just another tasteless put-on is far less important than a fact associated with the living. For now, lucky readers could split their attention between *two* attractive Kennedy widows, both of whose husbands had been gunned down by psychopaths. *Modern Screen* granted autumnal honors to Robert and Ethel Kennedy by permitting them to share the cover with—you guessed it—the Lennon Sisters ("THE BABY WHO MAY BREAK UP THE LENNONS")—and an account of Bobby's and Ethel's love story, which "couldn't be told until now!" Also aware that there were now two Kennedy stars (even if one remarried shortly, the other would make an eligible widow), *TV Radio Mirror* bracketed "Jackie" and Ethel in a little miracle play by Carmel Berman, "How God Spoke to Each in Her Hour of Need."

Movie Life alone kept faith with normal folly and clouded perception through the horoscopes of Madame Calliope St. George, a sibyl who interpreted destiny, as written in the stars, with advice in the areas of love, marriage, divorce, or finances. To wit:

> I have a crush on a very important movie star, and have written to him, and he's replied that if I'm ever in Hollywood he will autograph a photo for me. I love him so much that when I look at his picture I lose my head and get dizzy. The trouble is: I'm married, have three children, and my husband is a laborer who never brings home enough bacon! Should I run away from my family and head for Hollywood? Please advise me what to do. I was born March 4, 1940.
>
> PAT, Wichita, Kansas

Madame Calliope minced no words in her reply. Pat was advised to get a grip on herself because she was in deep psychological trouble and in immediate need of "clinical advice or the help of your local clergy."

For her "celebrity horoscope" that month, Madame Calliope chose—guess who?

> Yes, Jackie's chart shows a powerful romantic attachment, but I note a surprising setback.

If Bobby Kennedy had been nominated by the Democrats for the Presidency of the United States, I have a
hunch Jackie would have held back any plans to marry so
that Bobby could have had the entire limelight to himself. But now that RFK is gone, Jackie will probably feel
it necessary to continue postponing her wedding—out of
respect, and of course her grief.

However, I wonder how this would make Lord Harlech
feel? I just hope Jackie won't jeopardize her future happiness by holding off any marriage too long.

As a Leo, born July 28, 1929, Jackie is very strong, and
what she decides is *it*. So I pray she makes the best decisions
for herself and Lord Harlech, because I, like everyone else,
want her to enjoy the blessing of Lord Harlech's bright
companionship.

In their continuing struggle for circulation, the survival of
lesser magazines than *Movie Mirror* depended on the use of the
most sensational covers community standards will permit.
Therefore, the October *TV and Screenworld* must not be denied recognition, for in addition to its offer of a voyeuristic
bonus in the pictorial form of uncensored scenes from *Candy,*
the editors also offered photographs of Jacqueline Kennedy,
Katharine Hepburn, Doris Day, and Barbara Stanwyck to push
their lead article, "HOW FAMOUS WOMEN OVER 40 FACE
LIFE WITHOUT A MAN!"

The murder of Robert Kennedy, his abrupt removal from the
political scene, his widow's pregnancy—all these presented problems for editors and publishers. Uncertain as to the ganglion of
low stimulus it should excite, *Motion Picture* tickled readers
with "The Vow the Lennons Made to Ethel," a biographical
trifle about the singers' first encounter with political action:
they signed a petition for more stringent firearms legislation.
Far more dramatic was the issue's companion piece, a catalog
of mishaps and accidents suffered by all the Kennedy children,
and how death, it seemed, had marked them for special attention.

Still bullish on brides, *Photoplay*—whose wedding-dress-for-"Jackie" poll had received a boffo response—designated its October number as a SPECIAL COLLECTOR'S ISSUE; bridal photographs of Ethel, "Jackie," and Joan—the most recent nominee for unsolicited stardom—graced the cover. Readers were urged to share the "Memories of Three Brides. AN ALBUM OF LOVE THAT WILL NEVER DIE: A portrait of three women . . . their unforgettable moments of triumph and torment . . ."

But it is not the story of three brides of three brothers that makes this issue of *Photoplay* a collector's item for social and behavioral scientists. Instead, such must turn to a seemingly innocuous article, at first glance hardly worth the reading. "SIX STARS—Dress Like Your Favorite," by Arlene Wanderman. It offered head shots of Nancy Sinatra, Jr., Faye Dunaway, Barbara Parkins, Sophia Loren, "Jackie" Kennedy, and Mia Farrow atop torsos of models in Simplicity patterns inspired by dresses once worn by the six famous ladies. There were specific instructions for readers capable of more advanced games: "Capture your favorite celebrity's fashion mood with a Simplicity pattern. . . . Echo Jackie's elegance in (#7283)."

Only after players turned to pages 58 and 59 did they discover that they were being invited to "UNDRESS LIKE THE STARS." Again there were photographs of the six subjects, beneath which were drawings of the "stars" as they might look in their undergarments. The excuse for so presumptive an exercise in imagination, not to mention an outrage to privacy, is expressed tidily: "Every star knows that the proper undergarments and the right hairdo are two very important fashion ingredients in her total appearance. Undergarments are the basis of a successful look. . . . Now you, too, can have the same beginning and same ending as your favorite star."

And how does *Photoplay* dress and undress the former First Lady? The Simplicity gown worn under the Simplicity coat (#7283) is strapless. Elegance "calls for Lovable's 'Zip-Front Dance Time' strapless longline bra with plunging V back and light boning for a flat waistline. Lace covers the satin foam contour cups and the controlling Lycra panels. The detachable garter straps make it a truly all-purpose garment."

The sketch is explicit, probably drawn so to ease the disappointment of cloddish Clydes who bought the X-Ray Specs (only $1.00) advertised in the last issue only to discover they revealed far far less than Lili St. Cyr's More Than Nude Bra (#104) of "sheer marquezette [*sic*] with circles of CUT-OUT Tips to show a dazzling bit of you."

If Jacqueline Kennedy left the United States and risked American displeasure because she chose to live and educate her children abroad, would the most xenophobic and Draconian judges censure her for leaving the land of *Photoplay* and *Modern Screen* and *Motion Picture* and *Movie Mirror* and *Movieland and TV Time* and *Photo Screen* and *TV and Screen World* and *TV Radio Talk* and *Movie TV Secrets* and *TV and Inside Movie* and *Screen Stars* and *Movie Life* and *TV Radio Mirror?*

Even *papparazzi* and photographers whose specialty is the use of telescopic lenses, invasion of beaches, and landings by parachute treated her better.

CHAPTER FIFTEEN

"It's the end of Camelot."

Common reaction, *Time,* October 25, 1968

P*ARADE, The Sunday Newspaper Magazine,* slightly larger than quarto size and of approximately thirty-six pages, is sold nationally to a number of newspapers for their Sunday editions. Contents are a potpourri of two or three articles of general interest, jokes designed to soothe the mind and ease digestion, cartoons, an "Intelligence" section of encapsulated news items in a teletype format, and Walter Scott's "Personality Parade" on the second page of each issue. Readers are encouraged to write Mr. Scott if they wish to learn all the truth about prominent personalities. Each issue presents between twelve and fifteen questions for answer, and of these slightly less than half are asked by readers who live in keyholes.

In the four issues of *Parade* for October, 1968, fifty-four questions of the thousands sent to *Parade* were chosen for reply by Mr. Scott. Twenty-four of the questions published and answered were in the genre of fan magazine queries. Therefore this indicated the topical interest of almost fifty percent of

Parade's readers, who get 12,612,913 copies (*Ayer Directory of Newspapers and Periodicals,* 1968).

What is the inside story of Sidney Poitier and a white chick named Linda Cristal?

There was a rumor floating around Hollywood in the late 1930s that to become a Howard Hughes star, a girl had to submit to sterilization. Any truth? How many Howard Hughes contractees subsequently had children?

Does Rock Hudson go out with girls?

Three years ago Mamie Van Doren married Lee Meyer, a 19-year-old baseball player. At the time I believe she was old enough to be his mother. How has the marriage worked out?

Is the Elvis Presley marriage washed up?

I have just completed reading an article about Hollywood stars in which it was said that many are homosexual. Is this true? If so, please list the homosexuals.

John Lennon, the No. 1 Beatle, has been condemned for leaving his wife for a Japanese kook. Isn't this true because Lennon was forced into a shotgun marriage from which he is only now just escaping?

I have been told that Brigitte Bardot is a compulsive nudist, that as soon as a handsome male tips his hat, she starts to undress? If it is not, how come all those pictures of her in the nude with her new lover, Luigi Rizzi?

Is it true that when Shirley Temple was 5 she signed a film contract which said that if she ever got drunk or pregnant, the contract was null and void?

Of the lot, however, the question submitted by a Jersey City querist and answered by Mr. Scott in the October 13 issue of *Parade,* conjures up a scrutator who makes the most of the trash that passes for important news in the United States.

Q. Hasn't Greek millionaire Aristotle Onassis fallen in love with Jackie Kennedy? Isn't that why Maria Callas, Onassis' old girlfriend left him this past summer when Jackie and her chaperone Ted Kennedy showed up on the Onassis yacht?

A. Onassis makes no secret of his admiration for Jackie Kennedy. . . . That the Onassis-Jackie Kennedy friendship will continue to grow in the more sequestered waters of the world there is little doubt at this time.

Where did this observant analyst get her information about a bona fide romance between Jacqueline Kennedy and Aristotle Onassis? If she turned to the standard reference works of ignorance—the fan magazines—October's *Photoplay* only made passing gossip-column mention of a dinner enjoyed by "Jackie" aboard the *Christina* when she and her brother-in-law Ted were guests (in August) of the Greek shipping magnate. For November, *Photoplay* offered nothing on "Jackie"; rather, its cover was devoted to Elizabeth Taylor because "Neither love nor liquor can help Liz now . . ." and inside dope about what the Lennon siblings "don't tell their sisters."

Motion Picture treated Onassis as a casual figure in an eccentric story devoted to Ted Kennedy's grief, Joan's distress over his suffering and her turning to Ethel and "Jackie" for psychological assistance. Only Linda Robert in *Modern Screen* analyzed correctly the significance of Ted acting as chaperone aboard the *Christina*. After Ted and his sister-in-law returned to New York, Miss Robert reported "the world was wondering whether Jackie had actually embarked, with Ted's blessing, on a new romance with that strange, wealthy, engimatic [*sic*] man to whom she had just said an affectionate goodbye."

Even December issues for 1968 dared not commit themselves firmly to Aristotle Onassis as the suitor most likely to succeed where Lord Harlech, a true blueblood, seemingly had failed. *Motion Picture* flatly ignored so awful a possibility and, ostrich-like, gave other principals the benefit of its pages. *Photoplay*, for once, put romance aside, lauded "Jackie's" Christian concern for Ted's health and applauded her ministrations to the young Senator as they cruised the Greek islands aboard Onassis's yacht. Lord Harlech still was first choice for *Modern Screen,* though they did not rule out Onassis, recently introduced to readers in the November number. However, as a popular reference work of obstetrication, the December number concerned itself with the bittersweet approach of "Jackie's" fortieth birthday and the relevant chirurgical question: "After her marriage will Jackie have another baby?" Answer gave good midwife Betty Ferguson opportunity to review "Jackie's" parturient history, neglected since 1963, when she had been widowed.

It is doubtful if the fan magazines suffered great despair or discomfiture whenever predating and early distribution had involved them in serious journalistic bloopers and lapses of taste, especially in articles about the Kennedys. But we can assume that the November and December datings caused them much anguish, for it was not until the January and February and March issues of 1969 that they could get around to the marriage of "Jackie and Ari." Of all the bumptious periodicals with self-assigned claims and rights to invade the privacy of Jacqueline Kennedy, only *Women's Wear Daily* kept pace with the nation's newspapers as all followed hard on their interpretation of the headline event first announced by the Boston *Herald Traveler* on October 16. Next morning the *WWD* published a photograph of Jacqueline over a headline, "SHE'S OFF . . . SHE'S LOVELY, SHE'S ENGAGED . . . SHE'S ALL SMILES." In addition to full two pages of available and conjectural news about the engagement and impending wedding, *WWD,* which offers itself as "The Retailer's Daily Newspaper," offered an almost correct sketch of the bridal dress by Valentino.

The wedding and celebration on Sunday, October 20, was covered fully by the world's press. They considered so important that Lou Woods (on a televised NBC News broadcast) informed listeners of the network's intent to present *first films* of the wedding later that evening on the "Phyllis Diller Show."

Whatever honeymoon "Jackie and Ari" enjoyed from the press was concluded by Sunday midnight. Monday was the first work day of the new week, and Joyce Haber for the Los Angeles *Times* offered one of the first examples of the orchestrated but cacophonous treatment the honeymooning couple could expect from abusive epithalamiasts. Miss Haber's unfelicitous discharge bore the provocative headline "Cast Your Vote for Oddest Couple" and suggested that readers of her waste-product improbities vote for "Jackie and Ari, Joanie [Cohn] and Larry [Harvey], Julie [Andrews] and Blakie [Edwards] . . . as the Oddest Couple." Max Lerner, also given some grudging space by Miss Haber's newspaper, admitted his surprise at the wedding and suggested that significant criticism would be directed at the former First Lady by the young people of leftist sympathy, "for whom the Kennedy name . . . was associated with the struggle of the poor and oppressed."

Most slants on the wedding were neither rational nor sympathetic, and editorial prose ranged between malicious and purely vicious. And the majority of letters written to editors were condemnatory and cruel. "Jackie" was vilified as a "public sinner" by many Christians who were not Catholic. After Richard Cardinal Cushing, Archbishop of Boston, attempted a compassionate defense of Jacqueline Kennedy Onassis, he was subjected to such insane abuse by telephone and letter that he offered his resignation to the Pope. "I've had it," the Cardinal told reporters, after he explained his rejection of demands to brand the former Mrs. Kennedy as a public sinner and excommunicate her. His moderation and charity led to "Many mail deliveries—some of which are in the language of the gutter." The press continued to quote blind, derogatory criticisms of the marriage and its principals by "an acquaintance," "a prominent Hollywood producer," "an Italian columnist," "a group of commentators," "a prominent Boston matron," "a well-placed Kennedy sympathizer and confidant" and "a Jet Set leader"—none of whom was identified.

Some of the international press also treated the newlyweds with scorn, derision, and limpest humor, but it is safe to say these would have been minimized if the American media had

truly wished the couple well and not behaved like fan magazines.

As reported by our secret agent in the Hollywood Women's
Press Club, its members "were furious, really out of their skulls
and wigs, because they'd given Jackie just millions and millions
of dollars of *free* publicity that real stars would have given *anything* for—and then been willing to pay the millions. So what
did that ungrateful woman do? She decided to marry Onassis
without telling anyone but Cardinal Cushing who was bound by
silly oaths, which ought to be outlawed, not to reveal confi-
dences. Many of the girls thought the wedding was shotgun and
they were busy counting on their fingers. And if they're right—
and how they pray they are—then they'll really sock it to her.
What Ingrid Bergman and Connie Stevens got from the mags
would be like heaven. Meanwhile, we're still publishing and
we'll keep the fans boiling."

If the fan and coffee-table magazines, the daily press could
make unpleasant references to Jacqueline Kennedy Onassis and
her *foreign* husband, and not be censured by the national conscience, the abjuration of anything resembling good wishes to
the recently married couple was expressed through a full-page
advertisement taken in the "Calendar" section of the Los Angeles *Times* on December 15, 1968. It offered a record, "Beware
of Greeks Bearing Gifts" by Bob Booker and George Foster on
the Musicon label: "20 hysterical bands tell the satiric story of
'the Newlyweds' from 'getting ready for the wedding' to 'a
quiet evening at home.' " Some examples of the twenty "hysterical bands" are in order:

> How does the "about-to-be groom" tell "Momma" that
> he's getting married—BUT—"She's not a Greek girl,
> Momma!"

> The Newlyweds hold their "First Press Conference." The
> result is a "million dollars" worth of laughs.

> Meet the Tailor who makes the Groom's "Baggy suits."

The Bride's answer to a press question, "What are you looking forward to in your life together?" is a BILLION DOLLARS WORTH OF LAUGHS!

Discounted from $5.79 to $3.99, the record was cheap enough if it would have given a dignified, compassionate citizenry only half a BILLION DOLLARS WORTH OF LAUGHS.

Did Bob Booker, George Foster, and the people at Musicon hope they might irritate "Jackie and Ari" into suing them? If they were lucky, might they not get her to do what Julie Andrews had done in the first week of January, 1969—sue *Screenland* and *Modern Movies* for the publication of false and malicious statements about her private life? Both offending magazines and four individual defendants were summoned to answer two $3,000,000 damage suits in Santa Monica Superior Court, just miles from Hollywood.

Past suits filed by screen stars were usually settled out of court and removed from courtroom calendars. However, the evident determination of Miss Andrews to prosecute the suits and attempt the collection of substantial financial judgments from the defendants shocked the Hollywood press community which gathered in punitive phalanxes to heap invective on the plaintive, as if this might intimidate her.

When Charles Champlin—already identified as the entertainment editor of the Los Angeles *Times*—told Walt Anderson (in March, 1967) that his paper would probably not replace Hedda Hopper, he may have had too optimistic an opinion of his readers, his personal clout, or editorial authority. Within months Joyce Haber replaced Miss Hopper; and as her daily column became increasingly gelatinous it seemed just right in its damp, morbid, and myxomycetous tone for the millions of fans who swore by Hedda, her big hats and even bigger hates. To prove she stood with *Screenland* and *Modern Movie* against Julie Andrews, a *foreigner* who had dared petition *our* courts for relief against innuendo, scandal, and forthright malice, Miss Haber devoted much of her January 15, 1969, column to the making of a plangent din against the English actress.

"If I were Sidney Poitier, I'd sue Julie Andrews," said a top industry executive.

He was uttering my sentiments, and most of Hollywood's, as well, I hope, as those of most America. . . .

People are saying that Miss Andrews' behavior is unsuitable for a lady—or star. Jacqueline Kennedy, the subject of more and more-notorious stories in fan magazines, never sued.

There you have it. "Jackie" would never sue the fan magazines. Which was absolute perversity on her part, for the "America," to whom Miss Haber reports, would have adored such a fracas. Wouldn't that have relieved the boredom of impeccant ladies under the dryer—or as they sat around, waiting patiently for washing machines to end their spin cycles?

On February 2, 1969, the Gallup poll reported the election of Mrs. Ethel Kennedy to be first of the ten women admired most by Americans. Mrs. Aristotle Onassis, who had been most admired in five such successive polls, now was a poor seventh. Whether Camelot came to an end in the mythic past or as recently as October, 1968, is unimportant. All mythologists, even the most abstract and sentimental, described a realm sans plumbing, adequate lighting, central heating or a paved road beautified by even one of McDonald's golden arches or a bucket of fried chicken in the sky thanks to Colonel Sanders. And the Merlins couldn't make strong enough medicine to keep Mordreds out of the realm. Indeed, they were unable to neutralize the villains or keep the First Lady of the place chaste and dedicated to her marriage vows.

Was there a Camelot? Did it decline and fall at some mythic time long past or a year or two ago? If the realm existed, is its terminal date important? Whether Camelot was a time of castles or penthouses, of country fairs or happenings, of Merlins or flying-saucer sighters, is of lesser importance than the nation's traditional optimism: in a mythopoeic land, new fantasies will replace those lost, stolen, destroyed, or too worn for continued use with profit. This applies to castles, palaces, and mansions too; so the new structures to replace those of Camelot will be considerable improvements over anything conceived by Dark Age or medieval architects. How will this be accomplished? Quite simply. Institutional press plans for the future will eliminate the traditional privacy granted to citizens in a democracy, especially of those men and their consorts who are foolish enough to believe in service to their communities and condemn themselves, thereby, to suttee.

Traditional privacy has not been surrendered without some protest by people in the news. One of the more literate defenses of this surety was made in 1955, when *Harper's* published William Faulkner's essay "On Privacy . . . The American Dream: What Happened to It." The Nobel Prize novelist wrote of his objections to a project undertaken by "a wealthy widely circulated weekly pictorial magazine" of a piece about him. Not about "his work or works, but about [him] as a private citizen, an individual." Faulkner "explained why" he thought the theme repugnant: ". . . my belief that only a writer's works were in the public domain, to be discussed and investigated and written about, the writer himself having put them there by submitting them for publication and accepting money for them; and therefore he not only would but must accept whatever the public wished to say or do about them from praise to burning. But that, until the writer committed a crime or ran for public office, his private life was his own; and not only had he the right to defend his privacy, but the public had the duty to do so since one man's liberty must stop at exactly the point where the next one's begins; and that I believed that anyone with taste and responsibility would agree with me."

How old-fashioned, even pixilated, Faulkner's statement reads when measured by the yardstick of new publishing practices. Problems of circulation, production costs, competition for advertising revenues, these have compelled every popular magazine to retool to new purposes. Unless a magazine can interest advertisers, or is subsidized by a continued expenditure of substantial cash by some group in need of a publishing voice, it cannot survive. Melodrama and Soapland—to put dolichorrhinos readers where the private action is—are the editorial purposes of our current popular magazines. To be on the inside of things, at the open window where everything can be seen and heard, are what readers demand. If this, and no less, is what they will buy, this is what will be offered for sale; and in a free economy, where purchasers are privileged to pick and choose in the marketplace, who can blame manufacturers for studying public tastelessness and producing products to suit it?

Magazines for men, with the robust stories of *Argosy* and its imitators, no longer exist. Most contemporary magazines for studs model themselves after *Playboy* and are inclined to leave stories of adventure to the *National Geographic*. The ladies' magazines, published for the softer sex, once devoted to almost every room in the home, were hermetically sealed off from bedchambers. Now, such modesty is out. Now such magazines concentrate on interpretations of their advertisements for feminine hygiene and feature articles that discuss, in lay language, hysterectomies, curettage, the subtle sinuosities of sex and the secrets of Semiramis. The living area given greatest attention is the bedroom, and good ladies are instructed in the subtleties of lighting, scents, and appropriate decoration to stimulate imagination. In addition, they are educated in the nuances of dress, preliminary behavior and postures—all guaranteed to turn the American home into the perfumed tent and garden of Sheik Nefzawi. And it would be a substantial oversight to ignore the "advice columns," which can compete with the *Illustrierte Sittengeschichte* and the *Ananga Ranga*.

Can even one moral reason be offered to excuse the major American press, whose mastheads proclaim their allegiance to social improvement, integrity, coherence, and rectitude, yet slavishly imitate the pulpiest of scandalmongers that they too may profit from the assassinations of a universally beloved President and his brother? The activity defies culture, ethics, communication, and literacy, and what normal people would identify as compassionate decency.

And to subject their widows and children to the murky coverage of fan magazines, because it is profitable to do so, establishes for everyone of conscience the current nadir of national taste as well as the impoverishment of Christian kindness. Jacqueline Kennedy suffered imprisonment for more than five years in the publishing hell of the "Jackie factories." Now that she has escaped, is her cell being readied for Ethel Kennedy? Or Joan Kennedy? Or at some latter time, for Caroline Kennedy? The future alone will answer these questions. But it is not too prejudiced to conclude that only in a nation where many of its institutions and citizens have become clinically psychopathic, would aggressors scream so loudly if even one of their innocent victims escaped persecution.

In his misanthropic contempt for mankind's civilized practices and institutions and its rabid responses to decency, Mark Twain stood second to no man; and his assessment of Eseldorf, the best placename for everywhere and everyplace, enabled him to observe at some other time that "all you need in this life is ignorance and confidence, and then Success is sure." Daily, hourly, every passing minute, Twain's conclusion is proved, especially by the low forms of information that now pass for average and normal in the United States. January, February, and March issues of fan magazines in 1969 raved at "Jackie" for scooping them on her wedding; other members of the American press, which use better paper, typeface, and format, wished the bride and groom well, with their fingers crossed.

In a land where viewers have become voyeurs, reading of anything, even trash, will not have to be proscribed as it was in Ray Bradbury's *Fahrenheit 451* (1953). People themselves will decide that printed matter is a waste of time. Why read about people when they can be better enjoyed, slobbered over, by becoming an on-the-site spectator?

Fan magazines have conditioned their readers to expect *everything*, but they settle for *nothing*. To give the voyeurs more would disappoint them, because more, rather than less, would destroy their imaginations' heightened sensitivity to sexual suggestion and the satisfaction derived therefrom. The setting and ceremonies would be an elaborate put-on. Psychologically, this would be most fulfilling for voyeurs.

But who will be minding the store? Guiding the ship of state?

Simple. Give the problems to IBM now and they'll have the Big Computer ready before the first show. Similar Peeping-Tom houses in state capitals, cities, and even the larger towns, with computers to service the communities, and a guaranteed annual wage for the lumpencreats would keep them from climbing the walls and making unnecessary trouble for the Big Computer as it ran the government.

Culturally, if this comes to pass, such houses would curtail, even eliminate, the fan magazines and their imitators. Genetically, such houses would improve the breed. To be President is the noblest, most honored of patriotic ambitions. If, during his term of office, the President is in fullest possible view of his people (television coverage for the culturally disadvantaged shnooks in the boondocks would ease the hotel-motel problem in our modern capital), no creature could be nominated, let alone elected, if he failed by even a lash to meet the American middle-class ideal of masculinity. Cary Grant? Disqualified because he isn't an American and that also takes care of Rex Harrison and David Niven. So—Jimmy Stewart? He's had legislative experience too. Remember him in *Mr. Smith Goes to Washington?* Not a bad suggestion—but isn't he too old? Advancing age also eliminates John Wayne. So how about Leonard Nemoy—Mr. Spock? He's got the cutest ears, very sexy, he's really not from outer space somewhere and he might even be able to do things with the Big Computer. But to balance the ticket find someone who's made it big in the movies, looks like Cary Grant, and is about forty because the New Candidates will be creatures with sexual glamour and the rest of the Mastroianni-Sharif-y stuff. Creatures will elect the best-hung studs to represent the other-directed electorate who can thank popular American media, especially the fan magazines, for making them insensitive to pity or the reasonable longing for privacy.

There is no quantitative relationship between the size of bacteria, of virus, and the harm they do. Such organisms are microscopic, but the plagues and epidemics they engendered have crippled and killed millions of people. This is beyond the abilities of every mythic giant and even larger tribes of Kongs and

Godzillas. To charge fan magazines as the principal agent of American normlessness oversimplifies the problem. However, such magazines are a dangerous virulence, for they have corrupted every branch of popular media.

The question presents itself: why can good people who have never broken a law, received a traffic citation, kicked a dog, stolen a garbage-can lid or cut across a neighbor's lawn, view with indifference innumerable foreign and domestic horrors? How can they feel, and believe, that they are just being normally curious when they read, discuss, and *hope* the fan magazines are telling the truth about all those people? That they have righteous reason to be angry with "Jackie" because she cheated them in more ways than one when she married Aristotle Onassis? How? Because the fan magazines and their better-class imitators have told them so.

Another answer, of course, lies in the last Gallup poll which revealed "Jackie's" fall from first to seventh place. Even before this poll was tabulated, there were press references to "Pat's good legs" and how she need do little more than give up her sensible suits for a glamorous wardrobe to—*voilà!*—become a sexy first-place doll. If she follows this unsolicited but sincere advice, all the fan magazines would be delighted to feature her on their covers. Look what they had done for "Jackie," that ungrateful thing.

Wouldn't, then, life be beautiful even without the Peeping-Tom houses? Especially for the fan magazines, whose ideologues could look forward to a golden future replete with so many good-looking politicians blessed with sexy wives and swinging kids that they would no longer have to depend on temperamental movie and television stars for even filler copy. And until that great come-and-see-it day, in that blessed future time just before the opening of the all-glass New Executive Mansion, with a keyhole for every citizen, editors and publishers of fan magazines could dismiss every actor and actress with two words. You can believe it; they won't be "Happy Birthday."